What people are saying about …

The Fresh Life Series

"I'm touched and blessed by Lenya and Penny's heart for His kingdom."

Kay Arthur, Bible teacher and
author of many best-selling Bible studies

"What a great way for women to learn to study the Bible: interesting stories, thought-provoking questions, and a life-changing approach to applying Scripture. Lenya and Penny provide a great method so women can succeed and grow spiritually in a short period of time. Kudos!"

Franklin Graham, president and CEO of Billy Graham
Evangelistic Association and Samaritan's Purse

"Skip and Lenya Heitzig have been friends of my wife, Cathe, and I for more than twenty years. Lenya loves to study God's Word and teach it to women in a way that is both exciting and accessible. I trust her latest book will be a blessing to you."

Greg Laurie, pastor and evangelist of Harvest Ministries

"Lenya and Penny's love for the Lord and knowledge of His Word uniquely equip them to help other women discover the pathway to God through these in-depth Bible studies."

Kay Smith, wife of Chuck Smith (Calvary Chapel)

"The Fresh Life Series is an insightful and in-depth look at God's Word. Through these Bible studies Lenya Heitzig and Penny Rose lead women to deeper intimacy with God."

K. P. Yohannan, president of Gospel for Asia

"Lenya and Penny have created another wonderful Bible study series that invites participants to spend time in God's Word and then see the Word come to fruition in their lives. What a blessing! These studies are perfect for small groups or personal daily devotions."

Robin Lee Hatcher, women's event speaker
and award-winning author

Live Abundantly

The Fresh Life Series

A
20-Minutes-a-Day
Study

Live Abundantly

A Study in the Book of Ephesians

Lenya Heitzig & Penny Rose

David C Cook®
transforming lives together

LIVE ABUNDANTLY
Published by David C Cook
4050 Lee Vance View
Colorado Springs, CO 80918 U.S.A.

David C Cook Distribution Canada
55 Woodslee Avenue, Paris, Ontario, Canada N3L 3E5

David C Cook U.K., Kingsway Communications
Eastbourne, East Sussex BN23 6NT, England

The graphic circle C logo is a registered trademark of David C Cook.

Unless otherwise noted, all Scripture quotations are taken from the New King James Version. Copyright © 1982 by Thomas Nelson, Inc. Used by permission. All rights reserved. Scripture quotations marked NLT are taken from the New Living Translation of the Holy Bible. New Living Translation copyright © 1996, 2004 by Tyndale Charitable Trust. Used by permission of Tyndale House Publishers. Scripture quotations marked NIV are taken from the Holy Bible, New International Version®, NIV®. Copyright © 1973, 1978, 1984 by Biblica, Inc™. Used by permission of Zondervan. All rights reserved worldwide. www.zondervan.com. Scripture quotations marked KJV are taken from the King James Version of the Bible. (Public Domain.) The author has added italics to Scripture for emphasis.

LCCN 2011936867
ISBN 978-1-4347-0330-9
eISBN 978-0-7814-0806-6

© 2001, 2011 Lenya Heitzig and Penny Rose
Published in association with William K. Jensen Literary Agency, 119 Bampton Court, Eugene, OR 97404
First edition published as *Pathway to God's Treasure* by Tyndale in 2001 ©
Lenya Heitzig and Penny Rose, ISBN 978-0-8423-4261-2.

The Team: Terry Behimer, Karen Lee-Thorp, Amy Konyndyk, Caitlyn York, Karen Athen
Cover Design: ThinkPen Design, Greg Jackson

Printed in the United States of America
Second Edition 2011

3 4 5 6 7 8 9 10

020813

Contents

Lesson Nine

Lesson Ten

Lesson Eleven

Lesson Twelve

Introduction

HEAVENLY SAINTS

Ephesians is an epistle from an apostle. Simply put, epistles are ancient letters between two or more parties. The apostle Paul wrote this letter to a group of believers within a city: Ephesus. (In the same way, he wrote to groups of believers in Corinth, Philippi, Colossae, Thessalonica, and Rome.) What makes this epistle different from most letters is that it includes a forwarding address. First, this document belonged to the believers in Ephesus. Second, it belongs to you and me, if we are "faithful in Christ Jesus" (Eph. 1:1). Paul addressed these two groups of people as saints.

You? A saint? It's true! *Saint* describes someone set apart for Christ's purposes. It refers to our status positionally "in Christ" rather than to our piety in action. It also implies "godly ones" or "holy ones." In other words, all those who are saved bear the title *saint*.

Believe it or not, God bestows a better title upon you, His follower. Paul revealed our adoption as children of God. That makes you His *daughter*. Adoption, in the Greek, carries greater meaning than our English word does. It literally means "placing as a son." The Hebrew custom and Roman law most often applied to an adult rather than a child. You get into His family by regeneration, the new birth. Adoption, then, becomes the act of God by which He gives those "born again" an adult standing in the family. This makes us eligible to immediately claim our inheritance and enjoy our spiritual wealth. Babies cannot legally access their inheritance, but an adult can. Paul told the Romans, "You received the Spirit of adoption by whom we cry out, 'Abba, Father'" (Rom. 8:15).

HEAVEN'S STASH

Did you know that Ephesians contains a spiritual blank check from God written directly to *you?* We'll discover that He "has blessed us in the heavenly realms with every spiritual blessing" (Eph. 1:3 NIV). Because they were ignorant of their inheritance, the Ephesian believers were living as paupers when in fact they possessed royal riches. Sadly, they had not possessed their possession. God's eternal wealth outlasts gold that corrodes and cash that crumbles. As heirs of Christ Jesus, you have things money can't buy: salvation, forgiveness, grace, peace, holiness, and acceptance.

United Way's "Day of Caring" turned into much more for volunteer Barbara Strong-Nelsen. Armed with mowers, pruners, weed whackers, and other tools, Barbara and the other volunteers were ready to give Celebration Park in Tacoma, Washington, some much-needed attention. While on an initial foray into dense undergrowth, Barbara found a forty-dollar gift certificate to Anthony's Restaurant. Whoo-hoo! This must be her lucky day! A few minutes later Barbara found an uncashed check for a large amount. Things got serious when she noticed that the check had a name on it along with an address. Barbara was on a mission. She drove down the street, discovered the address, and was met at the door by an elderly woman. Delighted to hear the news, the woman explained that her car had been vandalized earlier in the week. Both the gift certificate and the check had been an anniversary present to her and her husband from their son. The certificate and check had been stolen.[1]

Just as Barbara discovered hidden riches, there are spiritual riches for you to receive as you dig into God's Word. Have you uncovered your spiritual riches? Do you possess all that God has bequeathed to you? As you study Ephesians you'll find riches beyond compare.

HEAVEN SENT

Our great inheritance comes not only from the Son but also from the other members of the Godhead. Paul reveals that the Trinity has made us benefactors of spiritual riches. Our salvation (standing as saints) was strategized by God, staged by the Son, and solidified by the Holy Spirit. God the Father decided to make you a saint before the foundation of the world (Eph. 1:4). God the Son saved you when He shed His blood on the cross (v. 7). God the Holy Spirit sealed you for the day of redemption (v. 13).

Not only is our salvation heaven sent, our new nature is as well. There's a tendency among some Christians to abuse the doctrine of predestination found in Ephesians (1:5). They mistakenly assume that if God has an eternal plan, they will be saved no matter how they live since God elected them. This mentality encourages people to indulge in sin. That's why the apostle included in the doctrine of predestination the idea of a new nature to make the saints holy and without blame before God in love (v. 4). Peter explains that the new birth demands a new nature. "That … you may be partakers of the divine nature, having escaped the corruption that is in the world through lust" (2 Peter 1:4).

It is our desire that as you complete this study, you, too, will know how to *Live Abundantly*. We pray that God will open your eyes to His wealth, your heart to worship, and your life to be worthy of His calling.

Author: Paul

Audience: Ephesians and those who follow Jesus

Theme: The spiritual wealth (chapters 1—3) and walk (chapters 4—6) of the believer

Timeline: About AD 60

Setting: Written by Paul in a Roman prison, the letter was intended for the believers living in Ephesus. Ephesus was a wealthy trade city that worshipped the pagan goddess Diana.

Scripture: "In Him also we have obtained an inheritance, being predestined according to the purpose of Him who works all things according to the counsel of His will, that we who first trusted in Christ should be to the praise of His glory" (Eph. 1:11–12).

How to Get the Most out of This Study

What makes you feel most alive? Looking at a beautiful sunset? Snuggling a newborn baby? Riding a roller coaster and feeling the rush of adrenaline as you defy gravity? These activities make life enjoyable ... even thrilling. But there is so much more to life than day-to-day activities.

God created all creatures with the capacity to live and breathe. But He gave humans an even greater gift—an eternal soul. Not only did God provide us with the chance to live forever, He designed us to live in intimate communion with Him. How amazing that the God who created the heavens and the Earth, the stars in the sky, and the fish in the sea wants to know *us* intimately. He wants us to truly live! It's been said that God doesn't add years to our life, He adds life to our years. Jesus said, "I have come that they may have life, and that they may have it more abundantly" (John 10:10).

Are you living life to the fullest, or are you just going through the motions? The secret to truly living rather than merely languishing is found in God's Word. We know that God reveals Himself through His Word. That's why doing a Bible study like this is so vital—because God's Word has the power to do His work in our lives. It is the catalyst that revives our hearts, renews our minds, and restores our souls. That helps make life worth living!

This particular Bible study focuses on Paul's letter to the Ephesians, where you'll discover that God has bequeathed to *you,* His beloved daughter, His treasures that allow you to *Live Abundantly.* God's purpose in sending the letter to the Ephesian Christians in the first century, and now to you, is so you would know "the riches of the glory of His inheritance" (Eph. 1:18). It is our prayer that, just like the early church, you will receive all that God has for you. If you're ready, then let's get started....

There are five elements to each day's lesson. They are designed to help you fully "live" as you apply the study to your life:

1. Lift Up ... Here we ask you to "Lift Up" prayers to God, asking Him to give you spiritual insight for the day's study.

2. Look At … This portion of the study asks you to "Look At" the Scripture text using inductive questions. These questions help you to discover *What are the facts?* You'll learn the basic who-what-when-where-how aspects of the passage as well as some of the important background material.

3. Learn About … The "Learn About" sidebars correlate to specific questions in order to help you understand *What does this text mean?* These sidebar elements offer cultural insight, linguistic definitions, and biblical commentary.

4. Live Out … These questions and exercises are designed to help you investigate *How should this change my life?* Here you are challenged to personally apply the lessons you have learned as you "Live Out" God's principles in your life.

5. Listen To … We finish with inspiring quotes from authors, speakers, and writers. You'll be able to "Listen To" the wisdom they've gleaned in their lives and relate it to your own.

"For you know the grace of our Lord Jesus Christ, that though He was rich, yet for your sakes He became poor, that you through His poverty might become rich" (2 Cor. 8:9). We pray that with God's grace you enjoy the incredible riches Christ offers. May you live abundantly,

Lenya Heitzig and Penny Rose

PERSONAL CHECKLIST

• Be determined. Examine your daily schedule, then set aside a consistent time for this study.

• Be prepared. Gather the materials you'll need: a Bible, this workbook, a journal in which to write your thoughts, and a pen.

- Be inspired. Begin each day with prayer, asking the Holy Spirit to be your teacher and to illuminate your mind.

- Be complete. Read the suggested Bible passage and finish the homework each day.

- Be persistent. Answer each question as fully as possible. If you're unable to answer a question, move forward to the next question or read the explanation in the "Learn About …" section, which may offer further insight.

- Be consistent. Don't get discouraged. If you miss a day, use the weekend to catch up.

- Be honest. When answering the "Live Out …" questions, allow the Lord to search your heart and transform your life. Take time to reflect honestly about your feelings, experiences, sins, goals, and responses to God.

- Be blessed. Enjoy your daily study time as God speaks to you through His Word.

SMALL-GROUP CHECKLIST

- Be prayerful. Pray before you begin your time together.

- Be biblical. Keep all answers in line with God's Word; avoid personal opinion.

- Be confidential. Keep all sharing within your small group confidential.

- Be respectful. Listen without interrupting. Keep comments on track and to the point so that all can share.

- Be discreet. In some cases, you need not share more than absolutely necessary. Some things are between you and the Lord.

- Be kind. Reply to the comments of others lovingly and courteously.

- Be mindful. Remember your group members in prayer throughout the week.

SMALL-GROUP LEADER CHECKLIST

- Be prayerful. Pray that the Holy Spirit will "guide you into truth" so that your leadership will guide others.

- Be faithful. Prepare by reading the Bible passage and studying the lesson ahead of time, highlighting truths and applying them personally.

- Be prompt. Begin and end the study on time.

- Be thorough. For optimum benefit, allot one hour for small-group discussion. This should allow plenty of time to cover all of the questions and exercises for each lesson.

- Be selective. If you have less than an hour, you should carefully choose which questions you will address, and summarize the edited information for your group. In this way, you can focus on the more thought-provoking questions. Be sure to grant enough time to address pertinent "Live Out ..." exercises, as this is where you and the women will clearly see God at work in your lives.

- Be sensitive. Some of the "Live Out ..." exercises are very personal and may not be appropriate to discuss in a small group. If you sense that this is the case, feel free to move to another question.

- Be flexible. If the questions in the study seem unclear, reword them for your group. Feel free to add your own questions to bring out the meaning of a verse.

- Be inclusive. Encourage each member to participate in the discussion. You may have to draw some out or tone some down so that all have the opportunity to participate.

- Be honest. Don't be afraid to admit that you don't have all the answers! When in doubt encourage ladies to take difficult questions to their church leadership for clarification.

- Be focused. Keep the discussion on tempo and on target. Learn to pace your small group so that you complete a lesson on time. When participants get sidetracked, redirect the discussion to the passage at hand.

- Be patient. Realize that not all people are at the same place spiritually or socially. Wait for the members of your group to answer the questions rather than jumping in and answering them yourself.

Are You in the Will?
Ephesians 1:1–14

Have you dreamed about inheriting treasures from a long-lost relative? To be "in the will" would change your life forever!

Consider the rags-to-riches story of Jack Wurm. In 1949, Mr. Wurm was unemployed and bankrupt. As he strolled along a San Francisco beach, he found a bottle with a scroll inside. He discovered that this "message in a bottle" was the last will and testament of Daisy Singer Alexander, heiress to the Singer Sewing Company fortune.

The faded paper read: "To avoid confusion, I leave my entire estate to the lucky person who finds this bottle, and to my attorney, Barry Cohen; share and share alike." The courts discovered that she had written the note and thrown the bottle into the Thames River in London. It had drifted across the oceans to San Francisco and reached a penniless Jack Wurm. Jack inherited over $6 million in cash and Singer stock.

Similarly, God has sent us a "message in a Bible." Within this book you'll find the "last will and testament of our Lord" with a different kind of inheritance—spiritual treasures. How will you respond? Will you walk past it? Or, like Jack Wurm, will you step out in faith and take action? Failure to take God's promises seriously leads to spiritual poverty. Jack's inheritance can't begin to compare with the spiritual wealth God offers His heirs! The book of Ephesians reveals the magnitude of your heavenly treasures.

Day 1: Ephesians 1:1	THE MESSENGER
Day 2: Ephesians 1:1–2	THE BENEFICIARIES
Day 3: Ephesians 1:3–6	THE BENEFACTOR
Day 4: Ephesians 1:7–12	THE REDEEMER
Day 5: Ephesians 1:13–14	THE GUARANTOR

The Messenger

LIFT UP ...

Father, I confess that this world tugs at my heart to go in directions that are not Your will for me. Use this study to transform my mind and direct my heart to follow You. In Jesus' name. Amen.

LOOK AT ...

Meet Paul, the author of the letter to the Ephesians. Paul wrote this letter while imprisoned in Rome for preaching the gospel. Though on trial for his life, Paul was concerned with the spiritual well-being of the churches he established on his missionary journeys. It was his honor and duty to deliver the "last will and testament" of our Savior to the church in Ephesus. Let's spend some time getting to know Paul, the messenger. As you study, ask yourself, "Am I in God's will?"

READ EPHESIANS 1:1.

Paul, an apostle of Jesus Christ by the will of God ... Ephesians 1:1

LEARN ABOUT ...

1 Apostle

In Greek, the word *apostle* literally means "a delegate"—one sent with a special message or commission.

---

3 Transformed

God took Saul, a murderous, vengeful man, and transformed him into Paul (Acts 13:9), the apostle who faithfully spread the gospel. Take comfort—God can rescue you from your "Damascus road" and transform your life for His glory.

---

5 Gentile

The Jews used the term *Gentile* to refer to all people who were not Jewish. In New Testament times this became a derogatory label filled with prejudice and disdain.

---

6 Prejudice

Prejudice is blinding. The Jewish leaders could not see that Jesus was their Messiah, and they crucified Him. They refused to acknowledge Saul's conversion and persecuted him. Don't let discrimination blind you— you may destroy something beautiful!

1. What did Paul call himself (v. 1)? What does this title tell you about his job description?

2. How did he become an apostle of Jesus Christ?

  Read Acts 9:1–31 to discover how Saul the Pharisee became Paul the apostle.

3. According to Acts 9:1–2, what was Paul like before he became a Christian?

4. Describe how Paul was converted to Christianity (Acts 9:3–18).

5. According to verse 15, to whom did the Lord call Paul to go?

6. Focus on verses 22–23. How did the Jews respond to Paul's conversion? Why?

7. According to verse 26, how did the disciples respond to Paul? Why?

LIVE OUT ...

8. We have seen that Paul knew God's will and purpose for his life. Write out what these verses teach you about God's will for your life.

SCRIPTURE	GOD'S WILL FOR YOU
1 Thessalonians 4:3	
1 Thessalonians 5:18	
1 Peter 2:15	

9. God's will includes our *sanctification*. Journal about some of the areas in which God has helped you separate yourself from sinful behavior.

10. It is God's will for us to be thankful. Journal a note of thanksgiving to God.

11. It is God's will for His followers to be doers of good deeds. Which of the good deeds below will you perform this week?

    ____ Phone an unbeliever

    ____ Visit an elderly friend

    ____ Babysit for a family

    ____ Prepare meals for the needy

    ____ Pray for a missionary

    ____ Other _____

○ ○ ● ○ ○

LEARN ABOUT …

9 Sanctification

Sanctification is the process of God's grace by which the believer is separated from sin and becomes dedicated to God's righteousness. Accomplished by the Word of God and the Holy Spirit, sanctification results in holiness or purification from the guilt and power of sin.

11 Doing Good

To be a Christian is to become Christlike—to imitate our Savior. "God anointed Jesus of Nazareth with the Holy Spirit and with power. Then Jesus went around doing good" (Acts 10:38 NLT).

Saul of Tarsus thought he was in God's will when, in fact, he was in bondage to his strict religious observance of the law. When God interrupted his life, Paul was transported from religion to relationship. He became a new creation in Christ. Paul learned to breathe the air of freedom by living in God's will. Jesus said, "If the Son sets you free, you are truly free" (John 8:36 NLT).

Henrietta Mears, a beloved Bible teacher, taught the secret to true freedom. She explained, "A bird is free in the air. Place a bird in the water, and he has lost his liberty. A fish is free in the water, but leave him on the sand and he perishes. He is out of his realm. So … the Christian is free when he does the will of God and is obedient to God's command. This is as natural a realm for God's child as the water is for the fish, or the air for the bird."[1]

LISTEN TO ...

All heaven is waiting to help those who will discover the will of God and do it.

—*J. Robert Ashcroft*

DAY 2
The Beneficiaries

A five-year-old named Justin heard the story of the monk Simon the Stylite, who attained sainthood by sitting on a lofty pillar for forty years. The boy was intrigued by the idea of literally climbing closer to God, so he decided to imitate Simon. Placing the kitchen stool on top of the table, he climbed his precarious perch and began his journey to sainthood. His mother saw him and cried, "Justin, get off that stool before you break something!" Justin jumped off his perch and marched out of the room saying, "You can't become a saint in your own home."

Paul called the Ephesians *saints*. It's easy to view some people as true saints—Mother Teresa or Billy Graham, for example. However, it's more difficult to comprehend that *all* believers (including you and me!) are saints in God's eyes. You don't have to stay perched on a lofty pillar to attain sainthood. A saint is simply a person who belongs to God and is set apart for Him. If Paul wrote a letter to you, a believer, he would call *you* a saint.

Lift Up ...

Thank You, Lord, for the riches of Your inheritance. Don't let the gold and silver of this world fool me. Remind me daily that my treasure is in heaven with You. In Jesus' name. Amen.

Look At ...

Yesterday we learned about Paul, the messenger of God's will. Today we turn our attention to the beneficiaries of his letter.

LEARN ABOUT ...

2 Faithfulness

Saving faith is ongoing and active. True faith goes beyond confession to implementation of God's Word. Faith must grow into faithfulness: "Just as the body is dead without breath, so also faith is dead without good works" (James 2:26 NLT).

4 Grace and Peace

These blessings are known as the "Siamese twins of the New Testament"—you can't have one without the other. Peace will follow grace, and only by experiencing the grace of God will you know the peace of God.

READ EPHESIANS 1:1–2.

To the saints who are in Ephesus, and faithful in Christ Jesus:
Grace to you and peace from God our Father and the Lord Jesus Christ.
Ephesians 1:1–2

1. How did Paul describe the Ephesians? Why do you think he chose this word?

2. What Christian attribute do the Ephesians display?

3. The Ephesians were described as "faithful." Look at the following verses, and write down what they teach about manifesting faithfulness in different areas of your life.

SCRIPTURE	FAITHFULNESS MANIFESTED
2 Chronicles 34:10, 12	
Proverbs 14:5	
Luke 16:10	
1 Corinthians 4:1–2	
3 John 5	

4. In Ephesians 1:2, Paul prayed for the Ephesians to experience grace and peace. Why would those be good things to pray for?

5. Who gives this grace and peace? Why is this important to remember?

6. Note the titles given to God and to Jesus in verse 2. What do these mean to you?

Live Out ...

7. a. In Ephesians 1:2 we learned that saints experience grace
    and peace. Check the boxes below that indicate ways you have
    attempted to create peace in your life.

    ___ Listened to music

    ___ Called a psychic hotline

    ___ Ignored my problems

    ___ Used drugs or alcohol

    ___ Stayed busy

    ___ Other_____

    b. Journal about whether or not these have been successful at giv-
    ing you lasting peace. Why or why not?

8. Jesus said, "I have told you all this so that you may have peace
    in me. Here on earth you will have many trials and sorrows. But
    take heart, because I have overcome the world" (John 16:33 NLT).
    Where (or with whom) can peace be found?

9. Paul revealed the way to restore peace in an anxious heart: "Be
    anxious for nothing, but in everything by prayer and supplication,
    with thanksgiving, let your requests be made known to God; and
    the peace of God, which surpasses all understanding, will guard
    your hearts and minds through Christ Jesus" (Phil. 4:6–7). Journal
    about the three steps that lead to peace:

    Step One: "Be anxious for nothing." Name your greatest fear, and
    then give that anxiety to the Lord.

Learn About ...

8 Peace

Jesus said His peace is
unique—it's "out of this
world!" "I am leaving you
with a gift—peace of mind
and heart. And the peace
I give is a gift the world
cannot give. So don't be
troubled or afraid" (John
14:27 NLT).

9 Anxiety

To be anxious means "to
be pulled in different
directions." The Spirit pulls
us in one direction—toward
hope and peace in the Lord.
Fear, anxiety, and worry
pull us in the opposite
direction—away from the
place of security and rest.

Step Two: "In everything by prayer … let your requests be made known to God." Write out a prayer about this fear or a situation that causes you stress.

Step Three: "With thanksgiving." Write your own psalm of praise, thanking God for setting you free from this fear.

○ ○ ● ○ ○

We have discovered that saints are people who are faithful to the Lord Jesus Christ. We have learned that a faithful Christian life exhibits ongoing and active faith. Faith is tested by the tough stuff in life—when the chips are down and the heat is turned up. I (Lenya) read about an elderly woman, badly crippled by arthritis, who was asked, "Do you suffer much?" She pointed to her hand and responded, "Yes, but there is no nail here. He had the nails; I have the peace." She then pointed to her head saying, "There are no thorns here. He had the thorns; I have the peace." Finally, she touched her side and declared, "There is no spear here. He had the spear; I have the peace." This faithful woman was a modern-day saint. She understood the incredible gift of grace given to her by God, and she was filled with "God's peace, which exceeds anything we can understand" (Phil. 4:7 NLT).

LISTEN TO …

A great many people are trying to make peace, but that has already been done. God has not left it for us to do; all we have to do is to enter into it.

—*Dwight Lyman Moody*

The Benefactor

Have you ever gotten one of those "too good to be true" sweepstakes envelopes in the mail with Ed McMahon's face on it? What do you do with the envelope? If you're like me, you throw it in the trash even though it says you may have already won $10 million. I've figured out the scam—I've read the fine print and learned my chances of winning are slim to none.

Ephesians reminds us that God *has* given us (past tense in the Greek) *every* spiritual blessing, and there is no catch. The tragedy is that some of us merely underline, quote, or frame the promises in the Bible, treating the treasures of God the same way we would treat a sweepstakes letter. Are you throwing away God's blessings? Today learn how to make withdrawals from your benefactor's heavenly bank account. It's all there waiting for you!

LIFT UP ...

Father, You have filled my life with immeasurable blessings. When I'm tempted to count my woes, help me to number my blessings. With a grateful heart, let my lips bless You, Lord. In Jesus' name. Amen.

LOOK AT ...

We have met the messenger and the beneficiaries of this letter. Now we turn our attention to God the Benefactor, Christ the Redeemer, and the Holy Spirit the Guarantor. Today we concentrate on God the Father and the blessings He has for His children.

READ EPHESIANS 1:3–6.

Blessed be the God and Father of our Lord Jesus Christ, who has blessed us with every spiritual blessing in the heavenly places in Christ, just as He chose us in Him before the foundation of the world, that we should be holy and without blame before Him in love, having predestined us

LEARN ABOUT ...

3 Heavenly Places

Why are your blessings stored in heaven? Jesus gave you the key to the storehouse when He said, "Wherever your treasure is, there the desires of your heart will also be" (Matt. 6:21 NLT). He wants to make sure your heart is in the right place.

_____

4 In Him

God is interested in the ins and outs of your life. Unless you are in Christ, in Him, and in the Beloved, then you are out of His will, out of His blessings, and outside of His family.

_____

5 Adoption

Roman law required that the adopting parent be male and childless. The one to be adopted had to be an independent adult, able to agree to be adopted. In the eyes of the law, the adoptee became a new person and was regarded as being born again into the new family.

to adoption as sons by Jesus Christ to Himself, according to the good pleasure of His will, to the praise of the glory of His grace, by which He made us accepted in the Beloved. Ephesians 1:3–6

1. What do you learn about God from this long sentence?

2. Describe the kinds of blessings God has given to us.

3. Where are these blessings?

4. Ephesians 1:4 ("just as He chose us …") moves from telling us about God's blessings to the conditions for receiving them.

    a. When were we chosen in Christ?

    b. Why has God chosen us?

    c. What should be our response to Him?

5. In verse 5 ("having predestined us …") we discover that God wants to bring us even closer to Him.

    a. How does God make us members of His family?

    b. Who has secured the right for our adoption as sons and daughters?

    c. Why has God adopted us?

6. In verse 6 God grants us another incredible grace: "He has made us accepted in the Beloved."

a. In whom is our acceptance found?

b. In your own words, what does this mean?

c. How did Paul say we should respond to what God has done for us?

Live Out …

7. We have learned that God has given us every kind of spiritual blessing.

Journal a list of some of the specific blessings God has placed in your life.

8. What a wonder that God chose us before the foundation of the world! Check the areas of your life where you have had the freedom to choose, thanks to our democratic society, which venerates freedom of choice.

_____ Spouse _____ Height

_____ Talent _____ Neighbors

_____ Friends _____ Hair color

_____ Family _____ Other_____

9. God wants you to become just like Him—a chip off the old block.

a. Since you became a Christian, in what ways have you chosen to become more like your heavenly Father?

Learn About …

7 Blessings

Out of God's richness, He bestows His blessings upon us. God's blessings to us are limitless—*every blessing* means every one! "The LORD will withhold no good thing from those who do what is right" (Ps. 84:11 NLT).

8 Choices

Life offers many choices, but God asks us to make the most important ones: "Today I have given you the choice between life and death, between blessings and curses. I call on heaven and earth to witness the choice you make. Oh, that you would choose life, … make this choice by loving the LORD your God" (Deut. 30:19–20 NLT).

9 Conformed

It is biologically impossible for people who are adopted to fully embody the attributes of their adoptive parents. However, as an adopted child of God, you are empowered by Him to become "conformed to the image of His Son" (Rom. 8:29).

b. What changes do you sense God wants you to make so you can become more like Him?

○ ○ ● ○ ○

A Sunday school teacher once had two new boys in class. When she asked their ages and birth dates for registration, the blond boy said, "We're both seven. My birthday is April 8, 1976, and my brother's is April 20, 1976."

"That's impossible!" blurted the confused woman.

The dark-haired boy piped in, "No it's not. One of us is adopted."

Before she could stop herself, the teacher asked, "Which one?"

The boys looked at each other and said, "We asked Dad a long time ago, but he just said he loved us both and couldn't remember which one was adopted."

God has only one begotten Son—the rest of us have been adopted. Your heavenly Father has not only adopted you but also completely accepted you in the Beloved. Your all-powerful, all-knowing heavenly Father has chosen to forget your past. He sees you just as He does His only begotten Son. You have become a coheir with Christ. You can now call the almighty God your Father: "You received the Spirit of adoption by whom we cry out, 'Abba, Father'" (Rom. 8:15).

LISTEN TO ...

Adoption ... is that act by which we who were alienated, and enemies, and disinherited, are made the sons of God, and heirs of his eternal glory.

—*Richard Watson*

DAY 4

The Redeemer

Potty training my son gave me insight into the meaning of redemption. When Nathan was a toddler, we were desperate to have him graduate from diapers to indoor plumbing. At first we bribed him with M&M's, but that didn't do the trick. Finally we discovered the ultimate motivator—a puppy. When the momentous dry-diaper day arrived, we headed to the Humane Society to set a puppy free. We chose Ginger, a bouncy cocker spaniel, paid the full price, and rescued her from captivity and death.

That's the essence of redemption: paying the price for another's freedom. That's what Jesus did for us. He redeemed us from bondage and death by paying the price for our sins with His blood.

LIFT UP ...

Jesus, before I met You, I was stuck in destructive patterns that enslaved me. Your blood has set me free to walk in newness of life. Thank You! In Jesus' name. Amen.

LOOK AT ...

Yesterday we focused on the blessings that God, our Benefactor, has given His children. Today we turn our attention to the Beloved Son, our Redeemer.

READ EPHESIANS 1:7–12.

In Him we have redemption through His blood, the forgiveness of sins, according to the riches of His grace which He made to abound toward us in all wisdom and prudence, having made known to us the mystery of His will, according to His good pleasure which He purposed in Himself, that in the dispensation of the fullness of the times He might gather together in one all things in Christ, both which are in heaven and which are on earth—in Him. In Him also we

have obtained an inheritance, being predestined according to the purpose of Him who works all things according to the counsel of His will, that we who first trusted in Christ should be to the praise of His glory. Ephesians 1:7–12

LEARN ABOUT ...

2 Debt Paid

Even the wealth of Bill Gates is insufficient to pay the debt your sin has incurred. Jesus owed no debt, yet He gladly paid the price for your sin—His blood: "The ransom he paid was not mere gold or silver. It was the precious blood of Christ, the sinless, spotless Lamb of God" (I Peter 1:18–19 NLT).

5 Gathered Together

"The fullness of the times" (v. 10) refers to the great gathering together of all things in Christ. This will happen in the future during Christ's reign in the millennial kingdom. God has given believers special insight into His plans for a time yet to come.

7 Predestination

Predestination is God's sovereign determination of a person's eternal destiny working together with a person's right to freely choose or reject salvation. In His omnipotent wisdom, God chooses those who will choose Him.

1. "In Him" refers to Jesus—the Beloved Son—from verse 6. What do we as believers have in Him?

2. By what means did Christ purchase our redemption?

3. Redemption and forgiveness are possible "according to the riches of His grace" (v. 7). How would you restate this phrase in your own words?

4. Why has God made known the mystery of His will to us (v. 9)?

5. What was the purpose of God's plan (v. 10)?

6. What more have we obtained in Christ (v. 11)?

7. What phrase confirms the idea that there are no accidents in a Christian's life?

8. What is the end result of a life that trusts in Christ (v. 12)?

LIVE OUT ...

9. Sin has left its stain on all our lives. With this in mind, follow the steps below, and journal your responses:

Step One: Write a list of some of the sins that have blackened your life.

Step Two: Write a prayer asking God to cleanse your sins with the blood of Christ. Thank Him that "the blood of Jesus, his Son, cleanses us from all sin" (1 John 1:7 NLT).

Step Three: Now take a red pencil, crayon, or marker and cover over the list of sins you listed above, just as the blood of Jesus has covered over your sins.

10. We have discovered that Christ has blessed us with an inheritance. Fill in the following chart to learn some elements of that inheritance.

SCRIPTURE	INHERITANCE
Titus 3:7	
Hebrews 1:14	
Hebrews 11:7	
James 2:5	
1 Peter 3:9	

11. God wants to reveal His mysteries—share His secrets—with His adopted children. As you journal today, include the following thoughts:

Write down some things that you now understand about God (things you may not have understood earlier in your life).

Write down some of the things you still don't understand or questions you still have.

Now journal a prayer of praise, thanking God for revealing the mysteries (secrets) of His will to you and asking for wisdom to understand more.

LEARN ABOUT ...

9 Forgiveness

God is willing to forgive any sin if you accept Christ's sacrifice in repentance and faith: "Though your sins are like scarlet, they shall be as white as snow; though they are red like crimson, they shall be as wool" (Isa. 1:18).

10 Inheritance

Inheritance is given only to those who have been qualified by Christ to be in God's will: "You are his heirs, and God's promise to Abraham belongs to you" (Gal. 3:29 NLT). With biblical inheritance, either you're a saint, or you ain't in the will.

11 Mystery

In the New Testament, *mystery* refers to a secret that is revealed by God to His servants through His Spirit. As such, it is an "open secret." Most of the occurrences of the word *mystery* are in Paul's letters and refer to the revelation of God's plan of salvation as that plan focuses in Christ.

· · ● · ·

I (Lenya) am a mystery buff, and I'm crazy about Sherlock Holmes books, movies, and trivia. I guess the attraction lies in trying to detect all the clues Holmes considered so obvious. As he would say to his sidekick, "It's elementary, my dear Watson." Because I love mysteries, I'm intrigued by the clues God has given us about the great mystery of His will. I've become a detective in the Word of God, where I find solutions to the mysteries of the universe.

Today's lesson has unlocked some of the mysteries found in God's Word: God's plan for redemption through Christ, His mysterious timetable for the gathering of His people into one, and His rich spiritual inheritance to all believers. These are significant discoveries for all Christians. But the greatest mystery to ponder is not *what* Christ has done but *why*. Why would Jesus pay for the penalty of my sin with His precious blood? Because "Jesus loves me, this I know." It's elementary, my dear.

LISTEN TO ...

The dying Jesus is the evidence of God's anger toward sin; but the living Jesus is the proof of God's love and forgiveness.

—*Lorenz Eifert*

DAY 5

The Guarantor

Do-it-yourself home-improvement projects are dangerous, especially if you're a novice like me. One day I (Lenya) decided to change the light fixtures in my bedroom. Without thinking, I grabbed the red and black wires at the same time. *Zap!* Not only did I get a free perm, but the breaker switch blew, and I was left standing in the dark. Since then I've become savvy about the concept of electric currents. Next time I'll tap into electrical currents with a proper conductor instead of my own two hands.

I found out the hard way that electricity needs a conduit, a safe channel to transmit the currents. God has made His incredible, electrifying power available to us. However, if we attempt to tap into that source without a conduit, we might get burned out. We need the Holy Spirit, our heavenly conductor, to ensure safe access into God's power source. The Holy Spirit is mentioned many times in this letter because He is the one who guarantees that our riches are channeled to us from the Father through the Son.

LIFT UP ...

God, thank You for sending the Holy Spirit to dwell in my heart as a guarantee that I belong to You. I eagerly await the day when You come to make me Your bride. In Jesus' name. Amen.

LOOK AT ...

As we complete this week's lesson, we turn our attention to the third person of the Trinity—the Holy Spirit, our guarantor of God's inheritance.

READ EPHESIANS 1:13–14.

In Him you also trusted, after you heard the word of truth, the gospel of your salvation; in whom also, having believed, you were sealed with the Holy Spirit of promise, who is the

guarantee of our inheritance until the redemption of the purchased possession, to the praise of His glory. Ephesians 1:13–14

LEARN ABOUT ...

I Trust

The biblical meaning of trusting God is that we have confidence and are fully persuaded in God. You may sometimes feel as if you're on shaky ground, but in fact, you stand on a firm foundation: "He alone is my rock and my salvation, my fortress where I will never be shaken" (Ps. 62:2 NLT).

3 Sealed

In the ancient East, a seal was an imprint pressed into wax. Like a brand, a seal indicated ownership and also was used to complete legal transactions. Being sealed with the Holy Spirit means that God has completed a transaction with us—He has placed His imprint upon us.

6 Praise

In a world that idolizes celebrities, it's easy to praise people who are unworthy of our devotion. Don't get caught up in a counterfeit religious experience—instead, praise God!

1. Verse 13 offers four steps in the process of salvation: You heard, trusted, believed, and were sealed. Describe your experience of one of these four steps.

2. Have you taken all of those steps in your faith journey? If not, and if you are ready, take the time now to walk through them with God in prayer.

3. Paul revealed that we are sealed with the Holy Spirit. Fill in the chart to discover more of what this means.

SCRIPTURE	HOW YOU ARE SEALED
John 14:16–17	
Romans 8:9	
1 Corinthians 6:19–20	

4. According to verse 14, what does the Holy Spirit guarantee for us?

5. What is the purpose of redemption?

6. How does Isaiah 43:21 confirm our purpose?

LIVE OUT ...

7. Look up Revelation 4:10–11. We read that those who stand before God's throne in heaven will cast their crowns before Him and worship.

Why is God worthy of praise? Think about any good or praiseworthy things in your own life—your "crowns"—and journal a prayer, casting those things down before God in worship.

8. Today we learned that the Holy Spirit lives in—indwells—believers. In which of the following ways do the outside actions of your life reveal what has taken place on the inside?

___ Daily prayer   ___ Reaching out to unbelievers

___ Regular church attendance   ___ Responding in love

___ Changed lifestyle   ___ Spending time in God's Word

9. We saw that to trust means to have full confidence in something or someone. Name three people you trust, and describe why.

10. Journal about a time when someone betrayed your trust. Did that misplaced trust in people damage or increase your trust in God? How?

11. What other areas in your life are causing you to doubt God today? Rewrite this prayer for your situation: "I do believe, but help me overcome my unbelief!" (Mark 9:24 NLT).

LEARN ABOUT ...

8 Indwelling

To have the Holy Spirit dwelling in you is an honor. Before Jesus' birth, the Holy Spirit visited only a few select people: prophets, priests, and kings. But Jesus opened the way for the Holy Spirit to dwell within all believers: "For He dwells with you and will be in you" (John 14:17).

9 Trustworthy

Put your trust only in someone who is trustworthy. *Webster's Dictionary* says that trust is an "assured reliance on the character, ability, strength, or truth of someone or something." Human beings are corrupt; God is incorruptible. People are weak; God is omnipotent. The psalmist tells us, "It is better to take refuge in the LORD than to trust in people" (Ps. 118:8 NLT).

∘ ∘ ● ∘ ∘

Have people ever told you they loved you, but their actions betrayed their words? When I (Lenya) was in seventh grade, I thought a boy loved me. The notes he passed to me in math class said so. In reply, my notes were always "sealed with a kiss." But one day my boyfriend saw me being silly with my friends, got embarrassed, and dumped me! When I grew up, I met Skip Heitzig. He also told me he loved me, but he showed me how much by sealing his love with a ring. That ring became my guarantee that Skip would do what he said. It represented the promise that one day Skip would take me as his bride.

Jesus loved you so much that when He made you His own, He put His "seal of approval" on your life. That seal is the Holy Spirit, who is your guarantee that God will do what He has promised. He is completely trustworthy. Paul said that when you believed, "you were sealed with the Holy Spirit of promise" (Eph. 1:13). The Holy Spirit's indwelling in your life is your engagement ring. God intends to marry you, His bride, at the marriage supper of the Lamb. God's love letter, the Bible, is better than any romance novel, and He made certain it was "sealed with a kiss."

LISTEN TO ...

Trustfulness is based on confidence in God, whose ways I do not understand. If I did, there would be no need for trust.

—*Oswald Chambers*

LESSON TWO

Secret Treasure

Ephesians 1:15–23

Growing up, I (Lenya) was enthralled with the book *Treasure Island.*

A poor boy named Jim Hawkins had no idea that the oilskin packet left by the dead pirate, Billy Bones, was indeed a map. But when Jim enlisted as cabin boy with Long John Silver on the *Hispaniola,* the eyes of his understanding were opened. He discovered that the oilskin map charted a path leading to secret treasure. On his adventure he would become rich beyond his wildest dreams.

As an adult, I read J. Wilbur Chapman's real-life story of another boy turned beneficiary. For over a year the young man was homeless, begging at the city train depot. One day he called out to a passerby, "Hey, mister, can you spare a dime?" When the person turned around, the young man was shocked to discover it was his own dad. "Father, do you recognize me?" he asked. Throwing his arms around his son, the father said, "At last I've found you! You want a dime? All I have is yours."[1] A homeless son begged his father for spare change, when for years his dad had been looking to give him everything he had.

The apostle Paul wanted Christians who are spiritually poor to know that their heavenly Father is searching for them to give them the key to His secret treasures. Too often believers lack knowledge of the riches God offers. What about you? Are you missing out on hidden treasure? God has left you a map that will chart a path to the adventure of a lifetime and open your eyes to "the riches of the glory of His inheritance."

Day 1: Ephesians 1:15–16	PAUL PRAYS
Day 2: Ephesians 1:17–18a	PRAYER FOR KNOWLEDGE
Day 3: Ephesians 1:18b	PRAYER FOR HOPE
Day 4: Ephesians 1:19–20	PRAYER FOR POWER
Day 5: Ephesians 1:20–23	PRAYER FOR POSITION

DAY 1

Paul Prays

LIFT UP ...

Lord, I believe You have spiritual treasures for me. Grant me the faith to see them and use them for Your glory. In Jesus' name. Amen.

LOOK AT ...

This week we gain insight into Paul's prayer life by exploring the first of two prayers written for the believers in Ephesus. As you study, ask God to teach you how to be a person of prayer.

READ EPHESIANS 1:15–16.

Therefore I also, after I heard of your faith in the Lord Jesus and your love for all the saints, do not cease to give thanks for you, making mention of you in my prayers ... Ephesians 1:15–16

1. What two things had Paul heard about the Ephesians?

2. Who was the object of the Ephesians' faith? Of their love?

LEARN ABOUT ...

I Reputation

The Ephesians had a reputation; Paul had heard about them. Be careful how you live—people will hear about you, too.

4 Persistence

To pray constantly does not mean we are to literally keep up an incessant verbal dialogue (they have places for people who do that, and the doors lock from the outside!). The idea here is persistent prayer rather than constant prayer—keep at it continually.

5 Heart Prayers

Many of us have the mistaken notion that if we ask God to do something, then He is obligated to respond. However, God listens to our hearts over the din of our words! A heart out of sync with God's Word speaks louder than the requests of a disobedient believer.

3. What does this teach you about your responsibility as a believer?

4. What did Paul persistently do?

5. We see in verse 16 that one requirement for an effective prayer life is giving thanks. Fill in the following chart to learn other keys to an effective prayer life.

SCRIPTURE	KEYS TO EFFECTIVE PRAYER
Psalm 66:18–19	
Matthew 21:22	
Mark 11:25	
John 14:13	
1 John 5:14	
Jude 20	

LIVE OUT ...

6. Today we learned that the Ephesians had a reputation of being faithful and loving. Lesson 1 taught us that before Saul was converted, he was vengeful and vindictive. After his conversion Paul became known for his love for the Lord. Using an acrostic format, fill in the blanks describing your reputation *before* and *after* you met Christ.

B (Example: bad temper)   A (Example: amiable)
E   F
F   T
O   E
R   R
E

7. Today we discovered the keys to an effective prayer life. Which attitudes below have hindered your prayer life at times?

____ There's a sin I'm not willing to surrender to God.

____ I haven't believed God and taken Him at His word.

____ I have been praying "my will be done."

____ I haven't forgiven others for trespasses against me.

____ I trust too much in myself, not Christ.

____ Other _____.

8. It's not enough just to check a box—we must also check our hearts. Journal a prayer of repentance for these destructive patterns in your life based on the definition of repentance provided in the sidebar.

b. As you give thanks to God for these people, write down the good things you know and have heard about them. Ask God to increase their faith.

○ ○ ● ○ ○

LEARN ABOUT …

7 Hindered Prayer

God has selective hearing. He won't tune in to a prayer distorted by disobedience. "The LORD's … ear [is not] too deaf to hear you call. It's your sins that have cut you off from God. Because of your sins, he … will not listen anymore" (Isa. 59:1–2 NLT).

8 Repentance

True repentance is a "godly sorrow" for sin, an act of turning around and going in the opposite direction. This type of repentance leads to a fundamental change in a person's relationship to God.

A mother once asked her son after the first day of school, "Did you learn anything today?" "No," he replied in disgust. "I have to go back tomorrow." With prayer, as in life, don't be discouraged if God doesn't answer your prayers immediately or in the way you expect. Remember that Paul prayed without ceasing—he kept going back to God. Jesus also prayed persistently and consistently. In Matthew we learn that "he went to pray a third time, saying the same things again" (Matt. 26:44 NLT). Prayer, like school, is a discipline that takes more than one day's attendance.

LISTEN TO ...

Keep praying, but be thankful that God's answers are wiser than your prayers!

—*William Culbertson*

Prayer for Knowledge

Knowledge is fleeting and is constantly changing. It has been estimated that the accumulated knowledge from the beginning of recorded history to the year 1845 could be represented by one inch, further accumulated knowledge from 1845 until 1945 would amount to three inches, and what we have learned from 1945 until 1975 would represent the height of the Washington Monument. Since 1975, that total knowledge has doubled! Who can keep up with such rapidly growing knowledge?

However, when it comes to biblical knowledge, it's not *what* you know but *Who* you know. Unlike the wisdom of the world, the knowledge of the Holy One never changes. He is the same yesterday, today, and forever. The knowledge of God is the only source of true wisdom: "The fear of the LORD is the beginning of wisdom, and the knowledge of the Holy One is understanding" (Prov. 9:10).

LIFT UP ...

Lord, my heart's desire is to know You intimately. Don't let me settle for just knowing about You. Take the knowledge out of my head and place it deep within my heart. In Jesus' name. Amen.

LOOK AT ...

We've seen that Paul was a man of prayer who prayed for the believers in Ephesus. Today let's examine Paul's prayer for believers to discover the kind of knowledge God wants us to have.

LEARN ABOUT ...

1 The Son

Although Jesus is equal with God, when He came to earth, "he gave up his divine privileges; he took the humble position of a slave and was born as a human being" (Phil. 2:7 NLT). Throughout His earthly life Jesus gladly submitted Himself to God the Father.

3 Wisdom

Wisdom is the ability to judge rightly and follow the best course of action based on knowledge and understanding. There is a difference between wisdom and knowledge. Wisdom is what you do with what you know.

4 Knowledge

Knowledge is the truth or facts that a person gains through experience or thought. The greatest truth that a person can possess is truth about God. God doesn't want us to merely know about Him in our heads. He wants us to know Him personally in our hearts.

6 The Spirit

"Without the present illumination of the Holy Spirit, the Word of God must remain a dead letter to every man.... It is just as essential for the Holy Spirit to reveal the truth of Scripture to the reader today as it was necessary for him to inspire the writers of it in their day."—William Law

---

READ EPHESIANS 1:17–18A.

... that the God of our Lord Jesus Christ, the Father of glory, may give to you the spirit of wisdom and revelation in the knowledge of Him, the eyes of your understanding being enlightened ... Ephesians 1:17–18a

1. What does the phrase *the God of our Lord Jesus Christ* teach you about the relationship between Father and Son?

2. What more do we learn of God's character in verse 17?

3. What are the first two things Paul prayed for God to give believers?

4. Describe the specific type of knowledge Paul prayed the Ephesians would receive.

5. What does it mean to have "the eyes of your understanding ... enlightened"?

6. Fill in the chart to discover the sources of true spiritual enlightenment.

SCRIPTURE	SOURCE OF SPIRITUAL ENLIGHTENMENT
Psalm 18:28	
Psalm 119:105	
Proverbs 6:23	
Matthew 5:16	
John 8:12	
John 16:13–14	

LIVE OUT ...

7. Read Matthew 5:16. Once we have received God's light, what is our responsibility toward others?

Journal about ways you are letting your light shine before others.

8. Jesus told His disciples not to hide the lamp of their faith under a basket but to let it shine for all to see. In the appropriate columns, place the following items that help your faith burn bright or can cause your faith to burn out: Bible study, watching TV, witnessing, shopping, prayer, humility, arguments, powerful teaching, busy schedule, fellowship, seeking God's kingdom, envy, self-pity, sacrifice, pride, love, lust, anger.

BURN BRIGHT   **BURN OUT**

LEARN ABOUT ...

7 Light Attracts

Light has a socializing effect—others are attracted to it like a moth to the flame. Well-lit places attract a crowd. Remember the movie *Field of Dreams?* The key message was, "If you build it, they will come!" When we turn on the light of God's love, others will come!

---

11 Revelation

Revelation is God's communication to people concerning Himself, His moral standards, and His plan of salvation. People, on their own, can never create truth about God. God has graciously unveiled and manifested Himself to humanity.

9. List some people who need the light of God's love and power. Commit to pray for these people.

10. Journal a prayer asking God to say to their hearts, "Let there be light" (Gen. 1:3).

11. We have learned that God desires us to have knowledge, wisdom, and revelation that will lead to a personal relationship with Him. With this in mind, work through the steps below:

Step One—Knowledge: Describe the things you knew about God in your head before you asked Him into your heart.

Step Two—Wisdom: Once God came to live in your heart, describe how He gave you the wisdom to live your life differently.

Step Three—Revelation: Describe what God has revealed to you recently that you never understood about Him before.

○ ○ ● ○ ○

We've seen that when it comes to spiritual knowledge, it's not *what* you know but *Who* you know. I (Lenya) experienced the value of knowledge that is up close and personal during the 1996 World Series between the Atlanta Braves and the New York Yankees. A pitcher for the Yankees, John Wetteland, is a close friend and gave my son and me tickets to attend a game in Atlanta. Because we knew John, his name was the key to untold opportunity wherever we went. It unlocked a hotel room in a city that was overbooked. It gained us entrance to the Yankee locker room. It even provided seats on the team bus right next to Reggie Jackson! My son, Nathan, and I kept pinching ourselves to make sure the whole experience wasn't a dream. But it was—a dream come true.

What personally knowing John Wetteland did for us in Atlanta, intimately knowing God does for a Christian in this life—it opens the entrance to eternity; it reserves a seat in heaven; and it unlocks the treasure house of God's wisdom.

LISTEN TO ...

Wisdom is the combination of honesty and knowledge applied through experience.

—*Denis Waitley*

DAY 3
Prayer for Hope

Life seemed hopeless in 1986. I (Penny) was a young wife and mother whose life was bleak. My husband's work was his mistress, my daughter was colicky, and we were mired in an ugly lawsuit. My plans to live the American Dream seemed like a nightmare. One day my mother came to my house, told me to get dressed, and drove me to a women's Bible study. She said, "You need this."

Mother knew best. My backslidden soul was thirsty for God. I soon rededicated my life to Jesus. For the first time in years I had hope. My circumstances didn't change, but my heart did. I clung to God's promise: "I know the plans I have for you ... plans to give you hope and a future" (Jer. 29:11 NIV). I developed a confident expectancy that things would work out God's way. I learned to trust His way as the best way. Things didn't turn out as I planned, but they worked out better than I hoped or dreamed. Though we lost the lawsuit, God used it to bring my husband into His kingdom and to turn us into a family of faith. Hope springs from the Eternal One.

LIFT UP ...

Lord, help me to realize that my hope is in You and is therefore unshakable. Send Your Spirit to fill my heart with hope like this. In Jesus' name. Amen.

LOOK AT ...

This week we have examined the reasons Paul prayed for his friends and one of the requests he made—that by knowing God they would become spiritually enlightened. In today's lesson, we explore two more aspects of Paul's prayer.

LEARN ABOUT ...

I Hope

Hope is confident expectancy. In the Bible, hope stands for both the act of hoping and the thing hoped for. Hope does not arise from the individual's desires or wishes but from God, who is Himself the believer's hope: "My only hope is in you" (Ps. 39:7 NLT).

---

4 Eternal Riches

God offers riches untold to those who believe. Yet often we think He is speaking of earthly treasures that will rust, rot, or be stolen. God's spiritual treasures can never be taken away from you. God promises eternal riches; make certain you don't settle for money.

READ EPHESIANS 1:18B.

... that you may know what is the hope of His calling, what are the riches of the glory of His inheritance in the saints ... Ephesians 1:18b

1. What is the first thing Paul prays the Ephesians will know?

2. In verse 18, Paul linked hope with the concept of God's "calling." In other words, he was praying for people to respond to God's call. Let's examine this concept. According to Matthew 9:13 ...

   a. Whom does Jesus call?

   b. To what does He call them?

3. Name the second request Paul prayed for the believers in Ephesians 1:18.

4. In whom is this glorious inheritance found?

5. Read Matthew 6:19–21.

   a. What two types of treasure does Jesus describe in this passage?

   b. What happens to the treasure in each of these places?

   c. Summarize in your own words the message of Matthew 6:21.

LIVE OUT ...

6. Fill in the chart to discover the different ways Christ called His disciples.

SCRIPTURE	WHOM HE CALLED	THEIR RESPONSE
Matthew 4:18–20		
Mark 10:17–22		
Luke 19:1–8		

LEARN ABOUT ...

6 Response

The call of God involves two important elements: (1) God calling us to follow Him and (2) our response. Many people hear Jesus calling but don't answer affirmatively. Sadly, they will discover that saying no means they're not one of His chosen few.

7 The Cost

To follow Jesus you must count the cost. For Simon and Andrew, it cost their careers. For the rich young ruler the cost was his cash, but his riches weighed him down. For Zacchaeus the cost was his business conduct. Jesus said, "You cannot become my disciple without giving up everything" (Luke 14:33 NLT).

7. Examine your heart. Have you heard Jesus' call to follow Him and answered it? If you have not, take some time to pray and listen for it now in your heart.

Journal a prayer in answer to the Lord's call.

8. People who live without Christ often place their hope in things that will ultimately leave them hopeless. Some people live in lust but end up lonely. Some hope in wealth but find themselves weeping.

Journal about some of the things you placed your hope in before you became a follower of Christ. How did those things leave you hopeless?

9. Rewrite the following verse into a personal prayer of hope in God: "I pray that God, the source of hope, will fill you completely with joy and peace because you trust in him. Then you will overflow with confident hope through the power of the Holy Spirit" (Rom. 15:13 NLT).

10. a. Today's lesson has helped us discover the spiritual treasures God offers. Have you personally experienced these riches? Check the boxes that indicate the riches you currently enjoy.

___ Riches of His grace (Eph. 1:7)

___ Riches of His goodness (Rom. 2:4)

___ Riches of the wisdom and knowledge of God (Rom. 11:33)

___ All my needs according to His riches in glory (Phil. 4:19)

b. If you have not received the riches that God so freely gives, journal a prayer of acceptance to receive your spiritual inheritance from God.

○ ○ ● ○ ○

Did you know that Jesus is a treasure seeker? He said, "The kingdom of heaven is like a merchant seeking beautiful pearls, who, when he had found one pearl of great price, went and sold all that he had and bought it" (Matt. 13:45–46). The church of Christ—you and I and all the saints—is the precious pearl for whom Christ gave His all. We are His inheritance (Eph. 1:18).

Pearls are the product of pain; an oyster that hasn't been hurt does not grow a pearl. When the shell of an oyster is pierced, a foreign substance—usually sand—gets inside. When this happens, the oyster's cells cover the grain of sand with layer after layer of nacre in order to protect the soft body of the oyster. The result is a beautiful pearl.

Not only is Jesus a treasure seeker, but He is also a treasure maker! He wants to transform our pain into pearls. When the grains of sand invade your life, let the soothing nacre of Christ's riches—His wisdom, His goodness, His grace, and His mercy—turn your troubles into treasures.

LISTEN TO ...

Hope means expectancy when things are otherwise hopeless.

—*G. K. Chesterton*

DAY 4

Prayer for Power

Think about the greatest manifestation of power you could witness. Perhaps a hurricane or tornado came to mind, or maybe an earthquake or an atomic bomb. I (Lenya) read about something more powerful than any of these. On May 18, 1980, there was an incredible explosion, estimated at five hundred times the force of the atomic bomb that destroyed Hiroshima. The blast ripped 1,200 feet off the top of a 9,700-foot volcano named Mount Saint Helens. Within one minute a cloud of ash blocked out the sun. *Sports Illustrated* reported that the "heat, blast and ash destroyed 26 lakes, 154 miles of resident trout streams and 195 square acres of wildlife habitat."[2]

That display of raw power is impressive. However, the Bible tells us that the presence of our God could make not only Mount Saint Helens crumble but also all the mountains known on earth. The psalmist wrote, "The mountains melt like wax before the LORD, before the Lord of all the earth" (Ps. 97:5 NLT). God is an awesome and *powerful* God, Creator of both heaven and earth. Ephesians teaches us that the greatest manifestation of God's power was not for destruction but for the resurrection of Christ from the dead!

LIFT UP ...

Thank You, Lord, that Your resurrection power is greater than any power I will ever know. Resurrect my heart with the power to follow You. In Jesus' name. Amen.

LOOK AT ...

We have seen how Paul prayed for believers to experience spiritual enlightenment, hope, and spiritual riches. Now we examine another element of his prayer about knowing God.

LEARN ABOUT ...

1 God's Power

It is important to remember that it is God's power that is given and not your own. There is danger in trusting in the power of self. On the contrary, God told Paul, "My power works best in weakness" (2 Cor. 12:9 NLT).

3 Power Equips

God's power equips you to use God's wealth. It is impossible to tap into God's riches without His power enabling us. Peter linked knowledge and power, saying, "His divine power has given to us all things that pertain to life and godliness, through the knowledge of Him" (2 Peter 1:3).

6 Jesus Is Life

There is no life apart from the Son of God. A saying goes: "No Jesus? No resurrection. Know Jesus? Know resurrection." Come to know Jesus, and let real life begin! "The Word gave life to everything that was created, and his life brought light to everyone" (John 1:4 NLT).

READ EPHESIANS 1:19–20.

... and what is the exceeding greatness of His power toward us who believe, according to the working of His mighty power which He worked in Christ when He raised Him from the dead. Ephesians 1:19–20

1. Continuing his prayer, what more did Paul pray the Ephesians would come to know?

2. Who is given "the exceeding greatness of His power"?

3. What word did Paul use to describe God's power? Why is this important?

4. What visible evidence of God's power did Paul point out?

5. Read John 11:43–44. How did Jesus manifest this divine power during His earthly ministry?

6. Read John 11:25–26.

   a. How does Jesus describe Himself?

   b. What does He promise those who believe in Him?

LIVE OUT ...

7. The hope of mankind is the resurrection of Jesus from the dead. He conquered death and gives resurrection life to all who believe in Him. Therefore, Paul told the Corinthians, "O death, where is your victory? O death, where is your sting?" (1 Cor. 15:55 NLT).

Journal about the loss of a Christian you have known. From what you've learned today, was death defeat or victory for your loved one?

LEARN ABOUT ...

7 Physical Resurrection

Before resurrection there must be a death. Jesus died literally and was resurrected. All Christians live in the hope of a literal resurrection too: "Since we believe that Jesus died and was raised to life again, we also believe that when Jesus returns, God will bring back with him the believers who have died" (1 Thess. 4:14 NLT).

8. When you die (or Christ returns), you will be reunited with those you love. How does this knowledge give you hope?

9. Believers can experience death and resurrection spiritually. Baptism represents death of the old nature and resurrection to a new spiritual life: "You were buried with Christ when you were baptized. And with him you were raised to new life because you trusted the mighty power of God, who raised Christ from the dead" (Col. 2:12 NLT). Which areas of your old life have you kept out of the water?

____ My will, wanting my own way.

____ My heart, seeking its own passions rather than God's.

____ My eyes, viewing things that are not edifying.

____ My hands, touching things I shouldn't.

____ My mouth, uttering words that displease God.

____ My thoughts, letting my mind wander.

10. This week, plan a funeral service for your old life. Write down a list of the things that you want to put to death, and then bury the list in your backyard. Don't be tempted to go back later and dig in the dirt!

11 New Clothes

Now that you've buried the old nature, it's time to take off your grave clothes and put on the garment of praise. God wants to update your wardrobe: "He will give a crown of beauty for ashes, a joyous blessing instead of mourning, festive praise instead of despair" (Isa. 61:3 NLT).

11. According to Romans 8:11, how can you experience the resurrection power of God in this present life?

Celebrate new life in the Spirit by writing out a psalm or prayer of praise to the Lord.

○ ○ ● ○ ○

The natives of the Fiji Islands have a hopeless custom known as "calling to the dead." The one who has suffered the death of a loved one climbs to a high tree or cliff. He mentions the name of the deceased, then cries out desperately, "Come back! Come back!" The eerie echo of grief fills the air. Those who have suffered the loss of their soul mate, companion, or beloved child can sympathize deeply.

The Christian does not need to climb to the top of a cliff, because Jesus climbed the hill of Calvary. You don't have to cry out, "Come back!" from a high tree, because Jesus cried out, "Father, forgive them," from a wooden cross. The resurrection power of Christ over death and hell brings a Christian hope in this life and the life to come.

LISTEN TO ...

Death to the Christian is the funeral of all his sorrows and evils, and the resurrection, of all his joys.

—*James H. Aughey*

DAY 5

Prayer for Position

There have been some powerful people throughout history: Napoleon, Alexander the Great, Caesar Augustus. But Jesus' power and dominion exceeds them *all*. God has seated Him "far above ... every name that is named, not only in this age but also in that which is to come" (Eph. 1:21).

Even one of the most powerful rulers in the nineteenth century understood Christ's sovereignty. The story is told that during Queen Victoria's reign in England, she once attended a performance of Handel's *Messiah*. Traditionally during the singing of the "Hallelujah Chorus," the audience would stand. However, Queen Victoria had been instructed not to behave like a commoner and to remain seated. As the choir reached the refrain, "Hallelujah! For the Lord God omnipotent reigneth," she could barely keep her seat. When the song reached its pinnacle, proclaiming Jesus as King of Kings, she rose to her feet despite protocol and humbly lowered her head in reverence to the One above every other name ... including her own!

Lift Up ...

Jesus, I humbly bow before You, my King of Kings and Lord of Lords. With my mouth I will glorify Your holy name. In Jesus' name. Amen.

Look At ...

Paul prayed for believers to experience the many blessings of Christ in their lives. He ended his prayer focusing on the One who is in the position to provide these treasures: Jesus Christ.

LEARN ABOUT ...

2 Over All

Principalities, powers, and dominions are terms used to describe the ranking of fallen angels. The power of Christ in the believer's life can't be defeated because it's greater than the hosts of Satan: "Greater is he that is in you, than he that is in the world" (1 John 4:4 KJV).

---

5 Head

The word *head* denotes a position of ultimate authority. It is a lovely thing to willingly pour out your life in submission to your loving head, Jesus. "A woman came in with a beautiful alabaster jar of expensive perfume made from essence of nard. She broke open the jar and poured the perfume over his head" (Mark 14:3 NLT).

READ EPHESIANS 1:20–23.

... and seated Him at His right hand in the heavenly places, far above all principality and power and might and dominion, and every name that is named, not only in this age but also in that which is to come. And He put all things under His feet, and gave Him to be head over all things to the church, which is His body, the fullness of Him who fills all in all. Ephesians 1:20–23

1. Where is Jesus seated now?

2. Over what is Christ exalted? How would you explain this in your own words?

3. How long will Christ reign supreme?

4. What is under Jesus' feet?

5. Over what is Jesus the head?

6. What word picture did Paul use to describe the church? Why do you think this word is appropriate?

7. Read further about the body of Christ in 1 Corinthians 12:12–27.

    a. How did the church become one body (v. 13)?

    b. Who ordains how each part of the body is to serve (v. 18)?

    c. How should the members of Christ's body treat one another (vv. 25–26)?

8. What final image of Jesus are we given in verse 27?

Live Out ...

9. Throughout the New Testament we are encouraged to care for one another because we are all members of one body. Which things below are you doing for other members of Christ's body, the church?

____ "Be kindly affectionate to one another" (Rom. 12:10).

____ "Be of the same mind toward one another" (Rom. 12:16).

____ "Through love serve one another" (Gal. 5:13).

____ "Forgiv[e] one another" (Eph. 4:32).

____ "[Submit] to one another in the fear of God" (Eph. 5:21).

____ "Comfort one another" (1 Thess. 4:18).

____ "Be hospitable to one another" (1 Peter 4:9).

____ "Above all things have fervent love for one another" (1 Peter 4:8).

10. Name a Christian whom you can serve with your gifts. Write down a "one another" action or attitude from the list above that you will perform for that person this week.

11. Journal a prayer asking Jesus to make you a servant by rewriting the following verse into a personal prayer: "Whoever wants to be a

Learn About ...

8 All in All

Jesus is the truth, the whole truth, and nothing but the truth! John tells us that Jesus was full of the truth. When you're completely filled with something, there's no room for anything else. "The Word became flesh and dwelt among us ... full of grace and truth" (John 1:14).

9 Serving

In God's economy, you get two for the price of one—when you do something for one of God's children, you have also served Jesus: "I tell you the truth, when you did it to one of the least of these my brothers and sisters, you were doing it to me!" (Matt. 25:40 NLT).

leader among you must be your servant, and whoever wants to be first among you must become your slave. For even the Son of Man came not to be served but to serve others and to give his life as a ransom for many" (Matt. 20:26–28 NLT).

12. a. Draw a picture of a person in some blank space in this workbook. (Stick men, cartoon characters, or works of art are all appropriate.) Label the parts of the body from head to toe. Beside each body part write the name of a church member who fulfills that role. (Example: Jesus is the head, your pastor is the mouth, etc.)

b. Perhaps you don't know yet how God has called you to serve in His body, the church. Journal a prayer asking Him to reveal this to you.

○ ○ ● ○ ○

Inspector Clouseau, the bumbling detective of the Pink Panther movies, was a master of disguise. At different times he transformed himself into the Hunchback of Notre Dame with an inflatable hump, a salty sea dog with a wooden peg leg, and a mafioso godfather with cotton balls stuffed in his cheeks.

When he was impersonating a godfather, someone asked Clouseau, "Hey! Where's your bodyguard?" He mumbled, "I don't need a bodyguard. I take care of my body, my body takes care of me."[3] Funny words, but good advice for the members of the body of Christ. A dysfunctional body becomes lopsided when one member takes more than its fair share, selfishly pursuing "What's in it for me?" All parts of a healthy body work together, sharing the load, asking, "What can I do for you?" You don't have to be a detective to figure it out: Take care of Christ's body, the church, and His body will take care of you.

LISTEN TO ...

A Christian church is a body or collection of persons, voluntarily associated together, professing to believe what Christ teaches, to do what Christ enjoins, to imitate his example, cherish his Spirit, and make known his gospel to others.

—R. E. Sample

LESSON THREE

The Greatest Gift
Ephesians 2:1–10

Divorce shattered my family when I (Lenya) was eight years old. The first Christmas without my father being home to string up the lights was dark. We hung our stockings and left out sugar cookies as usual for Santa's late-night arrival. But on the night before Christmas all through my house, the only creature I longed to see stirring was my dad, not a mouse.

The next day we went to my uncle's home for Christmas dinner with all the trimmings. We arrived dressed up in our Sunday best, toting the toys we'd found under our tree. During dinner we heard a knock at the door, and in walked the skinniest Santa I'd ever seen. He said, "Sit on my lap and tell me what you want for Christmas." I thought, *Santa can't give what I really want—my father's presence.* As I climbed onto Santa's lap, his eyes twinkled as he pulled off his white beard. Underneath the disguise I discovered the loving face of my dad! My father's presence was the best present he's ever given me.

In this week's lesson, Ephesians describes how God gave the world the gift of His presence—in a baby wrapped in swaddling cloths and laid in a manger. God understood how empty and alone we were, so He visited our dark world, lighting our lives with His presence. He gave us the greatest possible gift—Himself!

Day 1: Ephesians 2:1–3   **THE LIVING DEAD**

Day 2: Ephesians 2:4–5   **THE DEAD WHO LIVE**

Day 3: Ephesians 2:6–7   **THE GOD WHO GIVES**

Day 4: Ephesians 2:8–9   **THE GREATEST GIFT**

Day 5: Ephesians 2:10   **THE GIFT THAT KEEPS ON GIVING**

DAY I
The Living Dead

LIFT UP ...

Heavenly Father, thank You for Your good gifts. They make Your love real to my heart. Thank You for Your greatest gift—Jesus. His presence fills my empty world. In Jesus' name. Amen.

LOOK AT ...

Paul moved on to discuss our lives before we came to know Christ. It is good to remember where we have come from so we can truly appreciate God's marvelous gift of grace.

READ EPHESIANS 2:1–3.

And you He made alive, who were dead in trespasses and sins, in which you once walked according to the course of this world, according to the prince of the power of the air, the spirit who now works in the sons of disobedience, among whom also we all once conducted ourselves in the lusts of our flesh, fulfilling the desires of the flesh and of the mind, and were by nature children of wrath, just as the others. Ephesians 2:1–3

LEARN ABOUT ...

1 Dead

Paul did not describe unbelievers as "sick," "searching," or "misguided." Instead, he said they are dead. Life without God is a death sentence, not only in the afterlife but also in this earthly life.

4 Satan's Power

Our children are taught to be environmentally conscious—beware of air pollution. In a spiritual sense Satan, the prince of the power of the air, has influenced our culture and media for evil—so beware of mind pollution.

5 Sinful Flesh

Paul said that in his flesh there was "nothing good." Too often society tries to rehabilitate the sinful flesh with self-help programs. That's about as effective as giving a pig a bath. In Scripture, there is one edict for the flesh—death! Only then can new life begin.

7 The World

This term denotes "the fleeting character of life's riches and pleasures and the folly of making them of central importance in life." "And what do you benefit if you gain the whole world but lose your own soul? Is anything worth more than your soul?'" (Matt. 16:26 NLT).

1. What words did Paul use to describe the unbeliever's spiritual condition? What do you think he meant?

2. What is the cause of this spiritual death?

3. Name the two influences under which believers once walked.

4. Where is the prince of the power of the air at work?

5. In what ways did we all once conduct our lives, and what desires were we enticed to fulfill?

6. What, by nature, are we all? What does this mean?

LIVE OUT ...

7. a. We've been warned not to walk according to this world. Fill in the chart to discover how to avoid the world's pitfalls.

SCRIPTURE	LESSON ABOUT THE WORLD
Romans 12:2	
Galatians 6:14	
James 1:27	
1 John 2:15–17	

b. Choosing one of the Scripture passages from the chart above, journal a prayer asking God to give you victory over the influence of the world.

8. a. This passage in Ephesians has made us aware of an Enemy who works in the sons of disobedience. Fill in the chart to find out ways to avoid the Devil's path of destruction.

Learn about …

9 The Flesh

The phrase *the flesh* refers to the earthly part of us, representing our human lusts and desires. The flesh is contrary to the Spirit. Those who are in the flesh cannot please God. Christ alone is our salvation, since by the works of the law "shall no flesh be justified" (Gal. 2:16 KJV).

Scripture	Lesson About the Devil
Ephesians 4:26–27	
James 4:7	
1 Peter 5:8	
Jude 9	

b. Choosing one of the passages from the chart above, journal a prayer to God asking Him to give you victory over the influence of the Devil.

9. a. The Devil takes advantage of an area of weakness in all of us— our flesh. Fill in the chart below to discover how to gain victory in this area.

Scripture	Lesson About the Flesh
Matthew 26:41	
Romans 8:5	
Romans 13:14	
Galatians 5:16	

b. Choosing one of the passages from the chart above, journal a prayer to God, asking Him to give you victory over the influence of the flesh.

○ ○ ● ○ ○

When I (Lenya) was in grade school, my friend Julie and I walked to the neighborhood market to peek at the candy aisle. Our pockets were empty, but our eyes were filled with the enticing confections on the shelves. Out of nowhere came this devious thought, *I can slip that piece of candy into my pocket. No one will ever know.* My fingers began to twitch. My flesh wanted that candy. My mind had figured out a way to get it. But my heart knew it was wrong. Mom had told me that stealing was wrong. The decisive moment came when Julie dared me to take a piece. I grabbed the candy and bolted from the store, followed closely behind by the sales clerk. Busted! I learned my lesson the hard way.

I wish I could say that I have outgrown the temptation to do things that are wrong, but I can't. The world and my flesh still dare me to follow a voice that is not my heavenly Father's. As a believer, you are not immune to evil influences either. The world, your flesh, and the Wicked One will constantly seek to entice you. But praise God, the allure of sin that made us "children of wrath" can be overcome by the power of God. Because of Christ's sacrificial death, "he calls us his children, and that is what we are!" (1 John 3:1 NLT).

LISTEN TO ...

God clothed himself in vile man's flesh so he might be weak enough to suffer.

—John Donne

DAY 2
The Dead Who Live

The city dump caught the attention of a young black woman named Mary McLeod Bethune in 1904. Mary didn't see just a dump; she saw a way to fulfill her dream that, with God's help, she could teach illiterate black women to read and write. She shared her dream, and others came alongside her to help build a shack on that desolate place. They built desks from wooden crates and used blackberry juice for ink.

If you wander among the tall buildings, classrooms, and dormitories of Bethune-Cookman College, you will find a headstone that commemorates where Mrs. Bethune was laid to rest after her death at the age of seventy-nine. The inscription on the stone tells her story: "She has given her best so that others might live a more abundant life."

It takes a unique personality to see ruins and dream of restoration. Paul reminded believers that God saw desolate lives and was delighted to send a Deliverer to restore souls. He gave His Son so that we, who were dead, might live.

LIFT UP ...

Jesus, before I met You, my existence was lifeless and without meaning. Since You've come into my heart, I'm alive! I give You my life to live for Your kingdom and glory. In Jesus' name. Amen.

LOOK AT ...

One phrase in today's passage has made an eternal difference in the lives of many: "But God." With these two words Paul turned the attention away from sinful man and toward the powerful God.

LEARN ABOUT ...

2 Mercy

Mercy is the outward manifestation of pity; it assumes need on the part of the one who receives it and resources adequate to meet the need on the part of the one who shows it. It is used of God, who is rich in mercy, and who has provided salvation for all men.

3 Love

We read in I John 4:8 that God is love. If you looked up the word *love* in a dictionary, a picture of God should be there as a full definition. Because God is love, His love for us is picture-perfect.

5 Rescue

Jesus is our life preserver! When we were drowning in a sea of sin and shame, God planned a rescue operation. He threw out a lifeline—Jesus! "Reach down from heaven and rescue me; rescue me from deep waters, from the power of my enemies" (Ps. 144:7 NLT).

READ EPHESIANS 2:4–5.

But God, who is rich in mercy, because of His great love with which He loved us, even when we were dead in trespasses, made us alive together with Christ (by grace you have been saved) ... Ephesians 2:4–5

1. What is the first attribute of God described in this passage?

2. How much mercy is in God's bank account?

3. How is God's love described?

4. When did God show His rich mercy and great love to us? What does this tell you about Him?

5. What did God do for us "even when we were dead in trespasses"?

6. Can dead things live again? Only God can bring life out of death and hope out of despair. Fill in the chart below to discover situations where God brought new life and hope.

SCRIPTURE	NEW LIFE
1 Kings 17:17–24	
Matthew 8:14–15	
John 11:41–44	
Acts 3:2–8	

LIVE OUT ...

7. Jesus can bring life from death. Draw lines from items in one column to the corresponding items in the other column to indicate how we see life emerge from death in the world God created.

Sunset	Spring
Barren trees	Butterflies
Caterpillar	Frog
Tadpole	Crops
Seeds	Sunrise
Winter	Budding trees

8. Our God is rich in mercy, which means He has pity or compassion on those in need. Keeping this attribute in mind, prayerfully do these exercises:

   a. Write down the name of someone who is in need of God's mercy. (Example: a loved one who has made unwise financial decisions and is suffering.)

   b. Consider the present circumstances this person is in and write down the consequences that may occur. (Example: Poor financial decisions could result in bankruptcy.)

   c. Journal a prayer of mercy on the person's behalf, asking God to withhold the consequence and to show mercy instead.

9. God wants you to be merciful also. Jesus said, "Blessed are the merciful, for they shall obtain mercy" (Matt. 5:7). Sometimes you get exactly what you give. Which will you give, mercy or judgment? Prayerfully do the following exercises:

   a. Have you been harboring bitterness or resentment toward someone who has wronged you? If yes, then write down that person's name.

   b. Take the time now to ask God to cleanse you from your sin of unforgiveness. Jesus said, "Forgive us our debts, as we forgive our debtors" (Matt. 6:12). Write out a prayer asking God to give you a heart of mercy toward that person—not giving them what they deserve.

c. Decide now to call, write, or visit that person and offer him or her the mercy God has so freely given you.

○ ○ ● ○ ○

While studying this lesson, I (Lenya) drove to meet a friend for lunch. I was meditating on the truth of God's mercy and wondering who I knew that might need this. As I entered the parking lot, I eyed a space right up front. *What a blessing*, I thought. I waited patiently while my blinker kept time to the praise music on my radio. Then, out of nowhere, a woman in a Mercedes pulled up and stole my spot. "Ughhhhh!" My first thought was, *I'll roll down my window and give her a piece of my mind*. Next, I imagined myself bumping into her shiny, silver Benz, my way of saying, "Thanks for nothing!" Then that still, small voice of the Holy Spirit said, "What have you been studying about, Lenya?" I answered, "Uh … Your mercy, Lord—not giving others what they deserve."

Why does God make things so personal? He always holds me accountable to live out the things I learn. Words are cheap when they are not followed by actions. How about you? Do you practice what you preach? When you leave the quiet place of study today, make sure you take the lesson of God's mercy with you. I'm certain He'll provide the opportunity for you to share His mercy with someone who needs it—"Don't just listen to God's word. You must do what it says. Otherwise, you are only fooling yourselves" (James 1:22 NLT).

LISTEN TO …

Among the attributes of God, although they are all equal, mercy shines with even more brilliancy than justice.

—*Miguel de Cervantes*

DAY 3

The God Who Gives

Long ago, Persia was ruled by a kind shah who concealed his identity and visited the public baths as a beggar. Seeking the lowest place and worker, the shah went to a cellar where a man stoked a furnace. The shah befriended him, and the man shared his simple food and conversation. Over time the worker grew attached to this stranger who visited him. When the ruler finally revealed his true identity, he expected the worker to ask for a gift. Instead, the furnace tender said, "You left your palace and your glory to sit with me in this dark place, to eat my coarse food, and to care about what happens to me. On others you may bestow rich gifts, but to me you have given yourself."

What an illustration of what Jesus did for us! He left His throne of glory and came to our place of labor and loneliness to befriend us. That's amazing enough, but it gets even better. Jesus has invited us to sit together with Him in "the heavenly places" (Eph. 2:6). As you sit by His side, you will discover He is the God who gives.

Lift Up ...

Heavenly Father, Your kindness has touched my life and softened my heart. It is that kindness that leads me to repentance. May I reflect Your kindness to the world around me. In Jesus' name. Amen.

Look At ...

The gift of God is new life in Christ—we have been saved by grace! Today we discover that there are marvelous benefits for those in Christ.

Learn about ...

2 Heavenly Places

Some people think of heaven as a future place, "the sweet by and by." The verbs in this passage—*raised* and *made us sit*—are in the past tense because they're already a reality. For the Christian, heaven is for the present as well as the future—it's a done deal!

4 Amazing Grace

What's so amazing about grace? We don't deserve it! We're all sinners under a death sentence. But our gracious Savior pardoned us at the cross: "For everyone has sinned; we all fall short of God's glorious standard. Yet God, with undeserved kindness, declares that we are righteous ... through Christ Jesus when he freed us from the penalty for our sins" (Rom. 3:23–24 NLT).

6 In Christ

One aspect of being in Christ is that we are intimate with Him. Jesus came to earth to obtain a bride for eternity—His church. What a concept! Jesus wants to spend all of His time "together" with us.

Read Ephesians 2:6–7.

... and raised us up together, and made us sit together in the heavenly places in Christ Jesus, that in the ages to come He might show the exceeding riches of His grace in His kindness toward us in Christ Jesus. Ephesians 2:6–7

1. What phrase did Paul use to describe the "life out of death" experience?

2. What position do believers occupy?

3. Why do you think Paul repeated the word *together* in this passage? What's the significance?

4. Why has God raised us up together in Christ?

5. How is God's grace described?

6. What more do you learn here about what it means to be "in Christ"?

Live Out ...

7. Today we learned that Jesus has raised us up from the dead. New life begins here on earth and continues in His kingdom to come. Have you found yourself downcast in heart instead of looking up? Check the boxes that describe circumstances that get you down.

___ Financial struggles   ___ Physical illness

___ Difficult relationships   ___ Unrealistic expectations

___ Busy schedule   ___ Unfulfilled dreams

8. David wrestled with a downcast soul and found three ways to lift his spirits: "Why are you cast down, O my soul? … Hope in God, for I shall yet praise Him for the help of His countenance" (Ps. 42:5). With this passage in mind, follow the steps below:

Step One—Hope in God! In lesson two we learned that hope is a confident expectancy. Our hope is not based on wishful thinking but in God. Journal a prayer of hope regarding that circumstance in life that gets you down.

Step Two—Praise God! Take time now to journal your words of worship, praising God for His mercy, love, grace, and kindness.

Step Three—Look to His countenance! Now look to God and away from your circumstance. Journal about one of God's attributes that gives you hope.

9. Since we are seated in heavenly places with Christ Jesus and our true citizenship is in heaven, we are to "seek those things which are above" (Col. 3:1). Place the following items into the appropriate column either of things that keep you tied to earth or of things that turn your heart toward heaven: *Bible study, financial investments, prayer, fashion magazines, church attendance, TV, fellowship, shopping malls, hospital visitation, hobbies, teaching Sunday school, sports, giving to missions, home remodeling, sharing the gospel, illness, volunteer work.*

TOWARD HEAVEN   **TIED TO EARTH**

LEARN ABOUT …

8 Lifted Up

Jesus raised us up spiritually, but He also wants to lift our spirits. Don't hang your head; let the Lord lift it up. "You, O LORD, are a shield around me; you are my glory, the one who holds my head high" (Ps. 3:3 NLT).

---

9 Heavenly Minded

It's been said, "Some people are so heavenly minded that they're no earthly good." Jesus debunks that idea. He had heaven on His mind when He came to earth to rescue us. When heaven is on your mind, you'll be conscious of your duty to do good deeds on earth, too.

o o ● o o

My (Lenya) friend Louise is a stargazer. She loves to drive far from the city lights to marvel at the heavens and worship the Creator. When the Hale-Bopp comet streaked across the sky, she would faithfully follow its course. One day my friend asked me if I had seen the comet yet. I glibly answered, "I've got too much to do here on the earth to be gawking at the heavens." As I said it, I realized my priorities were out of orbit. It had been a dark time in my life; illness and disappointment had eclipsed the glory of heaven. I had become so "earthly minded" that I was no "heavenly good."

About this time, another stargazer helped turn my eyes upward. My stepfather, Richard, named a star "Lenya" to brighten my life. I received a certificate from the Star Registry with a detailed map showing the exact location of *my* star. If you look out into the night sky, you'll see me, seated in a "heavenly place." Now my eyes sparkle when I gaze at the stars, reminded that God is faithful and my true home is in heaven.

You don't need a star named after you to remind you of your heavenly home—you have the bright and morning star, Jesus Christ, to point the way: "I, Jesus, have sent my angel to give you this message for the churches.… I am the bright morning star" (Rev. 22:16 NLT).

LISTEN TO …

By His Ascension Our Lord enters heaven and keeps the door open for humanity.

—*Oswald Chambers*

DAY 4
The Greatest Gift

A headline in the *Grand Rapids Press* read, "Conversion to Hindu Faith Is Tortuous." The article stated that a German businessman had completed his conversion to the Hindu faith by piercing himself through the cheeks with a quarter-inch-thick steel rod and pulling a chariot for two miles by ropes attached to his back and chest by steel hooks. Other converts had walked through long pits of fire, donned shoes with soles made of nails, or hung in the air spread-eagle from hooks embedded in their backs.[1]

Aren't you glad that conversion to Christianity is not accomplished by self-inflicted torture? In contrast, Jesus Christ was afflicted with one of the cruelest forms of torture ancient Rome could devise so that He could freely give you the gift of salvation. Jesus paid the price for your conversion so that you could not and would not have to do a thing to earn it. The only requirement is for you to receive the greatest gift God gave.

Lift Up ...

God, thank You that Your Son opened the way of salvation for me. Forgive me for trying to enter through the gate of works and religion. In Jesus' name. Amen.

Look At ...

Two key components make salvation available to all: God's grace and our faith.

Read Ephesians 2:8–9.

For by grace you have been saved through faith, and that not of yourselves; it is the gift of God, not of works, lest anyone should boast. Ephesians 2:8–9

1. What is the "gift of God" given to you?

2. By what means have you been saved?

3. What response is necessary on your part?

4. Read Romans 10:9.

   a. What are two important components in expressing a saving faith?

   b. What is the result of your confession and belief?

   c. If you have not taken these steps of faith, take the time now to do so: "Behold, now is the day of salvation" (2 Cor. 6:2).

5. What two phrases in these verses tell what you are *not* saved by?

6. Why is salvation a gift rather than the result of merit or effort?

7. According to 1 Corinthians 1:31, what should believers boast or glory in?

LIVE OUT ...

8. We've seen that being good enough or working hard enough does not achieve salvation. Using the letters from the acronym WORKS, write about the ways you have mistakenly tried to earn your salvation.

W

O

R

K

S

9. As you think about God's gracious gift of salvation, journal your thoughts below.

   a. Describe the best gift someone has ever given you. Did you *do* anything to earn the gift?

   b. How might the giver feel if you offered to reimburse him or her for the gift through work or money?

10. Journal a prayer of thanks to God for His "indescribable gift" of salvation (2 Cor. 9:15).

11. Salvation comes through faith in Jesus Christ. Faith is key in the life of every Christian. Fill in the chart below to discover ways to strengthen your faith.

SCRIPTURE	WAYS TO STRENGTHEN FAITH
Romans 4:20	
Romans 10:17	
1 Corinthians 2:5	
1 Corinthians 16:13	

∘ ∘ ● ∘ ∘

We live in New Mexico near the city of Roswell, where aliens are said to have crash-landed back in the 1940s. Recently I (Lenya) looked up "Roswell" on the Internet. I was astounded to find thousands of sites that reported the story about the aliens as if it were true. Literally millions of people believe "the truth is out there—we're not alone." They actually put their faith in UFO conspiracies.

One site explained the Roswell incident, which is supposed to have happened in July 1947. According to reports, a UFO crashed, and four dead aliens of the so-called gray variety were found near the ship. Mac Brazel found portions of the ship on his ranch and reported it to the local sheriff, who contacted the local nuclear air base in Roswell. Several officers from the base investigated the site and sent out a press release. But the next day the United States Air Force contradicted the report.

Over five decades later, this incredible myth lives on, fueled by books, television, and movies. If so many otherwise intelligent and responsible adults can put their faith in "little gray men" based on inconclusive evidence, why can't you put your complete trust in the "God Man," who unquestionably came to earth and changed the course of history? "Have faith in God" (Mark 11:22 NLT).

LISTEN TO ...

Salvation is worth working for; it is worth a man's going round the world on his hands and knees, climbing its mountains, crossing its valleys, swimming its rivers, going through all manner of hardship in order to attain it. But we do not get it in that way.... It is "to him that worketh not, but believeth."

—*Dwight Lyman Moody*

The Gift That Keeps on Giving

While on a trip to Paris, I (Lenya) visited the Louvre Museum. I stood speechless in the presence of so many priceless paintings. I saw the *Mona Lisa,* up close and personal. My mother and I stood in awe, whispering in hushed tones, "Can you believe we're looking at her? She's the real thing, not a cheap imitation!" Leonardo da Vinci had no idea when he painted the portrait that it would be a gift to the entire world—a gift that inspires generation after generation.

God is *the* Master Artist; all of creation declares His handiwork. Each sunset is a stroke of the Master's brush. And *you* are His living masterpiece. *Mona Lisa* can't hold a candle to you. As God's work of art, you are not intended to hang on a wall in a museum, gathering dust. He created you with a purpose—His purpose: to do good works that reflect His artistry.

LIFT UP ...

Father, I praise You for creating me in Your image, for Your glory. Help me to shine the light of Your beauty to the world around me. In Jesus' name. Amen.

LOOK AT ...

Yesterday Paul reminded us of the indescribable gift of new life in Christ. Today we discover that we must not be selfish with this gift.

READ EPHESIANS 2:10.

For we are His workmanship, created in Christ Jesus for good works, which God prepared beforehand that we should walk in them. Ephesians 2:10

LEARN ABOUT ...

1 Workmanship

The word translated "workmanship" comes from the Greek word *poiema*, from which we get the English word *poem*. God views your life as poetry in motion.

3 Good Works

"A Christian should always remember that the value of his good works is not based on their number and excellence, but on the love of God, which prompts him to do these things."—St. John of the Cross

5 God's Work

It's all God! God planned your good works before you were born. He guarantees that His work in you will be completed. Praise God, who goes before and behind you! "I am certain that God, who began the good work within you, will continue his work until it is finally finished" (Phil. 1:6 NLT).

1. How are believers described here? How is this description significant to you?

2. In Revelation 4:11 the apostle John records words that shed more light on God's workmanship: "You are worthy, O Lord our God, to receive glory and honor and power. For you created all things, and they exist because you created what you pleased" (NLT).

   a. Who is the Master Creator? What has He created?

   b. Why did He do this?

   c. How should we respond?

3. We (the church) are God's corporate workmanship created in Christ Jesus. According to Ephesians 2:10, what purpose does God have for His workmanship?

4. Fill in the chart below to discover some examples of good works God has for us to accomplish.

SCRIPTURE	GOOD WORKS
Acts 9:36, 39	
1 Timothy 5:10	
Hebrews 10:24–25	
James 2:14–17	

5. When did God prepare the good works for us to accomplish?

Live Out ...

6. As God's workmanship, you are His masterpiece. Do you really believe that? The psalmist said that God made you "wonderfully complex" and "marvelous" (Ps. 139:14 NLT). Journal about your perception of yourself and God's perception of you.

Step One: Describe your physical appearance. What is your stature, shape, hair and eye color, features, etc.?

Step Two: Evaluate your physical appearance. What are your assets and deficits? What do you like? Dislike?

Step Three: God designed and created you exactly the way you are because it brings Him joy. You—His masterpiece—are perfect just the way you are. Journal a psalm of praise, thanking God for each aspect of your physical appearance—the good and the bad but beautiful to Him!

7. a. God planned your good works before time began. He designed them to suit you perfectly. God told the prophet Jeremiah, "I knew you before I formed you in your mother's womb. Before you were born I set you apart and appointed you as my prophet to the nations" (Jer. 1:5 NLT). Check the talents and gifts that God has created within you:

___ Good sense of humor	___ Great singing voice
___ Aptitude in mathematics	___ Writing ability
___ Heart of compassion	___ Sewing ability
___ Cooking skills	___ Athletic skills
___ Patience with children	___ Love for books
___ Multitasking abilities	___ Organizational skills
___ Green thumb	___ Other_____

Learn About ...

6 Beautiful

Beauty is in the eye of the beholder. If you don't see yourself as beautiful, perhaps you should look at yourself through God's eyes. Your not-so-secret admirer has something to tell you: "Listen, O daughter, consider and incline your ear; ... the King will greatly desire your beauty; because He is your Lord, worship Him" (Ps. 45:10–11).

7 Willingness

People don't do good works for one of two reasons: either they can't (no ability) or they won't (no desire). Since we all have gifts or talents, we are all equipped to do something. You are able, but are you willing?

b. Journal some ideas of ways to bless God by blessing someone else with one of your talents this week.

c. Rewrite this verse into a personal prayer: "For God is working in you, giving you the desire and the power to do what pleases him" (Phil. 2:13 NLT).

○ ○ ● ○ ○

What do a disabled woman and peanut butter and jelly sandwiches have in common? God used them both to reach hundreds of kids. In the summer of 1990, Bea Salazar didn't consider her life a work of art. She was unemployed with five kids, no money, and little hope. Then she found a crying boy digging for food in a Dumpster. She took the boy home and made him a peanut butter and jelly sandwich. Good news about the peanut-butter lady spread through the neighborhood, and more kids showed up on her doorstep. Today, she influences hundreds of kids through her organization, Bea's Kids, which offers tutoring, clothes, medical assistance, food, and counseling. Bea Salazar has received numerous awards for her good deeds. When Oprah gave Bea the Use Your Life Award, Bea said, "It gives me a purpose to live, it gives me life.… There is no greater joy."[3]

There is no greater joy than doing good works for others in the name of the Lord. Won't you give the gift that keeps on giving, the gift of yourself, for God's honor and glory?

LISTEN TO …

To me it seems when God conceived the world, that was poetry; he formed it, and that was sculpture; he colored it, and that was painting; he peopled it with living beings, and that was the grand, divine, eternal drama.

—*Charlotte Cushman*

Share the Wealth

Ephesians 2:11–22

When Mahatma Gandhi was a student, he became intrigued with the Bible. Reading the gospels touched his heart, so he considered becoming a convert. Christianity seemed to offer real solutions to the caste system that divided India's population. One Sunday he attended a church to seek the way of salvation. An usher refused him a seat and said, "Go and worship with your own people." Tragically, he left and never came back. Gandhi said, "If Christians have caste differences also, I might as well remain a Hindu."[1]

Ancient Israel suffered from a similar form of prejudice, a caste system of its own. Religious Jews treated the Gentiles with scorn. Gentiles were regarded as unclean—diseased. Any association with a Gentile was unlawful for a Jew. Israel mistakenly believed that Gentiles would not be included in God's family or inherit any of God's blessings.

Jesus changed all that! He broke down the social barriers that separated Jews and Gentiles, and His life removed the great divide. God invites both Jew and Gentile into His house to worship together as one family. This week's study reveals that these two groups (and all believers) must learn how to share the wealth of God's great treasures.

Day 1: Ephesians 2:11–12   THE GREAT DIVIDE

Day 2: Ephesians 2:13   THE TIE THAT BINDS

Day 3: Ephesians 2:14–17   LET THE WALLS FALL DOWN

Day 4: Ephesians 2:18–19   EQUAL ACCESS

Day 5: Ephesians 2:20–22   COMMON GROUND

DAY 1
The Great Divide

LIFT UP ...

God, I am certain that nothing can come between me and Your love. I pray that nothing will come between me and Your people. Thank You for a love that is unstoppable. In Jesus' name. Amen.

LOOK AT ...

In lesson three, Paul reminded us that we were once spiritually dead, but that now we have received new lives through Christ. Today's passage looks more closely at the contrast between then and now.

READ EPHESIANS 2:11–12.

Therefore remember that you, once Gentiles in the flesh—who are called Uncircumcision by what is called the Circumcision made in the flesh by hands—that at that time you were without Christ, being aliens from the commonwealth of Israel and strangers from the covenants of promise, having no hope and without God in the world. Ephesians 2:11–12

LEARN ABOUT ...

1 Therefore

A good rule of thumb in Bible study is that when you see a "therefore," find out what it's there for. Therefore is a connecting word; it joins what has been said with what is about to be said.

---

3 Circumcised Flesh

The physical sign of God's covenant with the Jews was circumcision "in the flesh," by removing the male foreskin. Since Gentiles didn't have the physical mark of circumcision to set them apart as God's people, many Jews considered them to be inferior and of no concern to God.

---

5 Alien and Stranger

An alien is a person of another family, race, or nation; a foreign-born resident who has not been naturalized; a person different in nature or character; a stranger. Aliens don't come from another planet, just a different place. Just because they're strangers doesn't mean they're strange.

1. Paul began by saying "therefore" and "remember." In other words, remember what phrases he used before from Ephesians 2:8–9: "by grace you have been saved; not of yourselves; through faith; lest anyone should boast; gift of God; not of works." Now write these phrases in the appropriate columns below.

SAVED BY	NOT SAVED BY
___	___
___	___
___	___

2. a. According to Ephesians 2:11 what were the Gentiles once called? By whom?

   b. What attitude do you think this term conveyed?

3. By what means was the circumcision accomplished?

4. Read Romans 2:28–29.

   a. What type of circumcision does God desire?

   b. How is this accomplished?

   c. What is the result of a circumcised heart?

5. Paul used five terms to describe the unbeliever's spiritual condition. What are they?

LIVE OUT ...

6. God is more concerned with the spiritual condition of your heart than the physical condition of your body. Look up the following verses to discover ways to develop a circumcised heart.

SCRIPTURE	CIRCUMCISED HEART
Deuteronomy 30:6	
1 Corinthians 7:19	
Galatians 5:6	

7. Which of the following need to be circumcised—cut away—from your heart? Please circle your answers.

Pride	Self-focus	Lack of love	Bitterness
Envy	Materialism	Stubbornness	Criticism
Ingratitude	Other _____		

8. Rewrite Ezekiel 36:26–27 into a personal prayer: "I will give you a new heart, and I will put a new spirit in you. I will take out your stony, stubborn heart and give you a tender, responsive heart. And I will put my Spirit in you so that you will follow my decrees and be careful to obey my regulations" (NLT).

9. God told the Israelites, "If a stranger dwells with you in your land, you shall not mistreat him.... You shall love him as yourself; for you were strangers" (Lev. 19:33–34). With this in mind, follow these steps:

    Step One: Journal about a time when you felt like a stranger.
        (Example: first day of school or moving to a new neighborhood.)

LEARN ABOUT ...

6 Circumcised Heart

Circumcision was intended to be an outward sign of an inward change. Cutting away your flesh without changing your heart is self-mutilation. There are those in our society who are caught up in tattooing and body piercing to change their looks. But changing your appearance won't change your heart and life.

9 Stranger

This means "a foreigner or alien"—what we might today call an immigrant. America, like Israel, is a land of foreigners. God says, "Neither mistreat a stranger nor oppress him, for you were strangers" (Ex. 22:21). Treat strangers kindly, and they'll become friends.

Step Two: Think about strangers "who dwell among you." Journal about how you will make them feel at home in a strange place.

· · ● · ·

When I (Lenya) was younger, I spent some time as a missionary on Oahu, where I worked in a coffeehouse ministry that reached out to prostitutes, drug addicts, and the homeless. Working the midnight shift meant the streets would literally be buzzing. One night someone shouted at me, "Hey, Haole, you go home!" It sounded as if he said "Howlie," and I would have been insulted if I'd known what a Haole was. A local friend explained, "That's what we call 'whitey' here on the islands." For once in my life, I was the outsider, and I didn't like it a bit!

The Gentiles were the "Haoles" in Israel, and the Jews wanted them to go home! But God is not prejudiced. Jews and Gentiles can all find a home in God's kingdom. Jesus Christ can bring all factions together into one big, happy family: "There is no longer Jew or Gentile, slave or free, male and female. For you are all one in Christ Jesus" (Gal. 3:28 NLT).

Listen To ...

To the frightened, God is friendly; to the poor in spirit, he is forgiving; to the ignorant, considerate; to the weak, gentle; to the stranger, hospitable.

—*A. W. Tozer*

DAY 2
The Tie That Binds

In 1936 a radio broadcast was transmitted to America from England. Just before King Edward VIII was to be on the air, someone stumbled over a wire in the New York radio control room and snapped the only line of communication between the two great countries. The engineers were frantic. Then, with only a few moments remaining before airtime, a quick-thinking apprentice grasped the two broken ends of the wire, one in each hand, and bridged the gap. Seconds later the king addressed the nation. In a real sense, his words were being transmitted literally through the body of that man!

In Paul's day, an ocean of rules and regulations separated the Jews and Gentiles. No matter how frantically they tried, the Gentiles could not make the connection with God and His people. On the cross, Jesus—the God Man—stretched out one hand to the Jews and the other to the Gentiles, uniting them with His own body. He became the tie that binds.

LIFT UP ...

Father, I look back to the time when I was Your enemy, and it grieves my heart. I rejoice that Jesus brought us together so I can call You my friend. In Jesus' name. Amen.

LOOK AT ...

We've seen the hostility that separated the Jew from the Gentile, as well as those things that separate unbelievers from God. Now we are introduced to a new state of affairs based on God's intervention.

READ EPHESIANS 2:13.

But now in Christ Jesus you who once were far off have been brought near by the blood of Christ. Ephesians 2:13

LEARN ABOUT ...

1 Then and Now

The past can rob you of the present and hinder your future. Paul believed in "forgetting the past and looking forward to what lies ahead" (Phil. 3:13 NLT). Christ frees you to live in the now.

3 Far Off

Is any place too far off for God to find you? Timbuktu? Kalamazoo? Katmandu? No! On the contrary, the psalmist said, "If I ride the wings of the morning, if I dwell by the farthest oceans, even there your hand will guide me" (Ps. 139:9–10 NLT).

7 Drawing Near

God wants to be closer to you; not just to your body but close to your heart and soul as well. Judas drew near to Christ with his lips—the kiss of betrayal. But his heart was drawn away for thirty pieces of silver. Jesus said, "These people honor me with their lips, but their hearts are far from me" (Matt. 15:8 NLT). Kisses from a hard heart are "lip service," not love.

1. What two key words transport us from the past to the present?

2. Who can change our focus from the past to the present?

3. How does Paul describe where we once were without Christ? Why do you think this is an appropriate description?

4. How are sinners brought near to God?

5. Fill in the following chart to learn how and why we can draw near to God through Christ's blood.

SCRIPTURE	CHRIST'S BLOOD AND SACRIFICE
Matthew 26:28	
Hebrews 9:12–14	
1 Peter 1:18–19	
1 John 1:7–9	

6. Three of the Scriptures in the chart above refer to the remission of our sins at salvation. Which of the verses offer cleansing of the sins a Christian commits *after* salvation?

7. According to James 4:8, how can you close the distance between yourself and God?

LIVE OUT ...

8. Our promise today was friendship with God. Pick an activity to do this week from the list below that will strengthen your friendship with Him and circle it.

Tell Him a secret.	Visit His house.	Take Him on a walk.
Give Him a gift.	Invite Him to dinner.	Call Him for advice.
Write Him a letter.	Show Him your photo album.	Make friends with His friends.

9. Just as there are things that strengthen friendships, there are things that will tear them down.

Journal about a time when a friendship failed or ended. What contributed to the breakdown? How did it make you feel?

10. We've seen that friendship with the world can distract us from our relationship with God. John divided friendship with the world into three categories: "For all that is in the world—the lust of the flesh, the lust of the eyes, and the pride of life—is not of the Father but is of the world" (1 John 2:16). With this Scripture in mind, journal about a specific way you have made "friends" with the world by participating in some aspect of each category.

Lust of the flesh: Something that feels good.

Lust of the eyes: Something that looks good.

Pride of life: Something to impress others.

LEARN ABOUT …

8 Friends

Solomon said, "A man who has friends must himself be friendly" (Prov. 18:24). In other words, friendships don't just happen; you make them happen by being friendly. God wants you to be a near and dear friend. Have you extended the hand of friendship to Him?

9 Friend or Foe?

Unhealthy friendships pull us away from stable ones. James warns us how our friendship with God can be jeopardized: "Don't you realize that friendship with this world makes you an enemy of God? I say it again: If you want to be a friend of the world, you make yourself an enemy of God" (James 4:4 NLT).

10 Lust

Lust is a strong desire for something that is forbidden or an obsessive sexual craving. Lust yearns for things that are contrary to the will of God. Christians can resist lust through the power of the Spirit. The flesh and its lusts are to be crucified: "Those who are Christ's have crucified the flesh with its passions and desires" (Gal. 5:24).

o o ● o o

I (Lenya) love the story of a little girl named Ruth who was sent on an errand by her mother. She was gone for such a long time that her mother became frantic with worry. When Ruth finally returned, her mother hugged her tightly, asking, "Where have you been? What took you so long?"

Ruth replied, "On my way home I saw Sally sitting in front of her house. She was crying because her doll was broken."

"So," said the mother, "you stopped to help her fix her doll?"

"Oh no!" replied Ruth. "I stopped to help her cry."

Jesus said, "There is no greater love than to lay down one's life for one's friends" (John 15:13 NLT). He saw that our sins caused great sorrow, so He stopped and shed not tears, but His blood, for our sins.

Listen To ...

You cannot say that you are friendless when Christ has said, "Henceforth I call you not servants ... but I have called you friends."

—*Billy Graham*

DAY 3

Let the Walls Fall Down

The politics of division separated Germany on August 13, 1961, when the residents of Berlin woke to a barbed-wire barrier between the communist East and the noncommunist West. The Cold War was most bitter. Soldiers quickly fortified the barrier, creating a concrete wall twelve feet high and over a hundred miles long. Loved ones were torn apart, and more than two million people attempted to escape East Germany by climbing, vaulting, tunneling, or crashing through checkpoints. Unsuccessful attempts resulted in more than four hundred deaths. In 1989, restrictions between the two Berlins were lifted. The Berlin Wall came down. The Cold War was over.

Celebrations around the world culminated with Germany's reunification as one country on October 3, 1990. Much work lay ahead to rebuild a city and a nation that had been divided by disagreement, laws, and treaties, resulting in a literal wall of separation. Bad laws lead to walls.

In the same way, laws and legalism kept the nation of Israel and other nations divided by a wall of prejudice. But two thousand years ago, a babe in a manger heralded the end of the Cold War between the Jews and Gentiles. Jesus tore down the spiritual wall of separation. Let the walls fall down!

LIFT UP ...

God, give me an undivided heart. If there are any walls of prejudice in me, let them fall down. Help me to be an instrument of Your peace in a troubled world. In Jesus' name. Amen.

LOOK AT ...

The blood of Christ is able to bring near to God all who are far off. Now let's see what Christ's role is in tearing down walls between us and God.

READ EPHESIANS 2:14–17.

For He Himself is our peace, who has made both one, and has broken down the middle wall of separation, having abolished in His flesh the enmity, that is, the law of commandments contained in ordinances, so as to create in Himself one new man from the two, thus making peace, and that He might reconcile them both to God in one body through the cross, thereby putting to death the enmity. And he came and preached peace to you who were afar off and to those who were near. Ephesians 2:14–17

1. How is Jesus described in the first phrase? What do you think this means?

2. What has Jesus done?

3. How has Jesus made both Jew and Gentile one?

4. What did Christ abolish? How would you put this in your own words?

5. What was the result of His abolishing this?

6. How were Jews and Gentiles reconciled to each other and to God?

7. What was the result of reconciliation?

8. Who were the recipients of Christ's message of peace?

LIVE OUT ...

9. a. Until you've surrendered your sinful nature (flesh), you remain at war with God. Circle any words from the passage below that describe sinful areas that reveal hostility toward God:

    > When you follow the desires of your sinful nature, the results are very clear: sexual immorality, impurity, lustful pleasures, idolatry, sorcery, hostility, quarreling, jealousy, outbursts of anger, selfish ambition, dissension, division, envy, drunkenness, wild parties, and other sins like these. (Gal. 5:19–21 NLT)

    b. Journal a prayer of surrender to God. Ask Him to forgive you for engaging in the sinful desires of your flesh. Ask Him to help you to crucify the flesh so that you no longer act on its cravings. Pray to be filled with His Spirit to walk in newness of life.

10. Today we learned that God wants you to be reconciled to other members of His family. Identify a person to whom you need to be reconciled and the cause of the division between you.

Journal a prayer of reconciliation, creating a "bridge" to that person's heart.

11. Jesus is the great reconciler! And He asks us to fulfill the same role, serving as His ambassadors of reconciliation: "Now all things are of God, who has reconciled us to Himself through Jesus Christ, and has given us the ministry of reconciliation" (2 Cor. 5:18).

    a. Identify two divided people who need reconciliation. (Example: Your brother refuses to speak to your parents.)

LEARN ABOUT ...

10 Bridges

Reconciliation builds bridges. The cross of Christ constructed a wooden bridge reuniting God with His creation. Forgiveness builds bridges between people who are separated. Jesus said, "If you ... remember that your brother has something against you, ... go your way. First be reconciled to your brother, and then come and offer your gift [to God]" (Matt. 5:23–24).

11 Forgive

Former US Senate chaplain Peter Marshall said, "If you hug to yourself any resentment against anybody else, you destroy the bridge by which God would come to you."[2] Jesus said, "If you forgive those who sin against you, your heavenly Father will forgive you. But if you refuse to forgive others, your Father will not forgive your sins" (Matt. 6:14–15 NLT).

b. Journal about how you can bridge the gap between these people, helping them to be reconciled. Ask God how you can serve as His ambassador of peace.

∘ ∘ ● ∘ ∘

The Hatfield-McCoy feud began in 1863, when the Hatfields fought with the McCoys on the Kentucky–West Virginia border. Historians disagree on the reasons for the feud; some say it began over a pig theft, others say it was because of a secret romance. Whatever the reason, the feud caused the death of more than one hundred men, women, and children. More than a century later, in May 1976, Jim McCoy and Willis Hatfield, the last two survivors of the original families, shook hands. The survivors came together to build a monument memorializing the victims of the feud. Jim McCoy died in 1984, at the age of ninety-nine. He bore no grudges, and the Hatfield Funeral Home handled his burial.

We know the reason for the feud between God and man: sin. But God was willing to meet us at a monument on the hill of Calvary. He was willing to bury His grudge in a tomb sealed with a stone. What about you? Are you still feuding with God? Perhaps it's time to accept the invitation to meet Jesus at the cross and bury your grudges along with your past.

LISTEN TO ...

Like the father of the prodigal son, God can see repentance coming a great way off and is there to meet it, and the repentance is the reconciliation.

—*Dorothy L. Sayers*

DAY 4

Equal Access

Over a century ago, the Supreme Court of the United States ruled that blacks and whites should be considered "separate but equal." However, white America focused on being separate, not equal. Black citizens were required to drink from separate water fountains, to eat at separate lunch counters, to sit in separate sections of schools, churches, and courthouses. This legislation stood unchallenged until 1955. One black woman in Alabama, a seamstress named Rosa Parks, refused to be treated separately and by her actions insisted on being treated with equality. Her choice not to give up her seat on a bus to a white person sparked a cultural revolution culminating in a federal court order for desegregation.

Over two thousand years ago, the Sanhedrin in Israel insisted that Gentiles were not only separate from the Jews but unequal as well. One Jewish man from Nazareth, a carpenter named Jesus, refused to treat Jews and Gentiles unequally. He reminded the world that in God's eyes, all people are created equal.

LIFT UP ...

Heavenly Father, thank You that in Your family You have no favorites. You see all of Your children, including me, as special and set apart. Help me to see others the way You do. In Jesus' name. Amen.

LOOK AT ...

This week we have been reminded what life was like apart from God. Today we will examine our new position as believers in God's kingdom.

LEARN ABOUT ...

1 Three In One

The members of the Trinity are distinct, yet all fully and equally God. This is hard for us to imagine. An egg has three separate parts: yolk, white, and shell. Each is distinct, yet they function together as a whole. God the Father, Jesus the Son, and the Holy Spirit are distinct persons, yet they are one God.

3 Together

God included both Jews and Gentiles in His nation and His family. But during Paul's day, God's children did not reflect His heart. Instead, God's kids had a bad case of sibling rivalry. Jesus was God's messenger telling His kids to "kiss and make up."

5 Fellow Citizens

"Can't we all just get along?" Read the news and the answer is, "Apparently not!" Look at a penny, and you'll find the solution: "In God We Trust." Only when citizens look to God's plan instead of their own agendas will there be true unity.

READ EPHESIANS 2:18–19.

For through Him we both have access by one Spirit to the Father. Now, therefore, you are no longer strangers and foreigners, but fellow citizens with the saints and members of the household of God ... Ephesians 2:18–19

1. Identify the three members of the Trinity named here.

2. Examine the process by which we have access to the Father by filling in the blanks provided: "For _____ we both have access _____ to _____."

3. Who is included in the phrase "we both" (Eph. 2:11–12)?

4. What are we no longer known as?

5. Instead of being outsiders, what two new positions do we possess?

6. What do you think are the implications of being members of God's household?

7. Verse 19 begins with a reference of time. When do we receive our new positions?

LIVE OUT ...

8. a. What special rights or privileges did you enjoy as a member of your household when you were a child? (Examples: food and clothing.)

   b. Journal a prayer thanking God for them.

9. God invites you to reside in His household of faith. Fill in the chart below to discover the privileges and joys you'll find in God's house.

SCRIPTURE	IN GOD'S HOUSE
Psalm 26:8	
Psalm 65:4	
Psalm 93:5	
John 14:2	

10. Journal a prayer of thanksgiving to your heavenly Father, who has prepared a place for you in His household filled with good things.

11. Using the chart, list the members of your current household, along with a description of their outlook on life. (For example, are they timid, outgoing, optimistic, negative?) Then put a smiling face by the people with a healthy outlook and a frowning face next to the people who need a new outlook. Finally, in the prayer box, write a prayer of thanks for the people who make you smile and a prayer of healing for the people who make you sad.

PERSON	PRAYER

12. If your home is unbearable, maybe you're the bear. Look in the mirror. Journal about the kind of attitude you display to others at home. Would you get a smiley face or a frown?

LEARN ABOUT …

6 Open House

Jews believed that Gentiles should be excluded from God's house—the temple. God made it clear in both the Old and New Testaments that His house was open to all nations: "Is it not written, 'My house shall be called a house of prayer for all nations'?" (Mark 11:17). God doesn't want anyone to be homeless.

9 At Home

God's household is full of glory, holiness, and goodness. Isn't that the kind of house you'd like to live in? Jesus said He was going to prepare a place for you in His house. Until then, the Holy Spirit has come to take up residence in you—His home away from home.

12 Smile

Smile and the world smiles with you. But even if you frown, God will smile back at you. God told Aaron to offer this blessing over His family: "May the LORD bless you and protect you. May the LORD smile on you and be gracious to you. May the LORD show you his favor and give you his peace" (Num. 6:24–26 NLT).

∘ ∘ ● ∘ ∘

In a *Peanuts* cartoon created by Charles Schulz, Lucy demands that Linus change TV channels and then threatens him with her fist if he doesn't.

"What makes you think you can walk right in here and take over?" asks Linus.

"These five fingers," says Lucy. "Individually they're nothing, but when I curl them together like this into a single unit, they form a weapon that is terrible to behold."

"Which channel do you want?" asks Linus.

Then Linus looks at his fingers and says, "Why can't you guys get organized like that?"

Weak things united become strong. Jesus took two weak and warring peoples, the Jews and the Gentiles, and brought them together to create a holy nation, the church, whose holy creed is love. Because of this unity based on love, Christianity became a powerful force in the ancient world and changed the course of history.

LISTEN TO ...

If your father and mother, your sister and brother, if the very cat and dog in the house, are not happier for your being Christian, it is a question whether you really are.

—*Hudson Taylor*

DAY 5

Common Ground

Back in 1957 the First Brethren Church of Sarasota, Florida, had a groundbreaking ceremony. Instead of using a silver shovel for VIPs to dig up the first clump of dirt, they brought a one-horse plow. Two strong ushers were harnessed to the yoke to break up the fallow ground. But the plow didn't budge an inch. Next, Sunday school officers and teachers were strapped in, but still the plow was immovable. Finally, all the church members present took hold of the rope, tugging with all their might. With every member pulling together, the plow moved forward, the ground was broken, and the church was built.

Our Savior was born in a barn, not Buckingham Palace. He was a blue-collar carpenter, not a blue-blooded aristocrat. His friends were commoners: fishermen, farmers, and homemakers. Jesus broke new ground in ancient Israel by using common people to build an uncommon community: His church. He is our firm foundation. We are all on common ground as members of His church.

LIFT UP ...

Jesus, the stability You've brought to my life is like a firm foundation. Help me to follow the blueprint of Your Word to build a life that is pleasing to You. In Jesus' name. Amen.

LOOK AT ...

We learned that Paul typified believers as "fellow citizens with the saints and members of the household of God" (Eph. 2:19). Today we discover a different metaphor for the body of believers.

LEARN ABOUT ...

1 Cornerstone

"Christ is called the 'cornerstone' in reference to His being the foundation of the Christian faith (Eph. 2:20), and the importance and conspicuousness of the place He occupies."—*The Unger's Bible Dictionary*

6 Dwelling Place

God is infinite; human beings are finite. Can the uncontainable be contained? Solomon said, "Will God really live on earth? Why, even the highest heavens cannot contain you. How much less this Temple I have built!" (1 Kings 8:27 NLT). Yet God has made us His dwelling place—filling the finite with the infinite through His Spirit.

7 In Spirit

God created us as a trilogy— spirit, soul, and body. Your body and soul are made for earth, to communicate with other people. Your spirit is equipped for eternity to worship God. "God is Spirit, so those who worship him must worship in spirit and in truth" (John 4:24 NLT).

READ EPHESIANS 2:20–22.

... having been built on the foundation of the apostles and prophets, Jesus Christ Himself being the chief cornerstone, in whom the whole building, being fitted together, grows into a holy temple in the Lord, in whom you also are being built together for a dwelling place of God in the Spirit. Ephesians 2:20–22

1. What do you learn here about the foundation and chief cornerstone of the household of God?

2. How much of the building is dependent upon the chief cornerstone?

3. Once this building is joined together, what does it become?

4. From beginning to end, upon whom is this growth dependent?

5. Where are you in this picture?

6. Why are we being built together?

7. How does God dwell in His holy temple, the church?

LIVE OUT ...

8. Read 1 Peter 2:5. What does this verse reveal about your role in God's holy temple? What should you offer in this temple?

9. Fill in the following chart to discover what spiritual sacrifices God desires.

SCRIPTURE

SPIRITUAL SACRIFICES

Psalm 51:17, 19

Psalm 141:2

Romans 12:1

Hebrews 13:15

LEARN ABOUT ...

8 Living Temple

God doesn't inhabit buildings of brick and mortar but bodies of flesh and blood. Your church building is dead until you fill it with the presence of God living in you. "Don't you realize that your body is the temple of the Holy Spirit, who lives in you and was given to you by God?" (I Cor. 6:19 NLT).

10 Living Sacrifices

We have seen that God desires unique sacrifices. The dictionary defines sacrifice as "an act of offering to a deity something precious." God doesn't want your hand-me-downs but your heart's delight! He loves you so much He gave His favorite thing—His Son.

10. a. Remember the scene in the movie *The Sound of Music* when Maria taught the von Trapp children to sing, "These are a few of my favorite things"? Make a top-ten list of some of your favorite things.

b. Write a prayer offering a sacrifice of praise to God for creating and providing one of these delightful things.

c. Journal about how, this week, you can offer to God one of your favorite things as an act of sacrificing your very best for Him. (Example: Instead of reading the latest novel, I'll take time to read God's Word. Be creative!)

o o ● o o

"There's no place like home" were the words Dorothy uttered as she clicked the heels of her ruby-red slippers. Her journey began in Kansas with ordinary folks like Uncle Henry and Auntie Em. But Dorothy was not content with her common existence on a pig farm and pictured herself "somewhere over the rainbow." An adversary on a bicycle, a carpetbagger in a wagon, and a journey through a tornado blew Dorothy into the land of Oz. At last she was living her dream: unusual sights, uncommon personalities, and unique encounters. But on the other side of the rainbow, all Dorothy could think about was the comfort of home sweet home.

"Father, forgive them" were the words Jesus uttered as His feet were nailed to the cross. His journey began in heaven with extraordinary company, the Father of lights. But Jesus was not content with our common existence on this clump of dirt and longed to bring all of us over the rainbow to our true home—seated with Him "in the heavenly places." His uncommon kindness opened the doors of eternity to all humanity, not just those who lived in the land of Israel. There's *no place* like His home!

LISTEN TO ...

"Where is the church at 11:25 on Monday morning?" The church then is in the dentist's office, in the automobile salesroom and repair shop…. It is in the hospital, in the classroom, and in the home. It is in the offices…. That is where the church is, wherever God's people are…. They are honoring God, not just while they worship in a building, but out there.

—Arthur H. DeKruyter

Trustee of God's Will

Ephesians 3:1–13

Before his conversion to Christianity, Paul had an impressive résumé: "I was circumcised when I was eight days old. I am a pure-blooded citizen of Israel and a member of the tribe of Benjamin—a real Hebrew if there ever was one! I was a member of the Pharisees, who demand the strictest obedience to the Jewish law. I was so zealous that I harshly persecuted the church. And as for righteousness, I obeyed the law without fault" (Phil. 3:5–6 NLT). Impressed? Paul wasn't. He learned that God is more concerned with what Christ had done for him than with what he had accomplished himself. He threw his résumé away, knowing it was "worthless because of what Christ has done" (Phil. 3:7 NLT).

After Paul had been on the job for God a few years, his résumé looked something like this: "I'm over fifty years old. I've never held down a pulpit position for more than three years. I had to leave some towns because I caused civil disturbances or riots. I have served time in jail at least three or four times, but I was innocent. My health isn't good either. I don't have letters of recommendation since I don't get along with most religious leaders. In fact, some have threatened me and attacked me physically." Based on this résumé, would your church hire Paul? Maybe not—but God did! This week, let's examine Paul's credentials and discover his qualifications as trustee of God's will.

Day 1: Ephesians 3:1, 13	PAUL THE PRISONER
Day 2: Ephesians 3:2–6	PAUL THE APOSTLE
Day 3: Ephesians 3:7–8a	PAUL'S POWER SOURCE
Day 4: Ephesians 3:8b–11	PAUL THE PREACHER
Day 5: Ephesians 3:11–12	PAUL'S APPROACH

DAY 1

Paul the Prisoner

LIFT UP ...

Father, though Paul was in prison, he experienced true freedom in You. There are areas in my life that hold me captive. Please set me free. In Jesus' name. Amen.

LOOK AT ...

Last week we learned that God desires unity and reconciliation rather than discord and division. In this lesson, we gain more insight into Paul himself—how he viewed himself, his circumstances, and his role in the kingdom of God.

READ EPHESIANS 3:1, 13.

For this reason I, Paul, the prisoner of Christ Jesus for you Gentiles ... Therefore I ask that you do not lose heart at my tribulations for you, which is your glory. Ephesians 3:1, 13

LEARN ABOUT ...

1 Prisoner

Paul was imprisoned because he believed in uniting Jews and Gentiles in the church. Paul did the right thing, but he was treated wrongly. Jesus will right the wrongs: "God blesses those who are persecuted for doing right, for the Kingdom of Heaven is theirs" (Matt. 5:10 NLT).

---

4 Intolerance

It's odd how the "tolerant" can be so intolerant. The Roman government tolerated many pagan practices but would not tolerate true religious freedom. Thus, to preserve the *pax Romana* (Roman peace), they imprisoned Paul and sent him to Rome to stand trial before Caesar.

---

5 Tribulation

The word *tribulation* means "great adversity and anguish, intense oppression, or persecution." Tribulation is linked to God's process for making the world right again. His Son underwent great suffering, just as His people undergo a great deal of tribulation from the world.

1. How did Paul describe himself?

2. Consider Paul's situation as a prisoner in a Roman jail. Why do you think he described himself as a "prisoner of Christ Jesus" instead of a "prisoner of Caesar"?

3. Paul revealed that he was a prisoner for the Gentiles. Read Acts 24:5–6 to understand better the charges against Paul.

   a. He was the creator of ...

   b. He was the ringleader of ...

   c. He tried to ...

4. According to Acts 24:12–13, how did Paul respond to the charges?

5. Paul asked his readers not to lose heart. What could have caused them to lose heart?

6. Whom did Paul say his tribulations were for?

7. What was the ultimate result of Paul's tribulations?

LIVE OUT ...

8. Paul considered himself a prisoner of Christ Jesus. In which of the following ways have you been "taken captive" by Christ?

   ____ Guarded my thoughts
   ____ Protected my heart

_____ Gave up rights to self

_____ Protected my emotions

_____ Restrained sinful actions

_____ Other _____

9. Behaviors such as gossip hold us captive. Activities like worship
    set us free. In the chart below, list behaviors that hold you captive
    (i.e., bad habits) and those that set you free.

HOLDS YOU CAPTIVE	SETS YOU FREE

10. a. Because of his relationship with Christ, Paul was able to find
       contentment and see God's purpose in his tribulations. Journal
       about a tribulation you are now experiencing.

    b. Write a prayer asking God for His perfect will to be done—
       either to remove the troubles or to strengthen you through
       them. Pray that however He responds to your prayer, He will be
       glorified.

∘ ∘ ● ∘ ∘

Experience is the best teacher. Paul learned through experience that
tough times could teach him even more than tranquil times. Suffering in
prison made him a better man, and he wanted to make certain that his

LEARN ABOUT ...

8 Look Up

Poet Frederick Langbridge
wrote, "Two men look
out the same prison bars;
one sees mud, and the
other sees the stars." The
difference? One looked
down while the other gazed
upward. When you're taken
captive by Christ you have
every reason to look up!
The captivity of the world
will only make you hang
your head.

10 Free Indeed

Paul was a prisoner physically,
but his knowledge of
God's freedom liberated
his heart and soul. You
may feel trapped by your
circumstances, but like
Paul, you can experience
spiritual freedom in Jesus:
"If the Son makes you free,
you shall be free indeed"
(John 8:36).

pain was for the gain of others. Jerry McAuley was another example of such an individual. A thief and a counterfeiter, he ended up spending seven years in Sing Sing Prison. After his conversion there, he began witnessing to other men who were imprisoned by sin. Later he started America's first rescue mission in New York City, where he befriended the worst sorts of criminals and street people.

Just before his death he said to his wife, "When I'm to die, and it may not be long, I want to die on my knees, praying for lost souls…. I would rather have some poor soul that I was the means of leading to the Lord put one little rose on my grave than have the wealth of a millionaire."[1] His wish was granted, for at his funeral an aged, shabbily dressed man appeared and placed a few flowers on the coffin, saying, "Jerry, who was my friend, 'll know … that they came from old Joe Chappy." Mrs. McAuley preserved that little bouquet for a long time in remembrance of the fact that her husband had been a true friend of sinners.[2]

LISTEN TO …

Jesus' guilt is our innocence; as his captivity is our freedom, and his death our life.

—*Malcolm Muggeridge*

DAY 2

Paul the Apostle

When I (Lenya) hear the word *apostle* or *prophet,* my mind conjures up visions of men in flowing white robes; sandal-clad feet; long, matted hair; and eyes blazing with zeal. I imagine Charlton Heston playing Moses in *The Ten Commandments* as the Red Sea divided. Or I envision Anthony Hopkins as he portrayed Paul the apostle in the movie *Peter and Paul.*

So what does the genuine article look like? Paul the apostle was probably a short, bow-legged man with a big hook nose and runny eyes. The Bible describes David, both king and prophet, as "dark and handsome, with beautiful eyes" (1 Sam. 16:12 NLT). Obviously, you can't judge a book by its cover or God's messengers by their looks. They come in all shapes and sizes.

What makes an ordinary person become an apostle or a prophet? God's call on their lives! A prophet was God's chosen messenger who courageously communicated His words to His chosen people—Israel. An apostle was a chosen messenger of Christ, specially sent out as an ambassador of the gospel.

Judging from his appearance, Paul was an unlikely candidate to be God's messenger. But Paul had everything he needed to be an apostle—Christ's call upon his life!

LIFT UP ...

God, I find security in the fact that all Your words of prophecy will come true. Your voice is the one true voice that can be trusted in a world full of pretenders. Help me to hear Your voice today. In Jesus' name. Amen.

LOOK AT ...

Yesterday we looked into Paul's role as a prisoner. Today we discover that he was also an apostle.

LEARN ABOUT ...

I Dispensation

A *dispensation* is a formal authorization or an act of dispensing. As an apostle, Paul was formally authorized by God to dispense the grace of God to the Ephesians—to Gentiles. Paul was like a vending machine; if you pushed his buttons, out came grace!

4 Mystery

The word *mystery* means "a secret untold; a hidden truth." God revealed a mystery to Paul: God was the Gentiles' secret admirer. Once the secret was told, the truth could come out. There is room in God's heart and His church for everyone.

5 Good News

Once the apostles and prophets heard the good news of reconciliation through Christ, they got busy telling others: "So they began their circuit of the villages, preaching the Good News" (Luke 9:6 NLT). Are you busy telling others the good news, or are you goin' nowhere fast?

READ EPHESIANS 3:2–6.

... if indeed you have heard of the dispensation of the grace of God which was given to me for you, how that by revelation He made known to me the mystery (as I have briefly written already, by which, when you read, you may understand my knowledge in the mystery of Christ), which in other ages was not made known to the sons of men, as it has now been revealed by the Spirit to His holy apostles and prophets: that the Gentiles should be fellow heirs, of the same body, and partakers of His promise in Christ through the gospel ... Ephesians 3:2–6

1. What dispensation was given to Paul for others?

2. Who gave this special dispensation to Paul?

3. What does "by revelation" mean?

4. What was revealed to Paul?

5. Who else was given this revelation, and how did they receive it?

6. What details of the "mystery of Christ" were revealed to Paul?

7. Of what are the Gentiles partakers? What does this mean?

LIVE OUT ...

8. a. Paul was a dispenser of God's grace. Use your imagination to assess yourself honestly: If you were a vending machine, what would you be stocked with? (Example: Stress, because your life's too busy? Fun, because life's a blast?)

TRUSTEE OF GOD'S WILL

b. We all have buttons: people, places, or positions that turn us off, ring our bells, or hit the jackpot. Journal about the things that really push your buttons.

9. a. We saw that Paul was God's messenger, faithfully conveying His words to His people. Journal about some messengers who have inspired you to follow Christ and how. Why were they effective?

b. Write a prayer of thanks to God for placing those messengers in your life. Ask Him to bless them in their ministries.

10. God used the prophetic Scriptures to reveal the mysteries of the church to the apostle Paul. Draw a line connecting the Old Testament prophecies to their corresponding New Testament fulfillment.

PROPHECY	FULFILLMENT
Genesis 12:3	Acts 10:44–48
Isaiah 49:6	Galatians 3:8
Joel 2:28–29	Acts 13:46–47

○ ○ ● ○ ○

Scientists report that one of the largest stars in our galaxy is about to self-destruct. Eta Carinae, which has a mass one hundred times greater than that of our sun, is giving signs that its life is almost over. Researchers say that it could become a supernova—a blazing, exploding star—anywhere from now to a million years from now.[3] What is especially interesting is that since light from the star takes at least 7,500 years to reach the earth, the actual explosion could have already taken place.[4]

This phenomenon reminds me of the nature of biblical prophecy. For example, the predictions found in the Bible are often written in the

LEARN ABOUT ...

9 Messenger

How do you know if a messenger is from God? It's not by their looks but by what comes from their lips. Messengers may come in many shapes and sizes, but the message reveals the authenticity of the messenger. "This is the message we heard from Jesus and now declare to you: God is light, and there is no darkness in him at all" (I John 1:5 NLT).

10 Prophecy

Prophecies are predictions about the future and the end time—special messages from God, often uttered through human spokesmen, which indicate the divine will for humanity.

past tense. This was done because even though the prophet was writing of a future event, he had already "seen" it. In the mind of God it's as if the event had already happened. God knows it all and has seen it all—past, present, and future. When God reveals future events to a prophet, though the event may have taken place in time (eternity past), it may take light-years until we can see the results here on earth (eternity present).

LISTEN TO ...

In God there is no was or will be, but a continuous and unbroken is. In him history and prophecy are one and the same.

—*A. W. Tozer*

DAY 3

Paul's Power Source

Abraham Lincoln had his share of setbacks on his way to success. He lost his position as captain in his short time of military service. His little country store "winked out," as he said, making him a failure at business. As a lawyer he was too impractical and unpolished to be very successful. And in politics he was defeated several times in bids for the legislature, Congress, and the vice presidency. At last, in 1861 he was elected president of the United States.

Lincoln viewed all of his frustrations and victories through the eyes of eternity, observing, "That the Almighty … directly intervenes in human affairs is one of the plainest statements in the Bible. I have had so many evidences of His direction, so many instances when I have been controlled by some other power than my own will that I have no doubt that this power comes from above."[5]

Paul also experienced a long list of catastrophes on the road to a power-filled life: "Five different times the Jewish leaders gave me thirty-nine lashes. Three times I was beaten with rods. Once I was stoned. Three times I was shipwrecked.… I have faced danger in the cities, in the deserts, and on the seas.… I have worked hard and long, enduring many sleepless nights. I have been hungry and thirsty and have often gone without food" (2 Cor. 11:24–27 NLT). In spite of these setbacks Paul could say that God had given to him "the effective working of His power" (Eph. 3:7).

LIFT UP …

Father, I know that trouble can make me rely on You and Your power in my life. Help me to see my circumstances through the eyes of eternity. In Jesus' name. Amen.

LEARN ABOUT ...

I Minister

Ministering is a distinctive biblical idea that means "to serve" or "to be a servant." Men and women who join the ministry shouldn't be trying to get ahead, but to stand behind.

---

3 Power

Power is the ability or strength to perform a task. Power is sometimes linked to authority. Power suggests physical strength; authority suggests a moral right. One can have power to perform a task but not authority to do it. Jesus Christ had both, and He bestowed these upon His followers. God gives His power to do His work.

---

4 The Least

God's kingdom runs contrary to our human ideas of power. He tells us the last will be first, the meek will inherit, and the humble will be exalted. God's philosophy of success? The way down is the way up. To prosper with God, ask yourself, How low can I go?

LOOK AT ...

We have gained new insight into Paul as a prisoner and an apostle. Today we examine another aspect of Paul, the trustee of God's will, and discover that he was a power-filled man.

READ EPHESIANS 3:7–8A.

... of which I became a minister according to the gift of the grace of God given to me by the effective working of His power. To me, who am less than the least of all the saints, this grace was given ... Ephesians 3:7–8a

1. How did Paul describe himself here?

2. What gift did Paul receive that enabled him to be God's minister?

3. How was that gift given to him?

4. Three phrases here reveal the humble way Paul viewed himself. Fill in the blanks below to discover his descending path:

   "To me, who am _____"

   "To me, who am less _____"

   "To me, who am less than the least _____"

5. Look back at verses 2, 7, and 8. What key word is repeated in reference to Paul's ministry? How is this significant?

LIVE OUT ...

6. Paul was truly a minister—a servant—of the people. Look ahead to Ephesians 4:12. Who else is equipped for the ministry? Why?

7. Journal a prayer to God by rewriting the following Scripture: "I have become a slave to all people to bring many to Christ" (1 Cor. 9:19 NLT).

8. To which of the following people have you been a servant this week?

___ Husband	___ Children
___ The homeless	___ Parents
___ Neighbors	___ The sick
___ Siblings	___ Coworkers
___ Friends	___ The elderly
___ Other	_____

9. You are called and equipped to be God's minister by His grace.

Journal about your experience in serving the person(s) you marked above. How did God empower and equip you for service?

o o ● o o

Shortly after I (Penny) rededicated my life to Christ, I developed a burning desire to serve the Lord but didn't know what He wanted me to do. I thought, *Maybe I should teach a Sunday school class.* But I really didn't feel qualified to teach—I was still learning. I thought about making meals for the homebound, but I could barely get meals on the table for my own family. Then one Sunday I read in the church bulletin: "Toy

LEARN ABOUT ...

8 Serving

You are most like Christ when you serve: "Even the Son of Man came not to be served but to serve others" (Mark 10:45 NLT). Serving Jesus has its benefits—intimacy with Him: "My servants must be where I am. And the Father will honor anyone who serves me" (John 12:26 NLT).

9 Supplies

When people join the army, they don't have to purchase their own gear or gun. They are fully equipped by Uncle Sam with all the supplies necessary. God's soldiers are also equipped with supplies for the task at hand: "My God shall supply all your need according to His riches in glory by Christ Jesus" (Phil. 4:19).

Washers Needed in the Children's Ministry." Immediately I thought, *I could do that*. So I volunteered to go in once a week to wash the toys in the nursery. I would take my kids and let them play as I washed buckets of toys week after week for two years. The service wasn't glamorous, but it was gratifying. As I stood at the sink, I had time to listen to praise music or think about the pastor's message. My time at the washbasin brought me closer to Jesus.

Teddy Roosevelt said, "Do what you can, with what you have, where you are." What could I do? I could use my hands. What did I have? I had a heart for service. Where was I? I was at home with my kids. And God used my limited resources to work for Him. Do you think you're not equipped to serve God? Then think again. He will take the smallest act of service and transform it into something sacred.

LISTEN TO ...

I am your servant! Everything I have is yours. But even as I say that, I know you are serving me more than I am serving you. At your command all of the resources of heaven and earth are at my disposal, and even the angels help me.

—*Thomas à Kempis*

DAY 4

Paul the Preacher

Unfortunately, preachers have gotten a bad name in recent history because some have behaved poorly. The PTL Network and ministry fell as the result of the indiscretions of Jim Bakker. Fast on the heels of the PTL collapse, the Jimmy Swaggart scandal rocked the evangelical world. Larry King wrote about Rev. Swaggart: "I would buy all of the sadness and tears and recriminations if, and this is a big if, Jimmy had come forward with his problem before somebody had pictures proving it. Anybody can be repentant when caught. Also, if he really wanted true forgiveness, he could donate his estate and all that property to some worthy charity. Give up all his earthly goods."

If you don't live what you've learned, then you are a liar. "Be doers of the word, and not hearers only, deceiving yourselves" (James 1:22). This week we have learned that Paul practiced what he preached. He was able to say with confidence, "You should imitate me, just as I imitate Christ" (1 Cor. 11:1 NLT). Being a preacher involves both doing what you say and saying words of truth. Since we already know some of what Paul did, let's look at what Paul the preacher had to say.

LIFT UP ...

Jesus, I'm grateful for the good examples You have put in my life—for the people who walk their talk. Help me to be a good example so when people see me, they see You, too. In Jesus' name. Amen.

LOOK AT ...

Today we examine yet another position this amazing man assumed in his ministry to the Gentiles: preacher of God's Word.

LEARN ABOUT ...

2 Endless Riches

Searching for buried treasure? You don't need a pirate's map; you need the Word of God. It holds the key to the unsearchable riches of Christ: "Oh, the depth of the riches both of the wisdom and knowledge of God!" (Rom. 11:33).

---

5 Manifold Wisdom

In his book *Be Rich*, Warren Wiersbe said, "This word [manifold] carries the idea of 'variegated' or 'many-colored.' This suggests the beauty and variety of God's wisdom in His great plan of salvation."[6]

---

6 Principalities

This refers to angelic beings. People believe that angels know everything, but they don't. Here we see something the angels were curious about: God's plan of salvation for the Gentiles—"things which angels desire to look into" (I Peter 1:12).

READ EPHESIANS 3:8B–11.

... that I should preach among the Gentiles the unsearchable riches of Christ, and to make all see what is the fellowship of the mystery, which from the beginning of the ages has been hidden in God who created all things through Jesus Christ; to the intent that now the manifold wisdom of God might be made known by the church to the principalities and powers in the heavenly places, according to the eternal purpose which He accomplished in Christ Jesus our Lord. Ephesians 3:8b–11

1. Paul was given grace for what purpose?

2. What was Paul supposed to preach to the Gentiles?

3. What did Paul want all to see through his preaching? How would you put this in your own words?

4. How long had this mystery been hidden? Where was this mystery hidden?

5. By whom was the manifold wisdom of God made known?

6. a. To whom was this manifold wisdom made known?

   b. What do you think about this?

7. What phrase lets you know that the mystery of the church was not an afterthought?

8. Who accomplished this eternal purpose?

LIVE OUT ...

9. Paul was a man who practiced what he preached. You may not be a preacher in the pulpit, but God expects your life to speak volumes.

Journal about a way your actions can speak God's love language this week. (Example: Give your time to a lonely neighbor.)

10. a. Sometimes your actions, public or private, can distort the message of God's grace to the world around you. List any behaviors in your life that are contradictory. (Example: I'm unethical in my business dealings, making promises I don't intend to keep.)

    b. Write a prayer confessing this conduct as sin. Ask God to empower you to turn away from it. Pray for a life that proclaims the goodness of God to those people you come in contact with.

11. a. Maybe your actions have made an impression on unbelievers, but they don't know about your faith. You've shown them the gospel—now it's time to tell them. Name someone who needs to hear the good news of God's love.

    b. Write a prayer asking God to give you the boldness and opportunity to witness to the person you named.

o o ● o o

Billy Graham has been called "America's Preacher." *Time* magazine included him in their list of "Heroes of the Twentieth Century," saying that Billy Graham exemplifies "courage, selflessness, exuberance, superhuman ability and amazing grace."[7] He's a hero admired not just for his achievements but, more importantly, for his character.

LEARN ABOUT ...

10 God Sees

My mother had eyes in the back of her head. If I (Lenya) misbehaved, she always found out. God has the eyes of eternity. Nothing escapes His view. If you misbehave, He'll always see. "For the eyes of the LORD run to and fro throughout the whole earth" (2 Chron. 16:9).

11 Great Commission

Some get the Great Commission backward. Instead of a "go into all the world" mentality, they develop a "come to our church service" mind-set. Christians are salt to a tasteless world. Pour the salt of your testimony out of the saltshaker and into your world. "Go into all the world and preach the Good News to everyone" (Mark 16:15 NLT).

Billy Graham has remained faithful while so many others have faltered because he determined that integrity would be the hallmark of his life and ministry. The foundation to that commitment came early in his organization when his team developed the "Modesto Manifesto" while at a crusade in California. In his autobiography, *Just As I Am*, Billy Graham shared the four commitments included in the manifesto:

Financial Accountability: "We determined to do all we could to avoid financial abuses and to downplay the offering and depend as much as possible on the money raised by the local committees in advance."

Sexual Purity: "We pledged among ourselves to avoid any situation that would have even the appearance of compromise or suspicion. From that day on, I did not travel, meet, or eat alone with a woman other than my wife."

Church Cooperation: "We were determined to cooperate with all who would cooperate with us in the public proclamation of the Gospel, and to avoid an antichurch or anticlergy attitude."

Publicity Integrity: "The tendency among some evangelists was to exaggerate their successes or to claim higher attendance numbers than they really had. This likewise discredited evangelism and brought the whole enterprise under suspicion.... In Modesto we committed ourselves to integrity in our publicity and our reporting."[8]

Like the apostle Paul, Billy Graham has been committed to practicing what he preaches. What about you? If you haven't been doing what you've been saying, maybe it's time to make a manifesto of your own.

LISTEN TO ...

There are many who agree with God in principle but not in practice.

—*Richard Owen Roberts*

DAY 5

Paul's Approach

"You kids are going to have to follow me down to the station," the police officer said as I (Lenya) dropped my head and shuffled my feet in the sand. At that moment I knew our little prank had gone too far. It was the middle of a long, hot summer, and we were bored. So a pack of my high school friends decided to take a midnight excursion to the wooded area known as the "twilight zone," where a crazy hermit lived in a dilapidated shack. We were young, stupid, and cocky enough to harass this mythical creature with toilet paper, rock throwing, and name-calling.

It all seemed perfectly innocent until the flashing lights and roaring siren rushed down the dirt road. We ran screaming into the bushes for shelter. The diligent officer of the Ludington Police Department found us anyway. I learned then that it's good to have friends in high places. When I told him my mother was married to Eugene Christman, the city attorney, he immediately changed his tone. Approaching him in my own name only made him scowl. Coming to him in the name of a man more powerful and influential than I was changed everything. Instead of taking us to jail, he sent us home with a stern lecture and a warning to keep out of trouble.

Paul knew the value of friends in high places too. He knew the only way to approach almighty God was in the name of His Son, turning judgment into justification.

LIFT UP ...

Lord, when I'm in trouble, I know that I can call on Your name to be saved. Forgive me for the times I've called out to others before calling on You. In Jesus' name. Amen.

LOOK AT ...

This week we have gained valuable insight into the life of Paul and have been challenged to a higher standard because of his example. Today we look at the manner in which Paul approached God.

LEARN ABOUT ...

1 Christ

Christ is sometimes translated "Messiah." It is a name that showed that Jesus was the long-awaited King and Deliverer. Jesus was clearly identified as the Messiah: "You are the Christ, the Son of the living God" (Matt. 16:16).

3 Boldness

Boldness is a courageous or daring spirit in the face of danger. Boldness is the courage to do something despite fear. Peter feared the storm but got out of the boat anyway, boldly going where only God had gone before.

6 Confidence

Paul's confident access to God was not the result of his bravery but of his belief. In the Old Testament only the high priest could enter God's presence once a year. Jesus changed that—now anyone can boldly approach God: "We can boldly enter heaven's Most Holy Place because of the blood of Jesus" (Heb. 10:19 NLT).

READ EPHESIANS 3:11–12.

... in Christ Jesus our Lord, in whom we have boldness and access with confidence through faith in Him. Ephesians 3:11–12

1. What two titles did Paul give Jesus?

2. Paul used the preposition *in* three times to describe his approach to God. Fill in the blanks to discover who opens the door of access.

   In _____

   In _____

   In _____

3. What words describe how we can approach God?

4. Why do you think being "in" Christ gives us confident access to God?

5. What's the connection between faith and access to God?

6. What four things motivated Paul to approach God?

   B_____

   A_____

   C_____

   F_____

7. According to Hebrews 4:15–16, to what do we have access?

LIVE OUT ...

8. Paul uses two titles to describe Jesus: *Christ* and *Lord*. Jesus wants to be much more than the Savior from your sins. He wants to be the Lord of your life. Fill in the chart below to discover ways to surrender to your Lord Jesus Christ.

SCRIPTURE	LESSON ON LORDSHIP
Matthew 9:36–38	
Mark 2:27–28	
Romans 14:8–9	
1 Corinthians 6:13–14, 19–20	
Colossians 3:17–21, 23–24	

9. God owns you. He is the Lord of your life and death, physical appetites, and relationships. The one thing you should never say is, "No, Lord." Lordship demands obedience.

   a. Journal about an area from the chart above where you have not surrendered to your Lord. What ways have you "just said no" to Him?

   b. Journal a prayer of repentance asking the Lord to forgive you for disobedience. Ask Him to help you "just say yes"!

10. We discovered that the role of subjects in relationship to their lord is obedience. The role of a lord in relationship to subjects is provision. Our Lord is a Good Shepherd who provides all our needs. Read Psalm 23, then circle the good things He has provided:

LEARN ABOUT ...

8 Lord

The word *lord* denotes ownership, implying absolute control. It applies to owners over slaves and kings over subjects. It is applied to God as owner and ruler of the earth. *Lord* also applies to Jesus since by His death He acquired a special ownership of mankind.

9 Lord of Life

Jesus taught His disciples that responding to His lordship is not just verbal, it's active. He doesn't want to be just the Lord of your lips, but the Lord of your life. "Not everyone who calls out to me, 'Lord! Lord!' will enter the Kingdom of Heaven. Only those who actually do the will of my Father in heaven will enter" (Matt. 7:21 NLT).

The LORD is my shepherd;
    I have all that I need.
He lets me rest in green meadows;
    he leads me beside peaceful streams.
He renews my strength.
He guides me along right paths,
    bringing honor to his name.
Even when I walk
    through the darkest valley,
I will not be afraid,
    for you are close beside me.
Your rod and your staff
    protect and comfort me.
You prepare a feast for me
    in the presence of my enemies.
You honor me by anointing my head with oil.
    My cup overflows with blessings.
Surely your goodness and unfailing love will pursue me
    all the days of my life,
and I will live in the house of the LORD
    forever. (NLT)

· · ● · ·

After applying for a marriage license in Detroit, a bachelor didn't return to the county clerk's office until eleven years later to pick up the important piece of paper. When the clerk asked why he and his bride had waited so long to get married, he admitted, "We had a few disagreements about the details." How tragic that this couple let years pass by because they were too stubborn to yield on minor details!

Christians have the same problem. Some waste years refusing to let the Lord Jesus arrange and govern the details of their agreement. A 1991 Gallup poll revealed that 78 percent of Americans expect to go to heaven. However, many of them hardly ever pray, read the Bible, or attend church. They admit that they live to please themselves instead of God. Today we learned that if He's not Lord of all, He's not Lord at all! To be your Savior, He must also be your Lord. When you surrender all to Him, you will experience the confidence and boldness to approach His throne in faith. You will discover that your Lord wants to be your provider and husband, too. Are you ready to sign on the dotted line?

LISTEN TO ...

What a great summary of the Christian life: "Christ died to be our Savior and lives to be our Lord." Why do we forget this? It's so simple!

—*Hank Hanegraaff*

LESSON SIX

Exceedingly Abundantly More
Ephesians 3:14–21

Danny Sampson used a hand-me-down Colt .45 to rob a bank in Canada, getting away with six thousand dollars. When the Mounties caught up with him, they confiscated the gun and sent it to their laboratory, where it was recognized as a collector's item. Danny discovered that he didn't have to rob a bank; his gun was worth $100,000!

As Christians, we are exhorted to have knowledge of all that we possess in Christ. Danny Sampson didn't realize the value of what was already his, so he did something foolish. When we don't take advantage of our resources in God's promises, we are tempted to fulfill our needs through fleshly means. It's human nature to look for power, love, and knowledge to make our lives rich. Through the "path of flesh," some find power in politics, love through lust, knowledge at a university, and fullness from a bottle. But these attempts to fulfill our needs are as futile as Danny's attempt to get rich by stealing. Paul said you don't have to rob a bank to get rich; you simply need to ask your heavenly Father.

This week we come to Paul's second prayer in the book of Ephesians. His first prayer was for believers to receive illumination—to see what treasures God has for us. Now Paul asks for inspiration—to use the wealth that is exceedingly, abundantly more than we can conceive.

Day 1: Ephesians 3:14–15   **BOWING DOWN—LOOKING UP**

Day 2: Ephesians 3:16   **GLORIOUS RICHES**

Day 3: Ephesians 3:17   **MANSION MAKER**

Day 4: Ephesians 3:18–19   **HIDDEN TREASURE**

Day 5: Ephesians 3:19–21   **THERE'S MORE?**

DAY 1

Bowing Down—Looking Up

LIFT UP ...

Father, I bow down to You because You alone are worthy of praise. I look up to You because You are the source of all that is good. Please inspire me to use all that You have for me. In Jesus' name. Amen.

LOOK AT ...

Paul gave us clues here about his view of the God to whom he prayed. As you study today, ask God to reveal Himself to you in a new and powerful way.

READ EPHESIANS 3:14–15.

For this reason I bow my knees to the Father of our Lord Jesus Christ, from whom the whole family in heaven and earth is named ... Ephesians 3:14–15

Learn about ...

2 Bowing

The practice of bowing was intended to convey an attitude of reverence, respect, humility, and homage toward others. A bent knee reveals a surrendered heart. "'As surely as I live,' says the LORD, 'every knee will bend to me, and every tongue will confess and give praise to God'" (Rom. 14:11 NLT).

4 Born of God

Biblical adoption cannot be rescinded—you are God's child now and forever. "You received the Spirit of adoption by whom we cry out, 'Abba, Father.' ... We are children of God" (Rom. 8:15–16).

5 Extended Family

"Family in heaven and earth" speaks of saints from every age—those presently in heaven and those who remain on earth. God is the Father of the living and the dead. The moment Christian loved ones leave your side they will find themselves by His side: "To be absent from the body and to be present with the Lord." (2 Cor. 5:8).

1. "For this reason" is a transitional phrase encouraging the reader to look back before looking forward. Look back at last week's lesson. What were the reasons for Paul's prayer?

2. What was Paul's physical posture as he prayed?

3. To whom did Paul bow?

4. Who is named after the Father?

5. What two locations are given for God's family?

6. According to John 1:12–13,

    a. Who makes up the family of God?

    b. Based on these verses, how do you know that you are a member of God's family?

Live Out ...

7. a. Paul's prayers were so passionate they brought him to his knees. How would you describe your prayer life?

    b. Journal how you see your prayer life now and how you would like to see it strengthened.

8. Think about a person who is a vital, confident prayer warrior. What qualities of that person's prayer life attract you?

9. Paul bowed down while he prayed. Fill in the chart to discover what other postures for prayer are recorded in Scripture.

Scripture	Person	Posture
Exodus 34:8		
1 Kings 8:22		
1 Chronicles 17:16		
Matthew 26:39		

10. How's your prayer posture? Which of the postures from the chart above have you practiced in your prayer life? Pick one that you've never experienced before, and try it now while reciting the Lord's Prayer:

> Our Father in heaven,
> Hallowed be Your name.
> Your kingdom come.
> Your will be done
> On earth as it is in heaven.
> Give us this day our daily bread.
> And forgive us our debts,
> As we forgive our debtors.
> And do not lead us into temptation,
> But deliver us from the evil one.
> For Yours is the kingdom and the power and the glory
> forever. Amen. (Matt. 6:9–13)

∘ ∘ ● ∘ ∘

Emperor worship began in the first century BC after the Roman senate voted to deify Julius Caesar. In his honor a temple was erected as a place

LEARN ABOUT …

7 Red-Hot Prayer

What's the temperature of your prayers? Lukewarm prayers are ineffective. James tells us to pray red-hot prayers: "The effective, fervent prayer of a righteous man avails much" (James 5:16). The word translated *fervent* means "to be hot or to boil." Is your prayer closet chilly? Then turn up the heat!

10 Posture

Don't be an imposter in your posture. You could have bent knees but a stiff neck, praying, "My will be done," instead of, "Thy will be done." Your posture is more than a physical position; it's a spiritual condition.

of worship. Under Augustus Caesar, emperor worship flourished and was incorporated into local religions. Under Emperor Trajan, Christians who would not renounce their allegiance to Christ and bow down to worship the emperor were often executed.

The penalties early Christians suffered were terrible beyond description. Christians were flung to the lions or burned at the stake. Caesar Nero drenched Christians in pitch and set them on fire, using them as living torches to light his gardens. They were tortured on the rack or scraped with pincers; molten lead was poured upon them; red-hot brass plates were affixed to the most tender parts of their bodies; their eyes were torn out.

There's a time to bow down and a time to stand tall. Christians have one true allegiance—to God. Jesus demonstrated the delicate balance between God and country when He said, "Render to Caesar the things that are Caesar's, and to God the things that are God's" (Mark 12:17). We may be called to honor king and country, but we, like Paul, must never bow down and worship anyone else but God.

LISTEN TO ...

Don't pray when you feel like it. Have an appointment with the Lord and keep it. A man is powerful on his knees.

—*Corrie ten Boom*

DAY 2

Glorious Riches

At a church meeting a very wealthy man rose to tell those present about his Christian faith. "I'm a millionaire," he said, "and I attribute it all to the rich blessings of God in my life. I remember that turning point in my faith. I had just earned my first dollar, and I went to a church meeting that night. The speaker was a missionary who told about his work. I knew that I only had a dollar bill and had to either give it all to God's work or nothing at all. So at that moment I decided to give my whole dollar to God. I believe that God blessed that decision, and that is why I am a rich man today."

There was an awed silence at his testimony. As he sat down, a little old lady sitting in the same pew whispered, "I dare you to do it again."

It's easier to give all that you have when you don't have very much. This man gave when the stakes were small. But would he be willing to give big when the stakes were raised? God is an extravagant giver—His riches and resources are limitless. He's got it all, and He's willing to share it all with His children, "according to the riches of His glory" (Eph. 3:16).

LIFT UP ...

God, Your Word says that You have given me everything I need to live a godly life. Help me to use the abundance You've given to perform good works that glorify You. In Jesus' name. Amen.

LOOK AT ...

Yesterday we learned of Paul's posture in prayer. Today we will examine the first petition in Paul's prayer for believers.

LEARN ABOUT ...

2 God's Riches

This term is used in a figurative sense to represent the gifts and graces of God's Holy Spirit: "Do you despise the riches of His goodness, forbearance, and longsuffering, not knowing that the goodness of God leads you to repentance?" (Rom. 2:4).

---

4 The Spirit

This is power in a person—the Holy Spirit. This is power with a purpose: "You will receive power when the Holy Spirit comes upon you. And you will be my witnesses, telling people about me everywhere" (Acts 1:8 NLT). With the Holy Spirit's power we will tell the world about Jesus!

READ EPHESIANS 3:16.

... that He would grant you, according to the riches of His glory, to be strengthened with might through His Spirit in the inner man ... Ephesians 3:16

1. What did Paul ask God to grant the Ephesians?

2. According to what resources does God grant prayer requests?

3. The riches of God's glory are a powerful resource. How can they help us, according to verse 16?

4. Through what means does God strengthen believers?

5. Where does God strengthen believers?

6. In 2 Corinthians 4:16–18 Paul contrasts differences between the "inward" and the "outward" person. Read the passage, then place the following key phrases under the heading that indicates where these things happen: *perishing, renewed, light affliction, eternal glory, seen, not seen, temporary, eternal.*

INWARD PERSON　　　　**OUTWARD PERSON**

LIVE OUT ...

7. We all need to be strengthened inwardly through God's Spirit. Mark an S by the items that *strengthen* you spiritually (i.e., inwardly) and mark with a W those activities that weaken you spiritually.

    ____ Reading the Bible   ____ Surrender

    ____ Prayer   ____ Entertainment

    ____ Worry   ____ Life-dominating habits

    ____ Godly counsel   ____ Seeking pleasure

    ____ Fellowship with others   ____ Jealousy

    ____ Adversity   ____ Other_____

8. Which of the above activities (or others) do you need to incorporate more into your life?

9. Which of the above activities (or others) do you need to eliminate from your life through God's strength?

10. Journal your thoughts about what keeps you from doing things that will strengthen you spiritually. How can you begin to make these changes in your life through the glorious riches of God?

11. Paul showed that it is God's will for us "to be strengthened with might through His Spirit in the inner man" (Eph. 3:16). Putting Ephesians 3:16 into your own words, journal a personal and specific prayer asking God to help you overcome the flesh through the power of His Spirit.

LEARN ABOUT ...

7 Spiritually Strong

Gold's Gym or God's Gym—where do you work out? Society is obsessed with the beautiful body; God is concerned with the strong soul: "Physical training is good, but training for godliness is much better, promising benefits in this life and in the life to come" (I Tim. 4:8 NLT).

9 Inner Turmoil

The inner person is made up of two entities: the spirit and the flesh. There is a constant battle between them. The one you surrender to is the one that will grow stronger and win the war. "Watch and pray, lest you enter into temptation. The spirit indeed is willing, but the flesh is weak" (Mark 14:38).

II Inner Strength

If you discovered a genie in a bottle and were granted three wishes, would "strength" make it to the top of your list? Probably not. But more than fame or fortune, God knows that supernatural strength is one of our greatest needs—as *Jesus Loves Me* says, "We are weak, but He is strong."

○ ○ ● ○ ○

Iris Bammert walked slower than most to the podium. Her face reflected a quiet confidence that, no matter how long it took, she would reach her goal. At last, she reached the microphone and spoke with gentle strength: "God has let me know that in this life we have tribulation, but be of good cheer. I have overcome the world."

Iris suffered a debilitating stroke in the prime of her life. Her whole world changed in a moment—from self-sufficiency to complete dependency. She can't drive a car anymore; instead, she's driven to her knees in prayer, seeking a strength that is not her own. She can barely speak, but God enabled her to remind the women in our Bible study, "This life is not so important. Don't forget the Lord is the One who does everything in and through us."

God does not ask you to walk in your own strength—He knows that is impossible. However, He does promise to give you the strength you need to walk in a way that is pleasing to Him. Philippians 4:13 reminds us, "I can do everything through Christ, who gives me strength" (NLT).

Listen To ...

Life … is a hard fight, a struggle, a wrestling with the Principle of Evil, hand to hand, foot to foot. Every inch of the way must be disputed. The night is given us to take breath, to pray, to drink deep at the fountain of power. The day, to use the strength which has been given us, to go forth to work with it till the evening.

—*Florence Nightingale*

DAY 3
Mansion Maker

It was a vintage home nestled among the tall trees near the University of New Mexico. Perhaps it was old-fashioned with its hardwood floors instead of carpet, but it suited our young family perfectly. The old furnace was noisy and inefficient, but that didn't matter. Our hearts were warmed by the love we felt toward one another. At least that's what I thought, until the day Skip called to say, "Would it be okay if I bring Franklin Graham home for dinner?"

"Franklin Graham!" I said. "Son of Ruth and Billy Graham? The president of Samaritan's Purse International?" As I switched into high gear, tidying up the place and putting dinner in the oven, the walls began to close in around me. I thought, *We don't have enough dining-room chairs for everyone. If that furnace acts up tonight, I'll be so embarrassed. Why did we buy an old worn-down house with only one bathroom?* When our guest arrived, he disarmed us with his genteel Southern charm and grateful spirit. He insisted on sitting on the floor with Skip while they ate. Franklin made me feel like our little house was more than an old home; it felt like a mansion.

Guess who's coming to have dinner with you? Jesus. He said, "If you hear my voice and open the door, I will come in, and we will share a meal together as friends" (Rev. 3:20 NLT). You may not have the latest fashion to wear, and perhaps you've got problems with the plumbing. Yet your humble Savior will come in, sit down, and make Himself at home. Your heart can become a mansion for the Maker of heaven and earth!

LIFT UP ...

Jesus, I am thrilled that You want to make my heart Your home. Thank You for making it possible for me to dwell with You in heaven and join You for a banquet. In Jesus' name. Amen.

LEARN ABOUT …

2 In Your Heart

God promises to take up residence in your heart. The God who can measure the universe with His hand is at home in your heart. "If anyone loves Me, he will keep My word; and My Father will love him, and We will come to him and make Our home with him" (John 14:23).

4 Rooted

This is an agricultural metaphor referring to the underground roots of a plant. To be grounded is an architectural term that speaks of a building's foundation. These two word pictures show that God's love toward a believer is both deep and strong.

7 The Owner

God is more than a houseguest. He is the rightful owner of your heart/home. You're not leasing the place to God—He holds the title deed. "For you were bought at a price; therefore glorify God in your body and in your spirit, which are God's" (I Cor. 6:20).

LOOK AT …

We know that we need to be strengthened inwardly by God's power. Paul's second petition was for Christ to dwell in us.

READ EPHESIANS 3:17.

… that Christ may dwell in your hearts through faith; that you, being rooted and grounded in love … Ephesians 3:17

1. Restate in your own words the two requests Paul made here.

2. Where did he pray for Christ to dwell? How?

3. Read John 14:17. What other member of the Trinity takes up residence in the heart of the believer?

4. What two words in Ephesians 3:17 describe stability in the life of a believer?

5. What are Christians to be rooted and grounded in? What do you think this means in practical terms?

6. According to Matthew 22:37–39, who are believers commanded to love?

LIVE OUT …

7. We've seen that the Trinity of God dwells within a believer's heart. Check the areas below that are evidence that your heart is God's home.

___ I believe Jesus is Messiah.

___ I believe Jesus died for my sins.

___ I have repented of my sins.

___ I asked Jesus to be Lord and Savior.

___ He has a place at our table.

___ We've cleaned out the closets.

___ He's rearranged the furniture.

8. Since your heart is Christ's home, journal through the exercise below.

   a. Ask God to reveal any closet space or dark corners that are not under His influence. (Perhaps you've been keeping a bad habit neatly tucked away—He sees it.)

   b. Acknowledge what other things have cluttered your heart and distracted your focus. (A good thing can become a bad thing if it keeps you from the best thing—Jesus!)

   c. Write a prayer and purposefully open each "room" in your heart to the fresh work of Christ. (Spring-cleaning includes airing out the place—let His Spirit blow through.)

9. A heart full of God's love needs to reach out. Jesus commanded us to love our neighbors as ourselves. Who are the people in your neighborhood? In the chart, name some of your neighbors, then list a way you will demonstrate God's love to them.

NEIGHBOR	HOW I WILL DEMONSTRATE GOD'S LOVE

LEARN ABOUT …

8 At the Center

Bible scholar Leon Morris said, "If Christ dwells in our hearts he is at the very center of our being and exercises his influence over all that we do and are."[1] That may mean it's time for spring-cleaning. Are there areas in your life that need to be washed, painted, or repaired?

9 In Love

The Greek word used for love is *agape*—love that is a matter of the will, not of the emotions. Thus, we choose to love whether we feel like it or not. "Love your enemies! … In that way, you will be acting as true children of your Father in heaven" (Matt. 5:44–45 NLT).

∘ ∘ ● ∘ ∘

James Hewett tells the story of a sailor shipwrecked on a South Sea island. He was seized by the natives, carried to the village, and set on a crude throne. He soon learned that it was their custom each year to make one man a king—for a year. He liked this until he discovered that every year each king was banished to an island where he starved to death. The sailor didn't like that, but he was smart—and he was king. So he put his carpenters to work making boats, his farmers to work transplanting fruit trees and crops, and his masons to work building houses. When his reign was over, he was banished, not to a barren island, but to an island of abundance. This sailor was wise. He learned to live for the future, not merely the present.

Foolishly, some people are so busy taking care of their earthly homes they neglect their heavenly dwelling place. Paul taught that while the deeds we perform now don't purchase a place in heaven, they do supply spiritual "building materials" for our heavenly homes. What will your mansion look like? "For no one can lay any foundation other than the one we already have—Jesus Christ. Anyone who builds on that foundation may use a variety of materials—gold, silver, jewels, wood, hay, or straw. But on the judgment day, fire will reveal what kind of work each builder has done. The fire will show if a person's work has any value" (1 Cor. 3:11–13 NLT).

LISTEN TO ...

Father! replenish with thy grace this longing heart of mine; Make it thy quiet dwelling place, thy sacred inmost shrine!

—*Angelus Silesius*

DAY 4
Hidden Treasure

There was a man in Wales who sought to win the affection of a certain lady for forty-two years before she finally said yes. The couple, both seventy-four years old, became man and wife. For those forty-two years the persistent, rather shy man had slipped a weekly love letter under his neighbor's door. But she continually refused to speak to him and mend the spat that had parted them many years before.

After writing 2,184 love letters without ever getting a spoken or written answer, the single-hearted old man eventually summoned up enough courage to present himself in person. He knocked on the door of the reluctant lady and asked for her hand. To his delight and surprise, she accepted.

Like these two senior citizens, we discover that the greatest treasure in life is true love. Gold loses its luster. Money sprouts wings and is gone. Eventually, we all concede, things don't really matter—relationships do!

Paul understood the value of a relationship with God. So he prayed that Christians would know the unknowable and discover His hidden treasure. God's letters of love were delivered over centuries by prophets and apostles to the hearts of His people. But when God did not get the desired response from His loved ones, He sent His Son. That was God's way of revealing to us the height, depth, width, and length of His love. Open the door of your heart and say "I do" to your persistent God.

Lift Up ...

Father, I am forever grateful to You for sending Your Son, Jesus, to knock on the door of my heart. I love You and gladly say "I do" to You now and for all eternity. In Jesus' name. Amen.

LEARN ABOUT ...

I Comprehend

To comprehend means "to lay hold of so as to possess as one's own, to appropriate; to seize upon, take possession of." Paul was praying for saints to grasp and possess the incredible love of Christ. This is the kind of love you can take to the bank!

4b Cross of Love

On a highway in Louisiana there's a billboard high above the city as you reach the Mississippi River bridge. On it is a picture of Jesus hanging on the cross, head bowed. The caption says, "It's Your Move!" If you reach up as far as you can, God will reach all the way down.

4c Reaching Out

The love of Christ reaches out in every direction, extending beyond the horizon. No matter which way you turn, you'll find God's love. "Your unfailing love is higher than the heavens. Your faithfulness reaches to the clouds" (Ps. 108:4 NLT).

LOOK AT ...

God's love is a firm foundation. In Paul's third petition, we discover just how great that love is.

READ EPHESIANS 3:18–19.

... [that you] may be able to comprehend with all the saints what is the width and length and depth and height—to know the love of Christ which passes knowledge ... Ephesians 3:18–19

1. What more did Paul want for the Ephesians?

2. Who else will be able to comprehend this knowledge? Explain in your own words.

3. Paul offered some insight into Christ's love. What are the four dimensions Paul used to describe the love of Christ?

4. a. Connect the dots from width to length, then separately from height to depth.

height
•

width •   • length

•

depth

b. How do these four dimensions illustrate Christ's love?

c. Now draw an arrow pointing outward from each of these dimensions. Label the arrows like a compass. What insight do you gain about Christ's love from this picture?

5. What did Paul pray believers will know?

6. What phrase leads you to believe this knowledge is beyond human comprehension?

7. Why do you think Paul made this seemingly contradictory request?

LIVE OUT ...

8. What is the most profound or creative way you have ever demonstrated your love for another person?

9. a. What is one of the best ways someone else has revealed their love toward you?

    b. Journal about how that action made you feel and what it meant to you.

10. a. Name some of those who desperately need to truly comprehend—grab hold of—God's boundless love.

    b. Journal a prayer that God will go knocking on the door of their hearts. Pray for your opportunity to go knocking on the door of their house and show God's love to them.

o o ● o o

God's love knows no limits; He has gone to great lengths to express His boundless love to us. It reminds me of the story Richard Selzer tells in his book *Mortal Lessons,* a story of a deep and wide kind of love.

LEARN ABOUT ...

6 Unknowable

Knowing the unknowable is possible only through the inspiration of the Holy Spirit. The Spirit of God is the best teacher to have. "The Helper, the Holy Spirit, whom the Father will send in My name, He will teach you all things" (John 14:26).

9 True Love

The evidence of true love is not in whispering sweet nothings but in showing sincere actions. Words of adoration that never lead to acts of devotion are empty. "This is My commandment, that you love one another as I have loved you. Greater love has no one than this, than to lay down one's life for his friends" (John 15:12–13).

10 Love's Journey

Comprehending God's love requires a trip of eighteen inches from the head to the heart. It's not enough to know God's love intellectually; we must feel it experientially and demonstrate it practically. "If we love each other, God lives in us, and his love is brought to full expression in us" (1 John 4:12 NLT).

I stand by the bed where a young woman lies, her face postoperative, her mouth twisted.... A tiny twig of the facial nerve, the one to the muscles of her mouth, has been severed.... The surgeon had followed with religious fervor the curve of her flesh; I promise you that. Yet, to remove the tumor in her cheek, I had cut the little nerve.

Her young husband is in the room. He stands on the opposite side of the bed, and together they seem to dwell in the evening lamplight, isolated from me, private.... [They] touch each other so generously, greedily.... The young woman speaks:

"Will my mouth always be like this?" she asks.

"Yes," I say, "it will. It is because the nerve was cut."

She nods, and is silent. But the young man smiles.

"I like it," he says. "It is kind of cute."

At once I *know* who he is, and I lower my gaze. One is not bold in an encounter with [God]. Unmindful, he bends to kiss her crooked mouth, and I am so close I can see how he twists his own lips to accommodate to hers, to show her that their kiss still works.[2]

Listen To ...

If we have got the true love of God shed abroad in our hearts, we will show it in our lives. We will not have to go up and down the earth proclaiming it. We will show it in everything we say or do.

—*Dwight Lyman Moody*

DAY 5
There's More?

When my husband and I (Lenya) were new to the ministry, our first dinner invitation came from Paul and Millie Ciaccio, an affectionate couple who had been raised in New York by old-world Italian parents. We arrived at their mountain home with big appetites. Paul ushered us into the kitchen as Millie set out chips and salsa.

"Hope you're hungry," she said. A bountiful salad and crusty Italian bread were the first course, and Millie beamed with pride as she served one of her mother's famous pasta dishes. "Do you want seconds?" she asked, heaping a mountain-sized portion on my plate. My eyes bulged and my waistband was getting tight, but I thought, *I'd better eat what's put before me; dinner is almost over.* At that moment Paul came in with the main course.

In disbelief I said, "There's more?" Oh yes, there was more—exceedingly, abundantly more: pot roast with potatoes and vegetables, followed by homemade peach pie á la mode along with fresh fruit and coffee. I learned that old-world Italians express their love by filling you with food, and the Ciaccios' love was so great I was ready to pop!

God loves to fill His children full of goodness too! God has sent His Spirit to fill our inner being, Jesus to fill our hearts, and still there's more—exceedingly, abundantly more. Paul prayed that we will be filled with all the fullness of God—what more could you possibly want?

LIFT UP ...

Lord, I cannot be full of You and full of myself at the same time. Help me to empty my life of self, and fill me to overflowing with Your fullness. In Jesus' name. Amen.

LOOK AT ...

We have learned so much from this beautiful passage. Today we examine the fourth and last element of Paul's prayer for believers.

LEARN ABOUT ...

1 Filled Up

When you're full of something, there's no room for anything else. A person filled with hostility has no room for peace; a person filled with love has no room for hate. Being filled with all the fullness of God means there's no room for self. All of God; none of me.

5 Power at Work

We often desire power to control others—a "power trip." God gives us power so we can control ourselves. The transition from having power to using power wisely is a trip worth taking. "God has not given us a spirit of fear and timidity, but of power, love, and self-discipline" (2 Tim. 1:7 NLT).

7 To Him Be Glory

Candles melt away, lightbulbs burn out, sunsets fade, but in the heavenly city God's glory will shine brightly forever and ever. "And the city has no need of sun or moon, for the glory of God illuminates the city, and the Lamb is its light" (Rev. 21:23 NLT).

READ EPHESIANS 3:19–21.

... that you may be filled with all the fullness of God. Now to Him who is able to do exceedingly abundantly above all that we ask or think, according to the power that works in us, to Him be glory in the church by Christ Jesus to all generations, forever and ever. Amen. Ephesians 3:19–21

1. a. Paul prayed for believers to be filled with what?

    b. What do you think it's like to be filled in this way?

2. At the conclusion of Paul's prayer, he shared the reasons he believed God could and would answer his prayer. How did Paul first describe God?

3. What words describe God's amazing ability to act?

4. Above what does God's power exceed?

5. Where is God's exceptional power at work?

6. a. Who receives glory?

    b. What do you think "glory in the church" means?

7. To whom is it revealed and for how long?

LIVE OUT ...

8. What are your days full of? On a sheet of lined paper, make a grid: In a column on the left, list the hours of the day from 6:00

a.m. to 10:00 p.m. In a row across the top, list the days of the week. Then fill in your activities and routines. If there's no room for God in your daily schedule, perhaps it's time to do some holy editing. Place an E by the activities that are essential, that cannot be removed (work, meals, church worship, etc.); place an O by the items that are optional (TV viewing, hobbies, phone calls, etc.).

Journal about the ways you can empty your schedule of distractions and fill it with devotion to God.

9. Paul concluded his prayer with an amazing declaration of God's overwhelming ability to answer our requests. God is "able to do exceedingly abundantly above all that we ask or think." With this in mind, work through the steps below.

Step One: Journal about the most difficult situation you face.

Step Two: Use your spiritual imagination to dream of the best possible solution to that situation. Journal about the solution you came up with.

Step Three: Now journal a prayer asking God to do something bigger and better than your wildest dreams. Ask Him to put His unlimited resources to work.

o o ● o o

Is there such a thing as an "impossible dream"? One small-minded man living in the nineteenth century believed so. When asked if he thought it would be possible for men to fly in the air like birds, he responded skeptically, "Flight is strictly reserved for the angels, and I beg you not to repeat your suggestion lest you be guilty of blasphemy!" Ironically, the

LEARN ABOUT ...

8 Daily Investment

What would you do if you were given $86,400? Would you fill your bank account or go to a boutique? You have been given 86,400 seconds in every day. Are you spending them wisely or squandering them? "Teach us to number our days, that we may gain a heart of wisdom" (Ps. 90:12).

9 Possibilities

How big is your God? Can He heal a cold as easily as cancer? Is He able to repair relationships as well as resurrect the dead? "Humanly speaking, it is impossible. But not with God. Everything is possible with God" (Mark 10:27 NLT). Don't put limits on a limitless God! Whatever box you've put Him in—it's too small.

man was Milton Wright, father of Orville and Wilbur—two men who dreamed big dreams. Only thirty years later near Kitty Hawk, North Carolina, they made their first flight in a heavier-than-air machine, the prototype for modern airplanes. They proved that impossible dreams can come true.

The apostle Paul wanted Christians to believe that the impossible is possible with God. He wanted them to understand that impossible prayers can come true through the ability of a God who can do exceedingly abundantly above all that you ask or think. Go ahead, dream big dreams; then pray impossible prayers. God can make them soar!

LISTEN TO ...

God calls us to live a life we cannot live, so that we must depend on him for supernatural ability. We are called to do the impossible, to live beyond our natural ability.

—*Erwin W. Lutzer*

Coming of Age

Ephesians 4:1–16

When a mother eagle builds a nest, she begins with broken branches, sharp rocks, and a number of other items that seem unsuitable for the project. Then she lines this prickly foundation with a thick layer of feathers, wool, or fur from animals she has killed, making a soft place to lay her eggs. When the baby birds reach flying age, this comfortable nest and the free meals the mother brings make them a bit reluctant to leave. That's when the mother eagle begins "stirring up the nest." She pulls away the soft layers, exposing the sharp rocks and branches. Eventually, this and other promptings force the young eagles to leave their once-comfortable home and move on to maturity.[1]

Coming of age isn't easy for eagles or human beings; there are dues to be paid all along the way. Like a mother eagle, God knows when you are fully equipped, ready to leave the nest and fly into adventures untold. This week in Ephesians, Paul urges you to grow up in Christ, because you "should no longer be children, tossed to and fro, … but, … [grow] up in all things into Him who is the head—Christ" (Eph. 4:14–15).

Day 1: Ephesians 4:1–3	THE FATHER'S BUSINESS
Day 2: Ephesians 4:4–6	ALL IN THE FAMILY
Day 3: Ephesians 4:7–10	DUES PAID
Day 4: Ephesians 4:11–13	FULLY EQUIPPED
Day 5: Ephesians 4:14–16	ALL GROWN UP

The Father's Business

LIFT UP ...

Dear Father, the work that You've given me to do has given purpose to my life. Thank You for including me in Your family's business. Please give me the time and energy to get the job done. In Jesus' name. Amen.

LOOK AT ...

In the first three chapters of Ephesians, Paul taught Christians what to *believe*. Beginning with Ephesians 4 and continuing through the end of the book, Paul taught Christians how to *behave* in light of their faith.

READ EPHESIANS 4:1–3.

I, therefore, the prisoner of the Lord, beseech you to walk worthy of the calling with which you were called, with all lowliness and gentleness, with longsuffering, bearing with one another in love, endeavoring to keep the unity of the Spirit in the bond of peace. Ephesians 4:1–3

1. What was Paul asking believers to do?

2. Of what should believers walk worthy?

3. Fill in the chart to discover more about our worthy calling.

SCRIPTURE	DESCRIPTION OF CALLING
Romans 11:29	
1 Corinthians 1:26–27	
Philippians 3:14	
2 Timothy 1:9	
Hebrews 3:1	

4. a. We must learn *how* to walk worthy of this high call. What four virtues characterize a worthy walk?

   b. Choose one of these and describe in your own words what it means.

5. What do these attributes help a believer do?

6. What kind of unity is described? What do you think this means?

7. How is this unity achieved?

8. What phrase lets us know that keeping unity requires effort?

LIVE OUT ...

9. Today we discovered there are godly virtues that help believers to "bear with one another." Jesus is the perfect example of forbearance because He exhibits all of these virtues in bearing with us. Fill in the following chart to discover His character traits.

b. Which phrase speaks of God's sovereignty?

c. Of God's ability to work out His purposes?

d. Of God indwelling believers?

LEARN ABOUT ...

10 One Another

There's another "one"
we shouldn't miss—one
another. Why? Because
you're not the only one in
the body. The Bible teaches
us to love, care, admonish,
and pray for one another:
"Be kindly affectionate to
one another with brotherly
love, in honor giving
preference to one another"
(Rom. 12:10).

LIVE OUT ...

9. a. Unity happens when two or more people join together for a
common purpose. Check the groups you are currently joined
with in some way. Then write the name of that group and how
you fit in.

___ Family name: (Example: Jane Doe, sister, wife, and daughter.)
___ Ethnic background:
___ Political party:
___ Church denomination:
___ Club or society:

b. Reflect on one of these groups to which you belong. What
things promote unity in that group? What kinds of things cause
disunity or problems? Journal your thoughts.

10. This week we've examined seven elements that unite all Christians.
Place a check next to the ones that you have experienced thus far
in your own faith journey. Then briefly write what your experience
has been.

___ One Lord: (Example: I accepted Jesus as Lord in 1992.)
___ One Body:
___ One Spirit:

Learn about ...

II One Lord

The Lord God is the "one Lord." He's One in quantity—unlike the numerous idols the pagans worshipped. He's One in quality—a cut above the rest. He's One in unity—the triune God. "Hear, O Israel: The LORD our God, the LORD is one!" (Deut. 6:4).

___ One Hope:

___ One Faith:

___ One Baptism:

___ One Father:

11. Christians are to unite together into "one body" as completely as the Father, the Son, and the Holy Spirit are joined as "one Lord" in the Trinity. Jesus prayed, "Holy Father, you have given me your name; now protect them by the power of your name so that they will be united just as we are" (John 17:11 NLT).

Reflect about a situation where the modern-day church has been fractured by disunity. (Example: the conflict between the Catholic and Protestant churches in Ireland.) Rewrite Jesus' prayer into your own petition for your brothers and sisters in Christ who are in conflict.

o o ● o o

United we stand, divided we fall. It is estimated that if the thirteen American colonies had been more unified at the time of the American Revolution, they could have won the war for independence in one year. Instead, because of division, it took eight bloody years of battle. As Christians, we're in a battle for souls, and the tragedy is that we fight one another instead of our common enemy. Imagine what the world would be like if the body of Christ would keep the unity and join forces for the kingdom of God.

Listen To ...

When men are animated by the love of Christ, they feel united, and the needs, sufferings, and joys of others are felt as their own.

—*Pope John XXIII*

DAY 3

Dues Paid

My father is a podiatrist; he heals hurting feet for a living. When I was in college, I needed to earn some money, so Dad invited me to come work in his office for the summer. I pictured myself happily typing letters, answering phones, and taking long lunches. Instead, I was given the unpleasant tasks of washing dirty feet and clipping gnarly toenails. As if that wasn't enough, my dad also expected me to show up early to wash windows and clean toilets—something the other office girls never did. "Don't they have janitors for that sort of thing?" I argued, thinking I was above that job. I guess my father wanted me to learn that I had to pay my dues in the work world so I'd grow into a productive adult.

God the Father created heaven and earth, and He heals hurting hearts for a living. His Son wanted to join the family business, and do you know what? He washed feet too! And He touched lepers. Slept without a bed. And if that were not enough, He endured the shame of the cross, descended to the lower parts of the earth, and then ascended far above the heavens. Jesus paid the dues for all of humanity's sin so we could grow into mature Christians.

LIFT UP ...

God, the penalty for my sin was too great for me to pay. Thank You for sending Your Son, Jesus, to pay my dues and ransom my life from bondage. In Jesus' name. Amen.

LOOK AT ...

In these verses Paul revealed the price Christ had to pay so each of us could be given the free gift of grace.

LEARN ABOUT ...

1 Each One

God addresses us as individuals. His knowledge of each one of us is detailed. He numbers the hairs of our heads, collects our tears in a bottle, and understands our thoughts from afar. "Such knowledge is too wonderful for me, too great for me to understand!" (Ps. 139:6 NLT).

5 Conquering Christ

Paul used military terms to depict Christ as a conquering hero returning from battle. In ancient times the victor rode triumphantly through the city, leading his victorious army, the bounty of war, and the shackled captives. An ancient ticker-tape parade!

READ EPHESIANS 4:7–10.

But to each one of us grace was given according to the measure of Christ's gift. Therefore He says:

> *"When He ascended on high,*
> *He led captivity captive,*
> *and gave gifts to men."*

(Now this, "He ascended"—what does it mean but that He also first descended into the lower parts of the earth? He who descended is also the One who ascended far above all the heavens, that He might fill all things.)
Ephesians 4:7–10

1. Who was Paul addressing here?

2. a. What has been given to each one of us?

   b. What does this word mean?

3. How is this grace given?

4. To where did Christ ascend? Put this in your own words.

5. What two things did His ascension accomplish?

6. To where did Christ descend?

7. What was His purpose for ascending far above the heavens?

Live Out ...

8. a. Christ has set us free from the captivity of sin. Yet Paul warned the Galatians of the danger of falling back into a lifestyle of bondage: "Stand fast therefore in the liberty by which Christ has made us free, and do not be entangled again with a yoke of bondage" (Gal. 5:1). What is a sinful habit you have conquered in the past but have fallen into once again? (Example: smoking, swearing, or gossiping.)

   b. Journal about how you got trapped by this habit again. What triggered it? How could you have avoided its snare? What can you do in the future to stay clear?

   c. Rewrite the following verses into a personal prayer. Make a fresh confession and commitment to Jesus, who will set you free and help you find victory over this habit.

   Let us lay aside every weight, and the sin which so easily ensnares us, and let us run with endurance the race that is set before us, looking unto Jesus, the author and finisher of our faith. (Heb. 12:1–2)

9. We've learned that Jesus descended to the lower parts of the earth and ascended far above all the heavens to set you free. He went low to bring you up. List things that make your heart sink and things that cause your spirit to soar.

   Makes You Sink
   (Example: fear)

   Helps You Soar
   (Example: friends)

Learn About ...

8 Captives

The phrase *led captivity captive* in Ephesians 4:8 is quoted from Psalm 68:18 and means "having conquest over your enemies," specifically those who had taken you captive. Being held captive can also refer to our spiritual enemies: Satan, sin, the world, and our flesh. Jesus conquered those spiritual enemies who had conquered us.

9 Down, Not Out

There are ups and downs in each of our lives. When King David was down, he didn't let it take him out. Instead he prayed, "From the end of the earth I will cry to You, when my heart is overwhelmed; lead me to the rock that is higher than I" (Ps. 61:2).

LEARN ABOUT ...

10 Uplifting

Don't throw drowning people a rock, or they'll sink. Instead lighten their load, and lift them up. Those drowning in a sea of sin need uplifting, not rock throwing. "If another believer is overcome by some sin, you who are godly should gently and humbly help that person back onto the right path. And be careful not to fall into the same temptation yourself. Share each other's burdens, and in this way obey the law of Christ" (Gal. 6:1–2 NLT).

10. Jesus meets us where we are; then He uses us to meet others who are sinking and lift them up. Think of someone who is overwhelmed and seems to be going down for the count.

Journal a prayer asking God to bring that person up out of despair and into His glorious light.

∘ ∘ ● ∘ ∘

I (Lenya) love a parade. It doesn't have to be Macy's Thanksgiving Day extravaganza; it can be a neighborhood pet parade or a high school homecoming march. They all have the same effect on me: misty eyes and a runny nose. I'm hopelessly sentimental.

It all began in my hometown, Ludington, Michigan, with the annual Fourth of July parade—a tradition that would make Norman Rockwell proud. The whole community gathers curbside to watch the action and wave Old Glory. Every emergency vehicle in the county roars by with lights flashing and sirens blaring. Closely behind follow tractors and trailers decorated like floats, carrying the Queen of Asparagus and the Cherry Queen. High school bands march in full regalia, and anyone with a horse rides proudly down the street. The entourage is sprinkled with children riding festive bicycles and senior citizens rolling along in wheel chairs decorated with crepe paper streaming in the wind.

There's a grand parade coming in the future that I can't wait to be a part of. I will stand at attention with my banner raised high as Jesus, the King of Kings, rides His white horse through heaven, crowned with glory. The hosts of heaven will cheer for the victory He's won over death and hell. Jesus invites all who will believe in Him to get in on the action. Don't let His parade pass you by.

LISTEN TO ...

In his life, Christ is an example, showing us how to live; in his death, he is a sacrifice, satisfying for our sins; in his resurrection, a conqueror; in his ascension, a king; in his intercession, a high priest.

—*Martin Luther*

DAY 4

Fully Equipped

When he was only six, (Lenya) our son Nathan thought his uncle Mike was the coolest guy to walk the earth. Mike could pitch an eighty-mile-an-hour baseball, beat Nate at Super Mario Brothers, and play ice hockey with an attitude. Nathan was putty in his hands. It was no surprise the day he walked in the door and said, "Uncle Mike signed me up for hockey at the ice arena. Can I play?"

"Sure, Nate," I said, completely ignorant of the details. I soon learned that first off he needed skating lessons. As the other kids glided and twirled past us, Nathan came shuffling by, clutching onto a chair so he wouldn't fall. Ice fees to cover practice and playing time cost two hundred dollars. Hockey requires more pads than football, and those rental fees were about one hundred dollars. Of course, he needed skates, and we found a used pair at a swap meet for seventy-five dollars. Nate shot with his left hand, so a special stick was purchased for forty-five dollars. Joining the hockey team was much more than signing on the dotted line: It required talent, teamwork, and tons of equipment and money!

When you join God's team, there are no hidden costs. God supplies everything you need. He assigns positions, gives you the necessary talents or gifts, and fully equips you for your place on the team.

LIFT UP ...

God, I'm not capable of doing Your work unless You equip me with the gifts of the Spirit. Thank You for providing me with everything I need to minister to others in Your name. In Jesus' name. Amen.

LOOK AT ...

We explored the depths and heights Christ went to in order to set us free. Now we will study some of the spiritual gifts He gives.

READ EPHESIANS 4:11–13.

And He Himself gave some to be apostles, some prophets, some evange-lists, and some pastors and teachers, for the equipping of the saints for the work of ministry, for the edifying of the body of Christ, till we all come to the unity of the faith and of the knowledge of the Son of God, to a perfect man, to the measure of the stature of the fullness of Christ … Ephesians 4:11–13

LEARN ABOUT …

1 Gift Giver

God is not like a great eBay in the sky. We don't order what we want. He chooses what gifts to give us—with a no-exchange policy. Paul lists not only the gifts but the gifted people of God. The next time you listen to your pastor, remember the Giver who gifted him.

2 Spiritual Gifts

A spiritual gift is a God-given ability to serve God and others so that Christ is glorified and believers are edified. Have you received God's spiritual gifts for you?

5 Equipped to Work

God's gifts aren't toys to play with; they're tools to build with. These "power tools" must be taken out of God's toolbox, plugged into His Spirit, and put to work in each believer's life and in ministry. "Do not neglect the spiritual gift you received" (I Tim. 4:14 NLT).

1. Match the gifts listed in verse 11 with the proper definitions.

   A_____ : "one who is sent with a commission"

   P_____ : "one who proclaims the Word of God"

   E_____ : "bearers of the gospel, the good news"

   P_____ : "one who shepherds God's people"

   T_____ : "a shepherd who feeds the flock the Word of God"

2. Paul's list here is not exhaustive. Fill in the chart below to discover the other spiritual gifts mentioned in Scripture.

SCRIPTURE	GIFTS
Romans 12:6–8	
1 Corinthians 12:4–11	
1 Corinthians 12:28	

3. What word repeated in Ephesians 4:11 shows that not everyone receives the same spiritual gifts? Why do you think this is important?

4. What two reasons does Paul offer as to why God gives spiritual gifts?

5. According to Paul, what will spiritual gifts equip believers to do?

6. What two things does Paul pray will be the result of the ministry of these gifts?

7. According to verse 13, what is the standard by which we measure our spiritual lives?

LEARN ABOUT ...

7 Perfect in Faith

When Mary Poppins pulled out a ruler to measure herself, she came up "Practically Perfect in Every Way." We all know that the only perfect man was Jesus Christ. But Paul uses the word *perfect* to mean spiritually mature and Christlike. How do you measure up?

---

8 Equal Gifts

What's the best shoe? It depends. Sneakers are best for athletics, but high heels are best for the prom. What's the best spiritual gift? Teaching if you're a pastor, mercy if you're a counselor, or hospitality if you entertain. "You should earnestly desire the most helpful gifts" (I Cor. 12:31 NLT).

---

9 Gift or Talent?

A spiritual gift is an extraordinary faculty operating for the benefit of the church. Gifts are given by the grace of God through the power of the Spirit to believers, whether the Holy Spirit imparts entirely new powers or stimulates those already existing to higher power or activity. With the touch of God's Spirit something ordinary becomes extraordinary!

LIVE OUT ...

8. God gives to His children diverse gifts that are appropriate for the ministry to which He has called them. With this in mind, complete the journal exercise below.

   a. List the areas of ministry you are currently fulfilling.

   b. List areas of ministry you feel God is calling you to in the future.

   c. Review the list of the gifts of the Holy Spirit found in question 2. Which of these gifts would enable you to fulfill your ministry with supernatural power?

   d. Write a prayer asking God to empower you with the gifts you need to serve Him.

9. Some of our abilities come naturally, and others come supernaturally.

   a. List some of the natural talents you possess. (Example: I'm a good cook; I am very sympathetic; I'm organized.)

   b. Reviewing the list of the gifts of the Spirit, which of your natural talents might be a manifestation of God's gifts? (Example: When I cook for others, I am offering hospitality. Caring and listening to others is being merciful.)

c. Write a prayer offering God your natural talents, and ask Him to transform them into supernatural abilities through the power of the Holy Spirit.

10. Gifts are good, but love is better. Listed below are the attributes of love described in 1 Corinthians 13. Place a ✔ by the ones you have and an ✗ by the ones you need.

___ Patient	___ Kind	___ Not Proud
___ Not Jealous	___ Not Boastful	___ Not Rude
___ Undemanding	___ Not Irritable	___ Forgiving
___ Rejoices in Truth	___ Enduring	___ Hopeful
___ Believes	___ Not Selfish	___ Faithful

○ ○ ● ○ ○

A church in Strasbourg, Germany, was destroyed during World War II. After the bombing, the members went to see what was left and found the entire roof caved in. Much to their surprise, a statue of Christ with outstretched hands was still standing. It was intact, except a falling beam had sheared off both hands. The people asked a sculptor if he could replace the hands on the statue. He was willing, and he even offered to do the work for nothing. The church officials met to consider the sculptor's proposition but decided not to accept his offer. Why? Because they felt that the statue without hands would be the greatest message possible that God's work is done with human hands through His people.

God gives gifts to believers so we can be His hands, His feet, and His mouth, fully equipped "for the work of ministry, for the edifying of the body of Christ" (Eph. 4:12).

LISTEN TO ...

No gift unrecognized as coming from God is at its own best; therefore many things that God would gladly give us ... must wait until we ask for them, that we may know whence they come: when in all gifts we find him, then in him we shall find all things.

—*George MacDonald*

DAY 5
All Grown Up

I (Lenya) read about a guy who catches live exotic fish for aquarium owners. His top-selling fish is the shark. He explained that if you catch a small shark and confine it to an aquarium, it would only grow in proportion to its environment. A shark can be a mere six inches long and still be an adult. Its growth is stunted by its surroundings. But if you turn that dwarfed shark loose in the ocean, he'll grow to his normal length of nearly eight feet.

The same thing can happen to Christians. I've seen some of the cutest little Christians who swim around in a little puddle of self-centeredness. They stay small and immature in their faith. But place them into a larger arena—the vastness of the body of Christ—and they can reach their full potential and "grow up in all things into Him who is the head—Christ" (Eph. 4:15).

LIFT UP ...

Father, please don't allow me to settle for the comfort of narrow surroundings or stunted growth. Stir up my heart and open the way to new horizons and greater growth in You. In Jesus' name. Amen.

LOOK AT ...

This week we have learned about some of the gifts given by Christ to the church. Today we learn how this supernatural equipping brings about spiritual maturity.

READ EPHESIANS 4:14–16.

... that we should no longer be children, tossed to and fro and carried about with every wind of doctrine, by the trickery of men, in the cunning craftiness of deceitful plotting, but, speaking the truth in love, may grow up in all things into Him who is the head—Christ—from whom the

whole body, joined and knit together by what every joint supplies, according to the effective working by which every part does its share, causes growth of the body for the edifying of itself in love. Ephesians 4:14–16

1. Paul gives another reason for becoming mature in faith. What is it?

2. What phrases describe the instability of these children?

3. What influences can cause us to be carried about?

   With _____

   By _____

   In _____

4. What type of speech is a sign of maturity?

5. What are we to grow "into"?

6. From our past study, of what is Christ the head (Ephesians 1:22)?

7. How does each part of the whole body work together most effectively?

8. What is the end result of this type of cooperation, according to verse 16?

LIVE OUT ...

9. This week we've learned some traits of childishness, but Jesus taught the value of being childlike: "Whoever does not receive the kingdom of God as a little child will by no means enter it" (Mark

LEARN ABOUT ...

2 Tossed About

To be tossed to and fro means "to fluctuate or roll up and down with the waves." Following a prevailing current will take you places you never intended to go—from bell-bottoms to bad behavior. Children get caught in the undertow of peer pressure. Maturity equips us to go against the flow!

4 Truth in Love

Truth without love is brutality—love without truth is hypocrisy. Maturity blends both to lead others to Christ. The truth? "For everyone has sinned; we all fall short of God's glorious standard" (Rom. 3:23 NLT). The love? "God showed his great love for us by sending Christ to die for us while we were still sinners" (Rom. 5:8 NLT).

9 Desire the Milk

Milk does His body good. God wants His children to be well fed so they can grow up into His image. If you're spiritually malnourished, open God's Word and drink up. "As newborn babes, desire the pure milk of the word, that you may grow thereby" (1 Peter 2:2).

LEARN ABOUT ...

II Truth Hurts

Truth hurts when someone who doesn't love you tells you your failures, hoping to make you bitter. Truth heals when someone who loves you tells you your flaws, hoping to make you better. "Open rebuke is better than love carefully concealed. Faithful are the wounds of a friend, but the kisses of an enemy are deceitful" (Prov. 27:5–6).

10:15). In the appropriate columns below, place the following attributes: *unstable, honest, gullible, trusting, boastful, humble, naive, eager, greedy, imitator, teasing, vulnerable, tender, weak, enthusiastic, impatient, teachable.*

CHILDLIKE   CHILDISH

10. a. Paul said, "When I was a child, I spoke and thought and reasoned as a child. But when I grew up, I put away childish things" (1 Cor. 13:11 NLT). With this Scripture verse in mind, review the columns above and examine your own life. Circle the childish attributes that you tend to display. Journal about how you can begin to turn these childish behaviors into more mature ones.

b. Some of us mistakenly put away our childlike *hearts* with our childish behavior. What childlike attitudes do you need to keep?

11. a. Mature believers develop mature speech by "speaking the truth in love" (Eph. 4:15). Write about a time someone told you the cold, hard truth about yourself. How did it hurt?

b. Write about a time someone told you the loving reality about yourself. How did it help?

∘ ∘ ● ∘ ∘

What is the one thing every mother wants for her children? To grow up! Picture your preschool child twenty years in the future. He or she has gone off to college or to begin a career. One day there's a knock at the door. When you open it, there stands your fully grown adult child, and the first thing out of his or her mouth is, "Mama, Dada, I want my baba." Your heart would drop, and tears would come at the tragedy of your child growing old without growing up.

Life is about progression. Plants mature from seedling to sapling. Musicians progress from "Chopsticks" to Chopin. Human beings grow from childhood to adulthood. Spiritual maturity, like physical maturity, is a growth process. Born-again believers are babies who must grow up.

Preacher and evangelist Leonard Ravenhill told a story about a group of tourists visiting a picturesque village: "They walked by an old man sitting beside a fence, and in a rather patronizing way one tourist asked, 'Were any great men born in this village?' The old man replied, 'No, only babies.'"[3] A frothy question yielded a profound answer. There are no instant adults either in this world or in the kingdom of God. Growth takes time.

LISTEN TO ...

Although we become Christians instantaneously by faith in Christ, knowing God and developing faith is a gradual process. There are no shortcuts to maturity. It takes time to be holy.

—*Erwin W. Lutzer*

Dress for Success

Ephesians 4:17–32

Some years ago CBC News reported that Imelda Marcos's legendary shoe collection had grown to nearly 3,000 pairs since her strongman husband was driven from his presidency. At the height of their power, Mrs. Marcos became known for lavish living despite extreme poverty in the Philippines. When Ferdinand and Imelda Marcos escaped the islands during a "people power" revolt, she left 1,220 pairs of shoes behind at the presidential palace—including one pair with lights that blinked when she danced. Her shoe collection, containing expensive foreign-made brands, astounded the world and became a symbol of excessive living.[1]

By the world's standards, if anyone was dressed for success, it was Imelda Marcos. Apparently no one ever told her that clothes don't make the woman. While the palace, presidency, and power crumbled all around her, she continued to buy more shoes. The Marcoses became exiles, literally fulfilling the saying "All dressed up with no place to go."

This week Paul lets us know that God is more concerned with godly behavior than gorgeous attire. God's standard for success looks different from the world's. Christian living is not about your shoes or the clothes you wear, but about the way you walk in holiness.

Day 1: Ephesians 4:17–19	WALKING SHOES
Day 2: Ephesians 4:20–21	MIRROR, MIRROR
Day 3: Ephesians 4:22–24	OFF WITH THE OLD, ON WITH THE NEW
Day 4: Ephesians 4:25–29	CLEAN OUT YOUR CLOSET
Day 5: Ephesians 4:30–32	DRESSED FOR SUCCESS

DAY 1

Walking Shoes

LIFT UP ...

God, forgive me when I try to clothe myself in my own righteousness. I know that in Your eyes it is just filthy rags. Clothe me in Your righteousness so I can make Your best-dressed list. In Jesus' name. Amen.

LOOK AT ...

Paul continued his teaching on how Christians ought to walk by contrasting fleshly vices and godly virtues. He used negative examples to encourage positive action. Today we are reminded of how sinful our lives are without Christ.

READ EPHESIANS 4:17–19.

This I say, therefore, and testify in the Lord, that you should no longer walk as the rest of the Gentiles walk, in the futility of their mind, having their understanding darkened, being alienated from the life of God, because of the ignorance that is in them, because of the blindness of their heart; who, being past feeling, have given themselves over to lewdness, to work all uncleanness with greediness. Ephesians 4:17–19

1. What phrase did Paul use to emphasize the importance of what he is saying?

2. Whom were the Ephesians no longer to emulate? Why?

LEARN ABOUT ...

3 Futility

To be futile means "to be full of emptiness, worthlessness, or vanity." A futile mind is full of nothing. Picture a hamster running on a wheel. It thinks it is going somewhere, and it is—nowhere fast. In their ignorance, unbelieving Gentiles were busy performing pagan religious rituals that would lead them nowhere. Paul wanted them to stop running around and start wising up.

---

4 Darkened Minds

Darkness is the absence of light. It is associated with the chaos before creation. It became a symbol of evil, affliction, or death. In hell there is only darkness. Darkness symbolizes man's ignorance of God's will and is associated with sin. "If the light you think you have is actually darkness, how deep that darkness is!" (Matt. 6:23 NLT).

---

7 Lewdness

Lewdness is a preoccupation with sex and sexual desires leading to indecent and disgraceful behavior. Those who have "given themselves over to lewdness" have recklessly abandoned themselves to sensual pleasure. Think of Sodom and Gomorrah, Studio 54, or Mardi Gras.

3. What phrase did Paul use to describe how the Gentiles (unbelievers) walk?

4. What is the result of their understanding being darkened?

5. What two things cause their alienation from God?

6. Why do you suppose ignorance and hard-heartedness lead to being "past feeling" (that is, callous and numb)?

7. Why do you suppose those who are "past feeling" give themselves to lewdness?

LIVE OUT ...

8. Paul said that to walk with God means to walk in the opposite direction of the "Gentiles," or the unbelieving world. Draw a line away from the specific ungodly behavior over to the opposite way we can walk with God.

WALK LIKE GENTILES	WALK WITH GOD
Futility of mind	United in Christ
Darkened understanding	Wise
Alienated from God	Valuable ideas
Ignorant	Generous
Blind hearted	Washed by the blood
Past feeling	Set apart for godliness
Given over to lewdness	Enlightened insight
Unclean	Sensitive to the Spirit
Greedy	Sees clearly

9. a. From the list above, circle one way you used to walk like the Gentiles. Then check below how God intersected your path to bring about change.

____ Stop sign
____ Dangerous Curve Ahead
____ Children at Play
____ Reduce Speed
____ Yield
____ Bump in the Road

    b. Journal about your experience of God's work in your life. (Example: My greed made me a spendaholic until God put up a Reduce Speed sign in my life.)

10. God is giving you a green light to let you know it's time to move forward. Journal about the steps you will now take to begin walking God's way in this area. (Example: God showed me it wasn't enough to stop spending on my own pleasures; I needed to generously invest in His kingdom.)

∘ ∘ ● ∘ ∘

The most unattractive part of the body has to be the foot. Thus, fashion designers throughout history have unleashed their imaginations in creating fanciful footwear to transform your body's greatest deficit into an asset. Elvis was protective of his blue suede shoes. In Oz, Dorothy walked the yellow brick road in her ruby-red pumps. Cinderella left a glass slipper as her calling card. My personal favorites were a pair of white go-go boots my dad bought me during the mid-1960s. They were more than a fashion

LEARN ABOUT …

8 Walk the Line
Johnny Cash sang, "Because you're mine, I walk the line."[2] For us as Christians, because we're His, we walk the line. "He tells us everything over and over—one line at a time, one line at a time, a little here, and a little there!" (Isa. 28:10 NLT).

9 Changing Habits
Bad habits are hard to break. The best way to beat a bad habit is to begin a good one. Don't just stop swearing; start sharing your faith with others. Instead of yielding to fear, give way to faith. "Hold on to what is good. Stay away from every kind of evil" (1 Thess. 5:21–22 NLT).

statement—they symbolized action. Nancy Sinatra's anthem said it all: "These boots are made for walking, and that's just what they'll do."[3]

I guess that's the point; shoes must be practical, not just pretty. Feet were made for walking, and your shoes should be as well. Isaiah, the prophet, reveals God's plan to beautify your less-than-lovely feet, and it's not with a new pair of shoes: "How beautiful on the mountains are the feet of the messenger who brings good news, the good news of peace and salvation, the news that the God of Israel reigns!" (Isa. 52:7 NLT). Paul wants believers to put their best foot forward. Instead of telling them to change their shoes, he asks them to walk in a different direction, out of the darkness and into God's wonderful light.

LISTEN TO ...

If I walk with the world, I can't walk with God.

—Dwight Lyman Moody

DAY 2

Mirror, Mirror

Mirrors don't lie—they merely reflect the truth. In the morning when the alarm sounds, I (Lenya) stumble to the bathroom, turn on the light, and take a good, long look in the mirror. Ughhh! It faithfully displays every flaw from wrinkles to warts. My mirror has neither chided me on a bad-hair day nor cheered me for having a beaming suntan. It's nothing personal—the mirror simply reveals the truth. After looking, I have the golden opportunity to *do something* about the truth staring back at me in the mirror.

The Bible says that Jesus is the Truth. When we take a good long look at Him, our impure thoughts, unbecoming attitudes, and inappropriate actions are exposed as glaring imperfections. Let's take advantage of this golden opportunity to look the Truth—Jesus Christ—in the face and do something about it. As you look in the mirror of God's Word, make it your goal to wear a beaming Son-tan.

Lift Up ...

Father, help me see myself as You see me. I know the changes You make are more than skin deep. Transform me from the inside out. In Jesus' name. Amen.

Look At ...

We've seen that walking in spiritual ignorance results in grave emotional, physical, and spiritual consequences. Now it's time to look in the mirror of God's truth.

Read Ephesians 4:20–21.

But you have not so learned Christ, if indeed you have heard Him and have been taught by Him, as the truth is in Jesus ... Ephesians 4:20–21

LEARN ABOUT ...

1 But You

Mothers hear the *but* word a lot: "But the other kids do it." "But everyone has one." Even God's kids justify inappropriate behavior. "But that movie won an Academy Award." "But all the cute guys go to the dance club." Paul gave us a great comeback: "But you have not so learned Christ." No ifs, ands, or buts.

4 Ears to Hear

There are none so deaf as those who will not hear. The first martyr, Stephen, wanted Saul and his countrymen to hear about Jesus but "they put their hands over their ears and began shouting [and] they rushed at him" (Acts 7:57 NLT). It took the audible voice of God on the Damascus Road to give Saul ears to hear.

6 Truth or Lie?

Who is Jesus? To the Jews a prophet. To Muslims the son of Abraham. To New Agers a miracle worker. None of them admit the whole truth: Jesus is God! Paul wrote, "Let God be true but every man a liar" (Rom. 3:4). The truth doesn't change because skeptics don't believe it. Jesus said, "I am ... the truth" (John 14:6).

1. *But you* are words that mark a contrast from the previous verses. Reflect on yesterday's lesson (Eph. 4:17–19). Who are the Ephesians contrasted with?

2. What would the Gentiles see if they looked honestly in the mirror of God's truth?

3. What had Paul's Ephesian readers learned that the Gentiles had not?

4. Paul dissected the elements necessary to learn Christ. Which of the five senses must we use in learning Christ?

5. What else is required to learn Christ?

6. What do you think it means to say that the truth is "in Jesus"?

LIVE OUT ...

7. We've seen that it's easy to justify inappropriate behavior using a *but* mentality. Look in the mirror of your life, and circle the excuses you've used for making bad choices.

   But I can handle it.

   But my friends do it.

   But they might reject me.

   But I've always done it.

   But it's not that bad.

   But my husband doesn't pay attention.

   But it's just this once.

   But no one will see.

But it's just the way I am.

But it's because of hormones.

But _____

8. Now that you've reflected on the ways in which you justify wrong behavior, you have the opportunity to make some improvements. Journal an "exchange" prayer in which you trade in one of your bad excuses for a better response. (Example: God, just because I'm hormonal doesn't mean I can treat people horribly. May Your holiness control my hormones.)

9. Today we discovered that the first step in learning Christ is to hear about Him. Journal some of the different ways you've heard about Christ. (Example: I watched a Billy Graham Crusade; a friend became a "Jesus freak"; I went to church, etc.)

10. a. Paul reminds us that we must not only hear of Christ, we must also be taught by Him. Which of the following tools has He used to teach you?

____ His Word   ____ Adversity

____ His Holy Spirit   ____ Success

____ Christian literature   ____ His people

____ Joy   ____ Mistakes

____ My pastor   ____ Sunday school

b. Reflect on one of these items and journal about how God used it to teach you the truth.

LEARN ABOUT ...

7 Excuse Me

Human beings have been making excuses and shirking responsibility since time began. God wanted to know who was to blame for eating forbidden fruit. Adam's excuse? "It's Eve's fault." Eve's excuse? "The snake made me do it!" Jesus told the truth: "They have no excuse for their sin" (John 15:22).

9 Break the Silence

By remaining silent, many Christians take only part of Solomon's advice in Ecclesiastes 3: There is "a time to be quiet and a time to speak" (v. 7 NLT). Paul urges us to speak up and share the gospel: "How can they hear about him unless someone tells them?" (Rom. 10:14 NLT). Let's break the silence!

○ ○ ● ○ ○

I (Lenya) read about a woman who, on the advice of her doctor, went to see a pastor to talk about joining the church. She had recently had a face-lift, and when her doctor dismissed her, he gave her this advice: "My dear, I have done an extraordinary job on your face, as you can see in the mirror. I have charged you a great deal of money, and you were happy to pay it. But I want to give you some free advice. Find a group of people who love God and who will love you enough to help you deal with all the negative emotions inside of you. If you don't, you'll be back in my office in a very short time with your face in far worse shape than before."

What happens on the outside is only a reflection of what's occurring on the inside. A face-lift won't disguise a faulty heart. Solomon said, "As a face is reflected in water, so the heart reflects the real person" (Prov. 27:19 NLT). God sees past your face and into your heart.

Listen To ...

Behavior is the mirror in which everyone shows his image.

—Johann Wolfgang von Goethe

Off with the Old, On with the New

Human beings are creatures of habit. I'm no exception to the rule. In grade school I (Lenya) choked down my first cigarette, trying to look cool. By my senior year I was blowing smoke on a daily basis. It's my belief that if you've got a habit, you should be the one paying the price—no bumming cigarettes or matches. I told my friends, "If you want to smoke, buy your own. I'm not sharing." That philosophy worked well until the day I needed a smoke. My friends threw my attitude back at me. "If you want to smoke, Lenya, then get your own." Then it occurred to me: *I don't want to smoke; it's not cool—it's a nasty habit.*

Mark Twain said, "A habit cannot be tossed out the window; it must be coaxed down the stairs a step at a time!"[4] Old habits—especially sinful ones—are hard to break. Paul teaches an all-important lesson: Replace bad habits with good ones. My new philosophy is, "Off with the old, and on with the new."

LIFT UP ...

Nothing is impossible for You, Lord. No habit is too great, no problem too big. Fill me with the grace and power to overcome the weakness of my flesh. Deliver me from evil. In Jesus' name. Amen.

LOOK AT ...

Yesterday we learned to look at the truth found in Christ. Today we learn that once we know the truth, we must be willing to make some other changes.

READ EPHESIANS 4:22–24.

... that you put off, concerning your former conduct, the old man which grows corrupt according to the deceitful lusts, and be renewed in the spirit of your mind, and that you put on

the new man which was created according to God, in true righteousness and holiness. Ephesians 4:22–24

LEARN ABOUT ...

2 The Old Man

This term refers to our sinful nature—the flesh. Putting off the old man is not deferring it for another day; it means putting it to death. "Our old sinful selves were crucified with Christ so that sin might lose its power in our lives" (Rom. 6:6 NLT).

4 Be Renewed

The phrase *be renewed* means "to make young or recent." Retin-A, face-lifts, and dermabrasion promise to peel away wrinkles; God's renewal plan offers a spiritual lift: "If anyone is in Christ, he is a new creation; old things have passed away; behold, all things have become new" (2 Cor. 5:17).

9 Battling Sin

Don't be discouraged if the old sin nature makes you feel defiled; Paul had the same struggle: "Oh, what a miserable person I am! Who will free me from this life that is dominated by sin and death? Thank God! The answer is in Jesus Christ our Lord" (Rom. 7:24–25 NLT).

1. Since we have learned about Christ, what is the first thing Paul said here that we are to do?

2. Paul called this former conduct "the old man." Why do you think this is an apt description?

3. How does our old nature grow? According to what?

4. After putting our old nature to death, what is an important part of our growing process as Christians?

5. What do you think it means to become renewed "in the spirit of your mind"?

6. What are we to "put on"?

7. Who was responsible for this new creation?

8. What are the two outstanding characteristics of the new man?

LIVE OUT ...

9. Paul makes it clear that our dirty old natures must be put to death. Have you tried to resuscitate your "old man" by falling back into old habits? Journal about any bad habits that are trying to come back to life. (Example: I was getting up early to have quiet time, but lately I've been sleeping in.)

10. The only way to become a new person is to be born again through faith in Jesus. If you have not placed your faith in Jesus, journal a prayer asking Him to forgive you of your sins and to make your life new in Him. If the "new man" in you is growing old, ask God to revive you.

11. Being renewed in the spirit of your mind begins by challenging negative thoughts with positive input. Follow the exercise below to discover ways to overcome negative thoughts with good ones.

    a. Ask God to reveal to you a thought or thought pattern that is not pleasing to Him. Write it down. (Example: I'm afraid of the future, so I don't sleep at night.)

    b. Using Philippians 4:8, write out biblical truths that will replace this unpleasing thought or pattern with a renewed spirit that exhibits your new, godly character.

       "Whatever things are true": (Example: God holds my future in His hands. I can rest in Him.)

       "Whatever things are noble": (Example: I will look forward to a future with Christ by my side.)

       "Whatever things are just":

       "Whatever things are pure":

       "Whatever things are lovely":

       "Whatever things are of good report":

LEARN ABOUT ...

10 A New You

God is not satisfied with outward, superficial change. He wants you to be completely transformed: to experience a new birth, take on a brand-new nature, and become a new you. Think of the difference between a snake and a caterpillar. A snake who sheds his skin is still a snake; but a caterpillar who sheds his cocoon becomes a butterfly.

"If there is any virtue":

"If there is anything praiseworthy":

○ ○ ● ○ ○

Two children, a boy and a girl, played together a great deal. One summer they attended a local vacation Bible school, where they both accepted Jesus as their Savior. One day the boy told his mother, "Mom, I know for sure that Emily's a Christian."

"How do you know?"

"Because she plays like a Christian. If you take everything she's got, she doesn't get mad. Before she was selfish. If she didn't get her way, she'd say, 'I won't play with you; you're an ugly little boy.'"

What an amazing promise that you are made new—He removes your ugliness and gives you His righteousness. What a mighty God, who re-creates His people! "Then He who sat on the throne said, 'Behold, I make all things new'" (Rev. 21:5).

LISTEN TO ...

No man can create faith in himself. Something must happen to him which Luther calls "the divine work in us," which changes us, gives us new birth, and makes us completely different people in heart, spirit, mind, and all our powers.

—*Nikolaus Ludwig von Zinzendorf*

DAY 4
Clean Out Your Closet

Everything I (Lenya) ever wanted to know about my friends, I learned by looking in their closets. Patty, the prayer warrior, has a closet that would rival Martha Stewart's, organized by color, season, and occasion. "A place for everything, and everything in its place" is her motto. Penny says, "If it's fun, then I'll do it." Looking in her closet is like going on safari, seeking out the next conquest—dressing is an adventure. Our women's ministry storage closet, tucked up in the rafters of our church building, is a scary place. Rats have been heard gnawing, boxes have mysteriously disappeared, and grown men have been known to say, "I'm not going in there!" What would I learn about *you* if I peeked inside your closet?

My personal philosophy of closet maintenance is simple: When I get a new item, I give away an old one. I can remain current but uncluttered. In the same way, the apostle Paul teaches us to keep our spiritual lives uncluttered. In the Christian life, before you can put on new actions that please God, you must strip away outdated, sinful habits. It's time to clean out your closets!

LIFT UP ...

Lord, what do You see when You look inside the closet of my life? Are there things that don't coordinate with Your Holy Spirit? Help me to do spring cleaning and clear away the clutter. In Jesus' name. Amen.

LOOK AT ...

Ephesians tells us we must not only put on the new man but also put away sinful vices. Today we examine four of these sins and the reasons Paul gave for clearing away the clutter.

LEARN ABOUT ...

1 The Whole Truth

"The essence of lying is in deception, not in words; a lie may be told by silence, by equivocation, by the accent on a syllable, by a glance of the eye attaching a peculiar significance to a sentence."[5]—John Ruskin

3 Anger and Sin

Anger in itself is not a sin since "God is angry with the wicked every day" (Ps. 7:11). Anger is sinful when it flares without reflection; when it is disproportionate to the offense; when it lasts too long and becomes revengeful.

6 Working Hard

Humanity was sentenced to life with hard labor: "The ground is cursed because of you. All your life you will struggle to scratch a living from it" (Gen. 3:17 NLT). But God turns curses into blessings. Hard work pays off with status, satisfaction, and sleep.

8 Good Words

Our words should be good, necessary, edifying, and gracious to those who hear them. *Think* before you speak. Ask yourself: Is it true, is it humble, is it inspirational, is it necessary, is it kind? "May the words of my mouth ... be pleasing to you" (Ps. 19:14 NLT).

READ EPHESIANS 4:25–29.

Therefore, putting away lying, "Let each one of you speak truth with his neighbor," for we are members of one another. "Be angry, and do not sin": do not let the sun go down on your wrath, nor give place to the devil. Let him who stole steal no longer, but rather let him labor, working with his hands what is good, that he may have something to give him who has need. Let no corrupt word proceed out of your mouth, but what is good for necessary edification, that it may impart grace to the hearers. Ephesians 4:25–29

1. What are we to put away? What should we do instead?

2. a. What should be our motivation for doing these things?

   b. Why do you think this motivation should lead to this act?

3. Verse 26 gives some dos and don'ts. We can be _____ as long as we don't_____.

4. What time limit does Paul give for dealing with anger?

5. How can sinful anger give place to the Devil?

6. a. Stealing is another item on Paul's "don't" list. Rather than stealing, what two things should thieves do instead?

   b. How does this benefit others?

7. What should not come out of the mouth of a believer?

8. What should proceed out of our mouths?

9. What does this kind of speech offer people who hear it?

LIVE OUT ...

10. This passage has exhorted us to stop lying and start telling the truth to our neighbors and fellow believers. Your closest "neighbor" may live in your own home. With that in mind, how have you compromised the truth with someone close to you recently?

____ pretending   ____ withholding information

____ hiding bad habits   ____ spending secretly

____ shading the truth   ____ looking the other way

____ exaggerating   ____ denying reality

____ blaming others   ____ other_____

11. To whom did you lie, and what were your reasons?

12. a. John gives the remedy for lying (as well as any other sin): "If we confess our sins, He is faithful and just to forgive us our sins and to cleanse us from all unrighteousness" (1 John 1:9). Journal a prayer confessing your sin of lying to God.

    b. Ask God for the strength to go to the person you lied to and seek forgiveness.

    c. Journal a prayer asking God to lead you to another Christian to whom you can confide your weaknesses and who can pray with you. "Confess your sins to each other and pray for each other so that you may be healed" (James 5:16 NLT).

LEARN ABOUT ...

10 Family Lies

The Day America Told The Truth reveals that 91 percent of Americans lie regularly.[6] A lie is a statement or act designed to deceive others. People lie to inflict pain or to protect themselves, usually out of fear or pride. "Do not lie to one another, since you have put off the old man with his deeds" (Col. 3:9).

12 True Confessions

Biblically, there are two types of confessions: admission of sins and profession of belief. Believers must not only confess what they've done wrong; they must proclaim what they know is right. "If you confess with your mouth that Jesus is Lord and believe in your heart that God raised him from the dead, you will be saved" (Rom. 10:9 NLT).

○ ○ ● ○ ○

A woman was married to a miserly man. One day she was going window-shopping, and he told her, "Look, but don't buy." A few hours later she came home with a new dress. Her husband said, "I thought I told you to look but not buy."

She explained, "I saw this dress and thought I'd try it on. When I did, the Devil said, 'It sure looks good on you.'"

"Right then you should have told him, 'Get thee behind me, Satan!'" her husband exclaimed.

"I did," she answered, "but when he got behind me, he said, 'It looks good from the back, too.'"[7]

Comedian Flip Wilson used to say, "The Devil made me do it," as a way of excusing sinful behavior. Satan will take advantage of every opportunity to promote sin. Lying, anger, stealing, and corrupt communication leave the door of our hearts wide open to Satan's influence—they "give place to the Devil." Don't give Satan a foothold in your life by allowing him to influence what goes into the closet of your heart. Instead, put away the old sinful behaviors and put on the characteristics of the new person God created you to be!

LISTEN TO ...

Temptation is the devil looking through the keyhole; yielding is opening the door and inviting him in.

—*Billy Sunday*

DAY 5
Dressed for Success

Parading down the red carpet of the annual Academy Awards, Hollywood's "royalty" are always dressed in hopes of success. These days every star has a team of stylists and designers for Oscar night, and the stars' fashions can be fabulous. Jane Fonda never looked better in her platinum colored gown by Vera Wang, with matching gloves and pearls. But Hollywood fashion can also be fickle. Uma Thurman once arrived in a stunning lilac slip dress by Prada. The next year there wasn't a slip dress in the crowd. Even those who were dressed in the height of fashion seemed outdated by the time the show was over. It's all about appearances, and if you didn't like this year's fashion look, don't worry—it's changed by now.

When the prophet Samuel was choosing a king for Israel, God gave him some good advice: "Do not look at his appearance or at his physical stature.... For the LORD does not see as man sees; for man looks at the outward appearance, but the LORD looks at the heart" (1 Sam. 16:7). Examine the inward attire of your heart. Are you a fashion victim adorned with bitterness, anger, and malice, or are you dressed for success in robes of kindness, tenderness, and forgiveness?

LIFT UP ...

God, don't let me be a slave to fashion or sin by imitating the world's pattern for success. Transform my thinking, to value what You value instead of what I wear. In Jesus' name. Amen.

LOOK AT ...

This week we have examined some of the attitudes and actions we should "put off" and "put on" as Christians. Now we discover that our sins hurt God as well as others.

LEARN ABOUT ...

1 Grieving the Spirit

To grieve means "to distress, make heavyhearted, or cause sadness." The Holy Spirit is a person who has feelings, intellect, and will. Whatever is unholy—contrary to the will of God—grieves the Holy Spirit. Every sin hurts God, but sin in His children breaks His heart.

6 Tenderhearted

The word *tenderhearted* means "easily moved by another's distress, or feeling a gnawing pain in empathy for another's suffering." The Greek word for tenderhearted literally means "having strong, kindly bowels." In the Bible the bowels are regarded as the source of kindness.

8 Personality

The Holy Spirit has a great personality, but this person is God. The Spirit (1) is called God; (2) exhibits divine attributes such as omniscience and omnipresence; (3) performs divine works such as creation and the new birth; (4) is offered worship and homage that belong only to God. "The Lord is the Spirit" (2 Cor. 3:17 NLT).

READ EPHESIANS 4:30–32.

And do not grieve the Holy Spirit of God, by whom you were sealed for the day of redemption. Let all bitterness, wrath, anger, clamor, and evil speaking be put away from you, with all malice. And be kind to one another, tenderhearted, forgiving one another, even as God in Christ forgave you.
Ephesians 4:30–32

1. What did Paul warn against in the first sentence of this passage?

2. What did he say the Holy Spirit has done for you? How would you put this in your own words?

3. a. Name the six sins Paul listed.

   b. What do you think "clamor" is?

4. What did Paul urge us to do with these sins?

5. How much of these sins should be put away?

6. What three virtues did Paul encourage among believers?

7. Why should we exhibit these virtues to one another?

LIVE OUT ...

8. We have discovered that the Holy Spirit is a person who has feelings, including grief. Fill in the following chart to discover some other personality traits of the Holy Spirit.

PASSAGE   HOLY SPIRIT'S PERSONALITY

Mark 13:11

Luke 12:12

Acts 9:31

Acts 15:28

Acts 16:6

LEARN ABOUT ...

10 Thick Skin

Here's a wise rule for living: "Learn to be thick-skinned while remaining tenderhearted." Developing thick skin in a world full of sharp tongues is essential for survival. However, thick-skinned people can be insensitive; a tender heart is imperative for revival.

9. In which of the above ways has the Holy Spirit interacted with you this week? How have you responded?

10. a. In order to please God, Paul exhorts us to put away *all* bitterness. *Bitterness* means "to cut or to prick." It is literally translated "pointed, sharp, or keen." In other words, our words can cut like a knife. Write about a time when someone pierced your soul with bitter words. How did it make you feel?

    b. Describe a situation when your bitter words stung another's heart. How did it make them feel?

    c. Take the time now to ask God through prayer and forgiveness to cut away the root of bitterness from your life and the lives of those you've injured.

11. a. *To be tenderhearted* means "to be moved by another's distress—to feel another's pain." Think of someone in your life who is in pain (physical, emotional, or spiritual). Write what you know about the situation that is causing their pain.

    b. Ask God to help you be tenderhearted and bear this person's burden through prayer. Write down a tangible way you can show you care this week.

○ ○ ● ○ ○

Before Louis XII of France came to power, he had been thrown into prison and kept in chains. Later when he became king, he was urged by others to seek revenge on those who imprisoned him. But he refused and instead prepared a scroll listing the names of all those who had perpetrated crimes against him. Next to each person's name he placed a cross in red ink. When the guilty people heard about this, they fled in fear for their lives. Then the king explained that the cross he had drawn beside each name was not a sign of punishment but a pledge of forgiveness extended for the sake of the crucified Savior, who upon His cross forgave His enemies and prayed for them.

Kindness, tenderheartedness, and forgiveness don't come naturally; they are acquired supernaturally through the redeeming power of the cross. King Louis XII had been completely transformed. Outwardly his clothes were upgraded from prison rags to palace robes, and inwardly his attitude toward his enemies changed from bitterness to blessing. He was dressed for success.

LISTEN TO ...

Do not keep the alabaster boxes of your love and tenderness sealed up until your friends are dead. Fill their lives with sweetness. Speak approving, cheering words while their ears can hear them and while their hearts can be thrilled by them.

—Henry Ward Beecher

In My Father's Footsteps

Ephesians 5:1–17

Bible teacher E. Stanley Jones told the story of a missionary who got lost in an African jungle. There was nothing around him but thick bush and a few cleared spaces. He came upon a local village and asked one of the men if he could lead him out of the jungle. When the African agreed, the missionary said, "Well, show me the way." The African man responded, "Walk." So they walked and hacked their way through unmarked jungle for more than an hour. The missionary began to get worried and asked, "Are you sure this is the right way? Where is the path?"

The man said, "Friend, in this place there is no path. I am the path."

It is a jungle out there—from pop culture to pop psychology, the path of life is overgrown with too many options and too little time. It's hard to see the forest for the trees. We need clear direction. Jesus said, "I am the light of the world. He who follows Me shall not walk in darkness, but have the light of life" (John 8:12). Jesus walked in His Father's footsteps, illuminating a path for others who desire to find their way. This week you will discover three ways to walk in His footsteps: in love, in the light, and in wisdom.

Day 1: Ephesians 5:1–2	**WALK IN LOVE**
Day 2: Ephesians 5:3–4	**DANGEROUS DETOURS**
Day 3: Ephesians 5:5–7	**OUT OF BOUNDS**
Day 4: Ephesians 5:8–14	**WALK IN LIGHT**
Day 5: Ephesians 5:15–17	**WALK WISELY**

DAY 1

Walk in Love

LIFT UP ...

Lord, hold my hand as I walk in this world. Guide my footsteps so I can go where You lead and walk as You walk. Keep me on Your path. In Jesus' name. Amen.

LOOK AT ...

Over the last few weeks we have learned to walk worthy of our high calling in Christ. We have also been challenged to no longer walk as the Gentiles walk. This week we'll learn how to walk in godliness and in love.

READ EPHESIANS 5:1–2.

Therefore be imitators of God as dear children. And walk in love, as Christ also has loved us and given Himself for us, an offering and a sacrifice to God for a sweet-smelling aroma.
Ephesians 5:1–2

1. This passage tells us to imitate God. Give an example of what this might look like.

LEARN ABOUT ...

2 Imitating God

To imitate means "to mimic or to act as." Children like to play dress-up and pretend they are adults like Mom or Dad. Christians should not pretend but actually become like our heavenly Dad. Imitation is the sincerest form of flattery.

---

5 Real Love

Love is not about getting, but giving. True love—the God kind—is sacrificial. When God showed His love, He gave His Son. When Christ showed His love, He gave His life. "For God so loved the world that he gave his one and only Son" (John 3:16 NIV).

---

6 Sweet Aroma

In the Old Testament, the Levitical sacrifices were a "sweet savor" to God. In the New Testament, Christ's sacrifice was a "sweet-smelling aroma." In heaven, the prayers of the saints are like incense ascending to the throne of God. "I will freely sacrifice to You; I will praise Your name, O LORD, for it is good" (Ps. 54:6).

2. What relationship compels us to become imitators of God?

3. How are we to walk as believers?

4. Whose love are we to model ourselves after?

5. What did Christ do to show His love for us?

6. In what two ways did Christ give Himself to God?

7. Fill in the chart below to discover how Jesus fulfilled Old Testament requirements of an acceptable sacrifice.

REQUIREMENT	FULFILLMENT
Without blemish = 1 Peter 1:19	
Outside camp = John 19:17	
With free will = John 10:18	
Perfect = 2 Corinthians 5:21	

LIVE OUT ...

8. Today we discovered that our goal as believers is to imitate God—to become like our heavenly Father. In order to become like Him, we must understand what He is like. Draw a line linking the attributes of God with the appropriate Scriptures.

GOD IS:	SCRIPTURE:
Faithful	Deuteronomy 4:31
Good	Psalm 145:17
Holy	Psalm 100:5
Just	Psalm 7:11
Love	Psalm 99:9

Merciful   1 Thessalonians 5:24

Righteous   1 John 4:8

9. a. Which of the attributes of God listed above has been most difficult for you to imitate?

    b. Write a prayer asking God to help you become like Him in this area of your life.

10. Paul revealed that one specific way to imitate God is to love as Christ loved—sacrificially.

    a. Journal about a time when someone sacrificed something to show his or her love for you.

    b. Have you ever loved someone sacrificially? What was the circumstance, and what did it cost you?

11. We should not only love others sacrificially, we should also love God sacrificially. Choose one of the following ways to pour out a sweet-smelling sacrifice to your heavenly Father. Describe how you will follow through this week.

    Fasting: I will fast from _____ so I can feed on God's Word.

    Money: I will tithe $_____ to support God's work.

    Intercessory Prayers: I will pray for _____ to show God's love.

    Time: I will offer time to _____ be God's hands on earth.

    Pleasure: I will abstain from _____ to obey God's commands.

LEARN ABOUT ...

8 God Is

God is called the great I AM because whatever you need, He is. If you need forgiveness, God is merciful. If you need discipline, God is just. Even if you are faithless, God is faithful. God is everything that is good and nothing that is bad. He is the "Lord God Almighty, Who was and is and is to come!" (Rev. 4:8).

_____

10 Costly Love

King David's philosophy was, "Give until it hurts." God told David to build Him an altar on Araunah's threshing floor. Araunah offered to donate the land, but David said, "I will not present burnt offerings to the LORD my God that have cost me nothing" (2 Sam. 24:24 NLT).

Friendships: I won't call _____, so I can talk to God instead.

○ ○ ● ○ ○

Love is the gift of oneself! I experienced a wonderful illustration of this truth. In 1984 my husband and I (Lenya) traveled to India with Gospel for Asia to train indigenous pastors and their wives. Nothing could prepare me for the experience. To know India is to smell its pungent aroma, to wilt in its humid air, to be overwhelmed walking its congested streets, and to see its slum villages drowning in poverty. Although the nation is poor economically, the people I met were rich in good deeds.

Finding food and drink that wouldn't upset our stomachs was challenging. We had been warned, "Don't drink the water, and limit your diet to foods cooked thoroughly and to fruits that have to be peeled." In one jungle village there was no bottled water, so a native climbed a coconut palm and gave us milk to drink from the shell. One morning we were served the sweetest pineapple. I gushed, "It's better than pineapple in Hawaii!" Incredibly, our host sent his son on a day's journey to pick another pineapple for dinner. When I learned of the boy's hike, I said, "You didn't have to walk so far for me." The boy smiled and said, "Long walk part of gift!"

Listen To ...

Love prompted God to send His Son, Jesus, on the long walk from heaven to earth to give you the best gift you could ever receive—Himself. True love is always costly.

—*Billy Graham*

DAY 2

Dangerous Detours

Hugh Hefner, founder of the Playboy empire, once said in an interview, "If Christ were here today and had to choose between being on the staff of one of the joy-killing, pleasure-denying churches [or *Playboy*], he would, of course, immediately join us." He has also written, "We reject any philosophy which holds that a man must deny himself for others."[1] The Playboy organization holds that we all should love ourselves preeminently and pursue our own pleasure constantly. Nowhere is the clash between Playboyism and the ways of Jesus any sharper than over how the good life is to be achieved. Hugh Hefner tells us to get all we can. Jesus tells us to give all we can.

Hefner's views are nothing new, but they will take you off course. Jesus said, "You can enter God's Kingdom only through the narrow gate. The highway to hell is broad, and its gate is wide for the many who choose that way. But the gateway to life is very narrow and the road is difficult, and only a few ever find it" (Matt. 7:13–14 NLT). It's important to avoid the dangerous detours found on the path of life and stick to God's righteous road instead.

LIFT UP ...

Father, when there's a fork in the road, please help me to choose the road less taken—the road that is pleasing to You. In Jesus' name. Amen.

LOOK AT ...

Yesterday we learned to walk in love. Today, we learn to distance ourselves from sinful desires.

LEARN ABOUT ...

I Bad Fruit

The way to heaven is too straight for a person who wants to walk the crooked road of unclean living. A crooked walk exposes a person who is bent on sin. "You will know them by their fruits.... Every good tree bears good fruit, but a bad tree bears bad fruit" (Matt. 7:16–17).

5 Bad Language

Filthiness refers to obscenities; *foolish talking* implies silliness or buffoonery; *coarse jesting* portrays a person who uses vulgar repartee or witticism. A good indication of a person's character is what makes him laugh. "Let your speech always be with grace" (Col. 4:6).

8 Safe Sex?

Sex-education classes teach kids that condoms and contraceptives make having sex anytime safe. This philosophy is full of holes. In God's Word, we discover that abstinence is the best policy until sex is in its safest context: the marriage of one man and one woman for a lifetime.

READ EPHESIANS 5:3–4.

But fornication and all uncleanness or covetousness, let it not even be named among you, as is fitting for saints; neither filthiness, nor foolish talking, nor coarse jesting, which are not fitting, but rather giving of thanks. Ephesians 5:3–4

1. The first two sins Paul listed here (fornication and uncleanness) are sexual. The third (covetousness) means greed. Does it surprise you that Paul thought greed is just as unspeakably bad a sin as sexual immorality? Explain.

2. What phrase cautions believers not to even speak of, much less participate in, those first three sins?

3. Why should the saints abstain from those sins?

4. What are the next three sins Paul warned against?

5. What area of life do these three sins deal with?

6. What reason did Paul give for avoiding these sins?

7. Rather than using our mouths in filthiness, foolishness, and coarseness—sinful speech—what should we be doing?

LIVE OUT ...

8. Paul exhorted believers to abstain from fornication, uncleanness, or covetousness. Read the definitions, then follow the instructions.

Fornication: Any sexual relationship outside the bond of marriage; unchastity. If you are currently engaged in sexual behavior that is unfitting for a saint, journal a prayer of repentance to God.

Uncleanness: Physical or moral impurity. If you have become defiled sexually, write a prayer asking God to wash you clean with His blood, making you white as snow.

Covetousness: An intense desire to possess something or someone that belongs to another person. If you have been coveting something or someone that belongs to another, write a prayer telling God what you covet and asking Him to help you renounce that desire and seek first His kingdom.

LEARN ABOUT ...

9 Thanks Living

Thanksgiving should become a way of living. We can be grateful to God for who He is, what He has done, and what He will do. We can give thanks in anticipation of answered prayer, knowing that God's answers are always in accord with His perfect will for our lives.

9. People who have base appetites usually develop disgraceful speech and humor. The Bible says to replace gross speech with giving thanks. Meditate on the following Scripture verses, then write prayers of thanksgiving.

"He has removed our sins as far from us as the east is from the west" (Ps. 103:12 NLT). Journal your thanks to God that your rebellious acts can cease once and for all.

"Though your sins are like scarlet, I will make them as white as snow. Though they are red like crimson, I will make them as white as wool" (Isa. 1:18 NLT). Give thanks that the stain of sin can be removed completely.

"Restore to me the joy of your salvation, and make me willing to obey you" (Ps. 51:12 NLT). Thank God that He can miraculously restore your joy.

• • • • •

Author and speaker Josh McDowell often speaks about sexual purity. He believes that in these last decades, contrary to popular opinion, we have been through not a sexual revolution but a revolution in the search for intimacy. He observes, "Most of our young people do not want the physical aspect of sex; they want someone who cares. They want to be able to care. They want intimacy. We have allowed our culture to dictate to us that the only way you find intimacy is through the physical—and that's an absolute lie!"[2]

Too many people get detoured by the idea that intercourse creates intimacy. One-night stands breed insecurity since there's no commitment for the future. But Scripture reveals that true intimacy is found in the bond of holy matrimony, not just the bedroom. "A man shall leave his father and mother and be joined to his wife, and the two shall become one flesh" (Matt. 19:5). When sex is on track with God's plan, it is beautiful. When it bypasses the bounds of marriage, it is sinful.

LISTEN TO ...

Things are seldom what they seem; that's why people mistake education for intelligence, wealth for happiness, and sex for love.

—Anonymous

DAY 3

Out of Bounds

Boundaries—in or out? The whistle blows when the football player runs out of bounds. The baseball player hits one outside the lines and hears, "Foul ball!" In snow skiing, out of bounds is a dangerous place to go. You might come face-to-face with a tree or be swept away in an avalanche. Boundaries are our friends—they keep us safe.

In the film series *Focus on the Family*, James Dobson told about a group of educators who decided to remove the chain-link fences from around the school playgrounds. They believed the fences promoted feelings of confinement and restraint. However, as soon as the fences were removed, the children huddled in the center of the playground to play. Conclusion: Children need boundaries.[3]

Adults need boundaries too. God has set loving parameters for His people, and those who choose to live "out of bounds" will find themselves outside of His kingdom.

LIFT UP ...

Father, thank You for setting safe boundaries that are pleasant to walk in. Throw up a red flag when I start to step out of bounds. In Jesus' name. Amen.

LOOK AT ...

This week we have received firm instruction concerning God's holy boundaries. Now we read about the consequences of purposefully, perpetually walking in disobedience.

READ EPHESIANS 5:5–7.

For this you know, that no fornicator, unclean person, nor covetous man, who is an idolater, has any inheritance in the kingdom of Christ and God. Let no one deceive you with empty words,

LEARN ABOUT ...

2 Idolatry

Idolatry is worshipping or paying divine honor to something created instead of the Creator. Idolatry may involve the worship of carved images, inanimate objects, animals, nature, people, or ideals. In Ephesus, the primary idol was Diana, a multibreasted fertility goddess.

5 God's Wrath

God's wrath is the manifestation of God's holy indignation against sin. God's wrath is not irrational or malicious. Rather, it is the just and proper expression of His righteousness. God offset wrath with love by sending His Son.

8 Don't Mix

To partake means "to join in partnership or cooperate with an activity." "Don't team up with those who are unbelievers. How can righteousness be a partner with wickedness?" (2 Cor. 6:14 NLT). Like oil and water, some things just don't mix.

for because of these things the wrath of God comes upon the sons of disobedience. Therefore do not be partakers with them. Ephesians 5:5–7

1. List the three kinds of sinful people Paul named in the first sentence.

2. a. Paul said the person who practices these sins is an idolater. Why is fornication (sexual immorality) a form of idolatry? What is the person worshipping?

   b. Why is covetousness a form of idolatry? What is the person worshipping?

3. What is the consequence of engaging in these sinful lifestyles?

4. What type of words are used to deceive believers?

5. Why do you think these sins invite God's wrath?

6. Who experiences God's wrath?

7. How should we respond to the deceit of the sons of disobedience?

LIVE OUT ...

8. Paul teaches that what a person does reveals who a person worships—creature or Creator. Fill in the following chart to learn more about the futility of idol worship in contrast to the fulfillment of worshipping God.

SCRIPTURE	CHARACTERISTICS OF IDOLS	CONTRAST TO GOD
Deuteronomy 4:15–19		
Psalm 135:5–7, 15–18		
Habakkuk 2:18–20		
Romans 1:20–25		

LEARN ABOUT …

10 Sons of Disobedience

Sons of disobedience habitually sin and encourage others to sin. Children of God are to be the opposite—obey God and help others obey. "We can tell who are children of God and who are children of the devil. Anyone who does not live righteously and does not love other believers does not belong to God" (1 John 3:10 NLT).

12 Sin Less

Less is more. When we sin less, we become more like Christ. "And the Lord—who is the Spirit—makes us more and more like him as we are changed into his glorious image. Therefore … we never give up" (2 Cor. 3:18—4:1 NLT).

9. a. Name some forms of modern idol worship (anything you give devotion to, from cars to stars).

   b. Journal about a situation in your life when you worshipped and served a created thing more than the Creator. What was the result?

10. Paul warned that the "sons of disobedience"—unbelievers—will try to deceive believers with empty words. Fill in the chart with ways you have been led astray by enticing propaganda. If these sources have been saturating you with fast talk, it's time to talk back. This week as you encounter any lies the media spouts, stand up and shout, "That's a lie, and I don't believe it!"

SOURCE	SPECIFICS	SOLICITATION
Ad Campaign	car company	New car = fulfillment
Ad Campaign		
TV series		
Movie		
Printed material		
Internet		

11. Review the previous chart. Write down the ways this enticing

propaganda has failed to deliver what was promised. (Example: My new car didn't bring fulfillment; instead it brought debt and dents.)

12. Bible teacher Warren Wiersbe once said, "A Christian is not *sinless,* but he does *sin less*—and less—and less!"[4] Journal about a time when you became aware that you were buying into a lie propagated by the world. How did you replace the lie with the truth? What was the result?

∘ ∘ ● ∘ ∘

A teenage girl wanted to join her friend's church. The pastor asked, "Were you a sinner before you received the Lord Jesus into your life?"

"Yeah, and it got me into lots of trouble," she replied.

"Well, are you still a sinner?" he asked.

The girl replied, "To tell you the truth, I think I'm a bigger sinner now than I ever was."

"So what difference has Christ made in your life?" the pastor responded.

She said, "I used to be a sinner running after sin, but now that I'm saved, I'm a sinner running away from sin!"

We all used to be sons or daughters of disobedience, running after sin. Learning to run away from sin is the right thing to do. However, sometimes we must learn to run away from sinners as well. Paul warned, "Do not be deceived: 'Evil company corrupts good habits'" (1 Cor. 15:33). Peer pressure is a powerful thing, for good or for evil. If you're running with the wrong crowd, perhaps it's time to turn around and "run with endurance the race that is set before us" (Heb. 12:1).

LISTEN TO ...

Idolatry: trusting people, possessions or positions to do for me what only God can do.

—*Bill Gothard*

DAY 4
Walk in Light

Years ago the Denver city zoo was offered the gift of a beautiful polar bear. Unfortunately there was no room for the animal. At the time of the gift the board of directors was in the middle of a fund-raising campaign to renovate the zoo. They changed the plans to include a magnificent habitat for the polar bear. In the meantime the bear was put in a temporary cage. The space was so small and cramped that it could only take three steps, turn around, and walk three steps back.

Due to countless delays the construction took three years, but the bear's new home was filled with waterfalls, caves, and lots of space. The bear entered its new home, looked around, took three steps, turned around, and took three steps back.

Like the polar bear given a new habitat, the Christian has entered a new realm too. You have been transported from darkness into His wonderful light. Now you must break out of your old habits, explore your new terrain, and learn how to walk as a child of the light.

LIFT UP ...

Lord, help me break out of the darkness that has confined me. Teach me to stretch my legs and walk in Your light. In Jesus' name. Amen.

LOOK AT ...

Walking on God's path means walking away from sin's path. Let's examine yet another aspect of the Christian journey—walking as children of light.

READ EPHESIANS 5:8–14.

For you were once darkness, but now you are light in the Lord. Walk as children of light (for the fruit of the Spirit is in all goodness, righteousness, and truth), finding out what is acceptable

LEARN ABOUT ...

4 Acceptable

The word *acceptable* means "what is agreeable or well pleasing to God." Humans were created with a purpose. "Our purpose is to please God, not people" (I Thess. 2:4 NLT). Crowd pleasers are often contrary to God pleasers. "Pilate, wanting to gratify the crowd, released Barabbas to them; and he delivered Jesus, after he had scourged Him, to be crucified" (Mark 15:15).

---

8 Rise and Shine

To sinners lulled to sleep by the dark world, Christ says, "Awake!" Spiritual awakening is to recognize and repent of sin. To those who are dead in trespasses, Jesus says, "Arise!" Spiritual resurrection means to be born again. "The day is at hand. Therefore let us cast off the works of darkness, and let us put on the armor of light" (Rom. 13:12).

to the Lord. And have no fellowship with the unfruitful works of darkness, but rather expose them. For it is shameful even to speak of those things which are done by them in secret. But all things that are exposed are made manifest by the light, for whatever makes manifest is light. Therefore He says: "Awake, you who sleep, arise from the dead, and Christ will give you light."
Ephesians 5:8–14

1. How does Paul contrast our lives before and after salvation?

2. Therefore, we should walk as "children of light." What do you think it means to be a child of light?

3. What three types of "soil" does the fruit of the Spirit grow well in?

4. What should children of light be seeking?

5. What two things are believers to do about unfruitful works of darkness?

6. What is shameful to speak of?

7. What happens to all things that are exposed?

8. Paul gives a symbolic gospel message to unbelievers.

   a. What two things does God exhort the unbeliever to do?

   b. Why?

   c. What condition are sinners in before they know Christ?

LIVE OUT ...

9. We are to walk as children of light. Fill in the following chart to discover how.

SCRIPTURE	HOW TO WALK
Deuteronomy 8:6	
Isaiah 30:21	
John 12:35–36	
Romans 6:4	
Romans 13:13	

10. Light exposes or manifests the things that are in darkness. With this in mind, journal through the steps below.

Step One: List some dark places in the world around you. (Example: adult bookstores, nightclubs, Internet sites, etc.)

Step Two: Imagine you've been given a powerful, portable spotlight. What would happen if you directed its beam on the dark places listed above? How would the people in those places respond?

Step Three: Rewrite this passage into a prayer for people dwelling in darkness:

"The people who sat in darkness
   have seen a great light.
And for those who lived in the land where death casts its
   shadow,
      a light has shined."

From then on Jesus began to preach, "Repent of your sins and turn to God, for the Kingdom of Heaven is near." (Matt. 4:16–17 NLT)

11. The apostle John warned that children of light can become blinded when they hate or reject other Christians: "Anyone who loves another brother or sister is living in the light and does not cause others to stumble. But anyone who hates another brother or sister is still living and walking in darkness. Such a person does not know the way to go, having been blinded by the darkness" (1 John 2:10–11 NLT).

Think of a Christian you have trouble getting along with. How have you rejected them in word or deed? Write a prayer asking God to help you shine the light of His love on them instead.

º º ● º º

Rose Crawford, who had been blind for fifty years, was recovering from a delicate eye surgery. "I just can't believe it!" she gasped as the doctor lifted the bandages from her eyes. She wept for joy when a beautiful world of form and color came into focus for the first time. The amazing thing about this story, though, is that twenty years of her blindness had been unnecessary. She didn't know it, but surgical techniques had been developed years before, and she could have had her sight restored much earlier.

Are there any Rose Crawfords in your life—people who are blinded by sin and have not yet heard that there is a cure in Christ? As a child of the light, reflect His glory to the dark world around you.

LISTEN TO ...

A single sunbeam is enough to drive away many shadows.

—*Francis of Assisi*

Walk Wisely

At one time our neighborhood was infested with pigeons—flying rodents, I (Lenya) called them. As I racked my brain thinking of ways to rid our roof of them, my son, Nathan, was making plans to capture one. One day we were bird-watching from the front porch and just burst out laughing at the way pigeons walk. They waddle from side to side like Charlie Chaplin, heads jerking back and forth like Egyptian dancers'. "Why do pigeons walk so funny?" Nathan asked me. I read an article explaining that a pigeon walks that way so it can see where it's going. Apparently it can't adjust its focus as it moves, so the pigeon brings its head to a complete stop between steps in order to refocus. The bird waddles along: head forward, stop, head back, stop, and so on.

It made me stop and think. In our spiritual walk we can learn something from the pigeon. Human beings can be haphazard, moving at a pace that blurs our vision. We should stop between steps to refocus on the Word of God so we can walk in the will of God.

LIFT UP ...

Father, help me to slow down so that I can consider what steps to take. Lead me in paths of righteousness for the sake of Your name. In Jesus' name. Amen.

LOOK AT ...

We are called to walk in love and in the light of God's Word. Now we see how to be wise in our steps as well.

LEARN ABOUT ...

2 Circumspect

To be circumspect means "to look around and walk carefully." The Greek word carries the idea of precision and accuracy. In other words, we should walk carefully or with exactness. Paul said, "But you have carefully followed my doctrine, manner of life, purpose, [and] faith" (2 Tim. 3:10).

7 God's Will

God's will is two-sided. One side shows what His will is; the other side reveals what His will is not. Peter taught, "The Lord is ... not willing that any should perish but that all should come to repentance" (2 Peter 3:9). Not in His will? Are you willing to repent?

8 Foolish

Fool in Scripture refers more to moral than to intellectual deficiencies. The fool does not lack mental powers but misuses them. He does not lack the ability to reason but reasons wrongly. The fool primarily casts off the fear of God and acts as if he could safely disregard the eternal principles of God's righteousness.

See then that you walk circumspectly, not as fools but as wise, redeeming the time, because the days are evil. Therefore do not be unwise, but understand what the will of the Lord is. Ephesians 5:15–17

1. Paul begins verse 15 with the exhortation "see then." What did we learn in yesterday's lesson that makes it possible for Christians to see?

2. As children of light, how are we to walk and how are we not to walk?

3. Fill in the following sentence based on the first sentence in today's passage: When I walk _____, God considers me to be _____.

4. What do you think it means to redeem the time?

5. Why is it important for believers to redeem the time?

6. What are believers cautioned not to be?

7. What should the believer understand?

LIVE OUT ...

8. a. Fill in the following chart to discover some characteristics of a spiritually foolish person. Then write a brief note evaluating whether or not you are exhibiting these.

SCRIPTURE	FOOLISH CHARACTERISTIC	SELF-EVALUATION
Psalm 14:1		
Proverbs 10:18		
Luke 24:25		
Galatians 3:1–3		
1 Timothy 6:9		

b. In which of these areas do you need to wise up?

9. a. Fill in this chart to find some of the ways you can walk wisely, and evaluate whether or not you are exhibiting these.

SCRIPTURE	WISE CHARACTERISTIC	SELF-EVALUATION
Proverbs 9:10		
Proverbs 14:1		
Romans 16:19		
2 Timothy 3:14–15		
James 1:5		

b. In which of these areas do you need to gain more insight?

10. Moses wrote this prayer: "So teach us to number our days, that we may gain a heart of wisdom" (Ps. 90:12).

Reword Moses' prayer into your personal prayer.

∘ ∘ • ∘ ∘

Imagine that you and Jesus are taking a walk. His footprints go consistently, rarely varying. But your footprints are a stream of zigzags. Gradually your footprints come alongside His—you and Jesus are walking side by side! As you continue, your footprints begin to fit precisely

LEARN ABOUT …

9 Wise Person

Jesus told of two builders: one wise and one foolish. Both built homes, endured storms, and heard God's Word. The difference? Obedience. It changes a fool into a scholar! "Whoever hears these sayings of Mine, *and does them*, I will liken him to a wise man" (Matt. 7:24).

10 Redeem the Time

The phrase *redeeming the time* means "taking advantage of or buying up the opportunity." If you're thirty-five, live a normal life span, subtract time for sleep, work, hygiene, chores, eating, traveling, and such activities, in the next thirty-six years you'll have about five hundred days left to live! Life is short, so spend your time wisely.

in His—you and He are becoming one. This goes on for many miles. But suddenly your footprints are back and it seems worse than before! Zigzags everywhere. Stops. Starts. Deep gashes in the sand.

Puzzled, you say, "Lord, I understand that at first You taught me to walk with You."

"That's true," He replies.

"And when my footprints were inside of Yours, I was learning to walk in Your steps—becoming one with You, right?" I ask.

"You've understood everything so far," He says and smiles.

"So, Lord, did I blow it or something? Why did the footprints separate?"

There is a long pause before the Lord explains, "Didn't you know? We were dancing."

God made people with hearts as well as minds. A wise mind will walk circumspectly; a happy heart will dance with joy. The wise King Solomon ruled with his intellect. The passionate King David ruled as a man after God's heart: "David danced before the LORD with all his might" (2 Sam. 6:14 NLT). It's wise to walk with the Lord; it's wonderful to dance with Him.

Listen To ...

A fool wanders; the wise man travels.

—*Thomas Fuller*

Change of Heart

Ephesians 5:18–33

Think of the heart. It weighs less than a pound, but it has a lot of work to do. On average, it pumps one hundred thousand times every day, circulating two thousand gallons of blood through sixty thousand miles of arteries, capillaries, and veins. This hollow muscular organ forces blood through the circulatory system, pumping life through every organ. However, when the arteries become clogged or the heart becomes diseased, there is a very real danger of heart failure and loss of life.

But the heart is more than an organ. The biblical meaning of *heart* represents our inner self—the source of emotions and deepest desires. The inner heart, when clogged and sickened by sin, can lead us into spiritual danger. Scripture tells us, "The human heart is the most deceitful of all things, and desperately wicked" (Jer. 17:9 NLT). There is only one cure: heart surgery. God says, "I will give you a new heart, and I will put a new spirit in you" (Ezek. 36:26 NLT).

This week we discover that God wants to replace our spiritually diseased hearts with Spirit-filled ones: hearts full of praise, thanksgiving, submission, respect, love, and unity. As you study this lesson, ask God to give you a new heart that is strong and ready to carry on the work of His kingdom.

Day 1: Ephesians 5:18–20   **SPIRIT-FILLED HEART**

Day 2: Ephesians 5:21   **HEART OF SUBMISSION**

Day 3: Ephesians 5:22–24, 33   **HEART OF RESPECT**

Day 4: Ephesians 5:25–28   **HEART OF LOVE**

Day 5: Ephesians 5:29–32   **HEART OF UNITY**

DAY I
Spirit-Filled Heart

LIFT UP ...

Father, the only way for my heart to be strong is to be filled with Your Spirit. Don't let me settle for worthless substitutes; instead, fill me to overflowing with Your Spirit. In Jesus' name. Amen.

LOOK AT ...

For the past few weeks we have studied what it means to live out our calling in Christ. This week we examine the inner heart attitudes that influence our outward actions. God wants us to be filled with His Holy Spirit and to exhibit hearts of praise and thanksgiving.

READ EPHESIANS 5:18–20.

And do not be drunk with wine, in which is dissipation; but be filled with the Spirit, speaking to one another in psalms and hymns and spiritual songs, singing and making melody in your heart to the Lord, giving thanks always for all things to God the Father in the name of our Lord Jesus Christ ... Ephesians 5:18–20

1. What did Paul tell believers not to do here?

LEARN ABOUT ...

2 Dissipation

The word *dissipation* means "indulgent or wasteful living, especially excessive drinking." People who live to "get wasted" end up wasting their lives like the Prodigal Son, who "packed all his belongings and moved to a distant land, and there he wasted all his money in wild living" (Luke 15:13 NLT).

3 Spirit-Filled

Filled here has three meanings—(1) filled: As wind fills a ship's sail, so God's Spirit fills us with power and direction; (2) permeated: As salt permeates food with flavor and preserves, so God's Spirit provides us with zest and permanence; (3) controlled: As one reins in a horse with a bit, so the Spirit guides and controls a life surrendered to Him.

6 All Things

Give thanks always in all ways. At work, give thanks for provision; at home, give thanks for family; on the road, give thanks for the occasion to practice patience with strangers. In all you say and do, let your life be a thank-you note to God.

2. Why should believers not do this?

3. Rather than being filled with wine, who are believers to be filled with?

4. This filling affects how we speak to one another. How are believers to speak to one another?

5. How does this filling affect what goes on in our hearts?

6. How often should we give thanks?

7. For what and to whom are we to give thanks?

8. In whose name are we to give thanks?

LIVE OUT ...

9. a. God wants us to be filled with the Holy Spirit rather than with artificial stimulants. Write down the name of a prodigal person who has filled his or her life with drugs or alcohol.

   b. Journal a prayer asking God to bring that person to his or her senses. Rewrite the following verses into a prayer: "When he finally came to his senses, he said to himself, ... 'I will go home to my father and say, "Father, I have sinned against both heaven and you"'" (Luke 15:17–18 NLT).

10. Fill in the following chart to discover people in the Bible who were filled with the Holy Spirit.

SCRIPTURE	WHO WAS FILLED	WHAT THE SPIRIT PROVIDED
Exodus 28:2–3		
Exodus 31:2–4		
Luke 1:67		
Luke 4:1		
Acts 4:31		
Acts 7:55, 59		
Acts 13:52		

LEARN ABOUT ...

8 In Jesus' Name

Shakespeare said, "A rose by any other name would smell as sweet." But there is no name sweeter than the one given by God to His only Son. "You are to name him Jesus, for he will save his people from their sins" (Matt. 1:21 NLT). What's in His name? The sweetness of salvation!

11. Paul's instruction to be filled with the Spirit applies to you, too. Before you can be filled with God, you must be emptied of self. Listed below are some of the "works of the flesh" and also the "fruit of the Spirit" taken from Galatians 5:19–23. Draw a line through the works of the flesh of which you need to be emptied. Then circle the fruits of the Spirit with which you desire to be filled.

11 Filled

The Greek word for *filled* means "to keep on being filled." The indwelling of the Holy Spirit is a onetime experience, but the filling of the Holy Spirit is an experience where believers are continually filled. There are two prerequisites for being filled with the Spirit: repentance of sin and yielding to God.

WORKS OF FLESH	FRUIT OF THE SPIRIT
Hatred	Love
Fits of Rage	Joy
Envy	Peace
Drunkenness	Patience
Hostility	Kindness
Jealousy	Goodness
Quarreling	Faithfulness
Selfish Ambition	Gentleness
Divisions	Self-control

12 Praise at Midnight

Spirit-filled Paul could sing praises when the night was dark and the walls were closing in. "Around midnight, Paul and Silas were praying and singing hymns to God.... Suddenly, there was a massive earthquake, and the prison was shaken to its foundations" (Acts 16:25–26 NLT). When you want to shake things up, sing songs of praise.

12. With the Holy Spirit's help, you can possess the graces of praise and thankfulness in the midst of difficult circumstances.

Journal about a time when you were able to praise the Lord or offer Him thanks only through the power of the Holy Spirit.

○ ○ ● ○ ○

In the late 1970s I (Lenya) was a preppie coed. Disappointment over my parents' divorce had made my heart calloused. Control became my way of coping. I controlled my appearance, every hair in place. I controlled my emotions with artificial stimulants, choosing partying instead of pain. And I controlled my relationships—dates but no commitments. Then my dad was saved and invited me to attend Calvary Chapel in Costa Mesa, California.

Pastor Chuck Smith reflected God's love as he entered the sanctuary. His Spirit-filled words disarmed my heart. His service ended with an invitation for prayer. I wanted to go forward, but I was terrified to relinquish control. The Holy Spirit compelled me to let go.

I told Pastor Malcolm Wild, "I believe in Jesus and I've been coming to church, but something's missing." He asked, "Have you repented of sin?" I had no idea what he meant. He explained, "Repentance means to have a change of heart, to turn from sin and toward God. Sin separates you from God, but confession brings forgiveness."

As he spoke, tears ran down my face. My "in control" veneer melted away. He led me in a prayer that changed my life, as I repented and asked God to fill me with His Holy Spirit. I sighed with relief. At last God was in control!

If your life is controlled by *you* instead of by God's Spirit, maybe it's time to let go and let God take charge.

LISTEN TO ...

A man ... should never give all his heart to anything which will end when his life ends.

—*C. S. Lewis*

DAY 2
Heart of Submission

You're in the army now! God has enlisted you "as a good soldier of Jesus Christ" (2 Tim. 2:3). The army, like the body of Christ, has a chain of command. Each member under the chain of command is equal in quality but differs in position. Generals are not better people than privates; generals just have a star instead of a stripe on their shoulders.

General Eisenhower once rebuked an officer for calling a soldier "just a private." Eisenhower thought the army could operate better without its generals than without its foot soldiers. "If this war is won," he said, "it will be won by privates." In the same way, simple Spirit-filled saints are the core of the church. Gifted evangelists run crusades; pastors lead large and small congregations; and parachurch ministries are headed up by charismatic leaders. But, if God's work is to be accomplished, if the Great Commission is to be fulfilled, it will be the "ordinary" Christians who will do it.

There are no "ordinary" Christians in God's army. He has developed an extraordinary chain of command in which we all submit to one another. The difference between human armies and the Lord's armies is that God, not the president, is the Commander in Chief. Soldiers surrender their will, serving their president out of compulsion. Christians surrender their hearts, serving their God out of love. Where do you fit in God's army? Have you gotten your marching orders from your Commander in Chief?

LIFT UP ...

Father, I'm ready to hear Your orders. Help me to be a good soldier who answers "Yes, sir!" when You call me to serve. In Jesus' name. Amen.

LOOK AT ...

We have found that the mark of a Spirit-filled believer is a heart of praise and thanksgiving. Today we find that God insists that believers possess a heart of submission to God and to others.

LEARN ABOUT ...

1 All Submit

Submission is not just for women. "One another" includes both sexes. Male children as well as female children are to honor their parents. Both genders are commanded to obey governing authorities.

---

2 Biblical Submission

The word *submission* means "humble obedience to another's will." This word in the original Greek denotes the idea of military ranking, to arrange in order. Biblically, submission means willingly relinquishing one's rights to another person based on the order God, in His wisdom, has established.

---

5 Fear of God

To fear the Lord means "to stand in awe of Him." Awe combines honor, fear, and respect before someone of superior office or action—primarily God. "Let the whole world fear the LORD, and let everyone stand in awe of him" (Ps. 33:8 NLT).

READ EPHESIANS 5:21.

... submitting to one another in the fear of God. Ephesians 5:21

1. To whom are believers to submit?

2. Fill in the chart to discover some "one anothers" we all must submit to.

SCRIPTURE	SUBMIT TO
1 Corinthians 16:16	
James 4:7	
1 Peter 2:13–14	
1 Peter 2:18	
1 Peter 5:5	

3. How does the definition of submission given in the sidebar influence or change your view of submission?

4. What actions or attitudes are the opposite of that definition?

5. According to verse 21, how should we submit to one another?

6. To discover more about the fear of the Lord, fill in the chart below.

RESULTS OF FEAR OF THE LORD	HAVE YOU EXPERIENCED IT?	SCRIPTURE
Deuteronomy 10:12–13		
Proverbs 1:7		
Proverbs 8:13		
Malachi 2:5		

7. How has your fear of the Lord enabled you to submit to others?

Live Out ...

8. When you hear the word *submit,* how do you respond?

    ____ "Submit on the outside, not the inside."

    ____ "I'll submit if _____."

    ____ "I'm willing to do that."

    ____ "You can't make me!"

    ____ "Women have been liberated."

    ____ "I'll submit joyfully."

9. a. Journal about your responses to question 8. What makes you respond that way? What do you need to change?

    b. Write a prayer asking God to supernaturally enable you to submit—to Him first of all, and then to one another. Confess and repent of the sin in your life that keeps you from submitting.

10. Submission and obedience to God are related. In Acts 5:24–32 the disciples found themselves in a situation where submission to God took precedence over submission to other people. Read this passage and answer the following questions.

    a. Who took the apostles captive (v. 26)?

    b. Before whom were they put on trial (v. 27)?

    c. What did the authorities command the apostles not to do and why (v. 28)?

    d. How did Peter and the apostles respond and why (v. 29)?

Learn about ...

8 God's Order

Submission isn't personal; it's practical. At creation, God subdued the elements, bringing order out of chaos (Gen. 1:1–3). At the fall in the garden of Eden, God established submission of wives to their husbands (Gen. 3:16). Part of submission is recognizing God's order of things—His chain of command. Are you the missing link?

10 Civil Disobedience

Chinese Christians disobey their government's ban on distributing Bibles. Israeli Christians disobey the official ban on evangelism. Commentator William Barclay wrote, "The Christian has a higher obligation than even his obligation to the state. While he must render to Caesar the things which are Caesar's, he must also render to God the things which are God's." When society's laws conflict with God's law, Christians must "obey God rather than men."[1]

11. Journal about a time when you or someone you love felt compelled to obey God rather than other people. What were the circumstances? What was the result?

○ ○ ● ○ ○

On a thirty-six-hour train ride from Beijing to Guangzhou, Vic and Colette Jury broke the law. They were traveling with a group of smugglers carrying illegal imports: over two tons of Bibles and gospel tracts. While the armed guards turned their backs to check travel documents, these "outlaws" extended their hands to pass out life-giving literature. In the dark of the night, a young woman covertly read the forbidden pamphlet, and the light of salvation broke through as she accepted the Lord. She became a lawbreaker too, acting as interpreter for this band of believers and recruiting other Chinese nationals to act as lookouts. Throughout the long journey, she whispered the good news to anyone who would listen. Eventually, she helped lead several others to faith in the Lord on this "gospel train" bound for glory!

What made Vic and Colette act in civil disobedience to China's governing authority at the risk of punishment or deportation? They realize a higher authority—Christ—governs them. He commanded, "Go into all the world and preach the Good News to everyone" (Mark 16:15 NLT).

Does this *true* story of civil disobedience imply that the Jurys don't know how to submit to "one another" as Paul instructed us? Definitely not! In our church I've seen them model humility and respect toward their pastor and the church leadership. Vic has generously submitted his time, energy, and support for worldwide missions. The key to godly submission is recognizing *whom* to submit to and *when* to submit.

LISTEN TO ...

In submission we are at last free to value other people. Their dreams and plans become important to us. We have entered into a new, wonderful, glorious freedom—the freedom to give up our own rights for the good of others.... We discover that it is far better to serve our neighbor than to have our own way.

—*Richard J. Foster*

DAY 3

Heart of Respect

When a man entered the hospital for tests, he never would have guessed what the doctors would find. At first they thought the X-ray technicians had put the film in backward. But then they discovered that nothing was wrong with the X rays; there was something wrong with the patient. The man's heart was in a reversed position. What was supposed to be on the left side of the man's chest was on the right side, and vice versa. He had a rare reversed-organ condition. His heart was not where it should be.

In many homes, women's hearts are not where they should be, either. Instead of respecting their husbands, these women are ruling the roost. The diagnosis? A reversed-*order* condition—role reversal where husbands and wives have gotten things backward. The cure? A heart of respect helps women turn their hearts and homes around.

LIFT UP ...

Lord, I want to be beautiful to You and to my husband. Right the wrongs in my heart so I can trust You and honor my husband's God-given authority. In Jesus' name. Amen.

LOOK AT ...

We now move into the realm of the marriage relationship, learning that the Spirit-filled home is a picture of the Spirit-filled church. Today we get some practical instruction concerning God's requirements for the wife in marriage.

READ EPHESIANS 5:22–24, 33.

Wives, submit to your own husbands, as to the Lord. For the husband is head of the wife, as also Christ is head of the church; and He is the Savior of the body. Therefore, just as the church is subject to Christ, so let the wives be to their own husbands in everything ... Nevertheless let each

LEARN ABOUT ...

I Submit As Equals

Wives aren't commanded to obey their husbands in the same manner as children obey their parents or slaves their masters. Submission may require obedience, but submission is not servitude. A wife should not be treated as a child, but an equal—bone of bones and flesh of flesh (Gen. 2:23).

---

3 Headship

The head is one who is "chief or exalted above." As the head governs the physical body, so Christ, the "head of the church," governs His body, the church. "The head of every man is Christ, the head of woman is man, and the head of Christ is God" (I Cor. II:3).

---

6 Subject To

Subjecting and *submitting* are similar terms meaning to relinquish one's rights. The word *relinquish* means "to yield, release, or surrender." In a healthy marriage the act of submission is not demanded by the husband; rather the wife freely offers it as a response to his love. Giving up rights isn't wrong.

one of you in particular so love his own wife as himself, and let the wife see that she respects her husband. Ephesians 5:22–24, 33

1. To whom should wives submit?

2. With what attitude are they to submit?

3. What further reason did Paul give for the wife to submit to her husband?

4. Whose headship is the husband's role compared to?

5. How else did Paul describe Christ, the head of the church?

6. How should a wife mirror the church?

7. In how many areas should the wife submit to her husband?

8. a. According to the last sentence of the passage, how does a wife exhibit a submissive heart toward her husband?

   b. What does he do to make it easy for her to submit?

LIVE OUT ...

9. a. R-E-S-P-E-C-T, find out what it means to *you*. It means a lot to your heavenly Head, Christ, and to your earthly head, your husband. Using the word HEAD as an acrostic, describe four qualities you respect about your husband, if you are married. Then write him a note telling him of your respect for him, and give it to him this week.

H
E
A
D

LEARN ABOUT ...

b. Author and theologian John Stott said, "[People] have equal dignity ... but different God-appointed roles."[2] Journal about how you have found dignity and fulfillment in your role as a submissive wife.

10. Respecting someone who is not respectable isn't easy, but it is possible. David was an example of this. Saul deserved respect from David because he was David's father-in-law and the king. Yet Saul was a proud, bitter, and vengeful man who attempted to murder David and who gave his wife to another man. Read 1 Samuel 26:7–11, 21.

a. What opportunity did David have (v. 8)?

b. What did David do with his opportunity and why (vv. 9, 11)?

c. How did David trust God to take care of Saul (v. 10)?

d. How did Saul respond to David's show of respect (v. 21)?

e. How did Saul describe David's respect (v. 21)?

o o ● o o

8 Love and Respect

"Each one of you" implies a universal duty from which no husband or wife is exempt. It applies to every (not some) Christian wife regardless of age, occupation, or spiritual maturity. It includes all (not a few) Christian husbands no matter their intelligence, character, or upbringing.

9 R-E-S-P-E-C-T

Respond prayerfully instead of reacting poorly. Exhibit compassion instead of contempt. Speak words of support instead of sabotage. Place his needs first instead of last. Expect God to intervene instead of taking things into your own hands. Cast all your cares on the Lord instead of complaining to others. Trust God to change your husband's heart instead of hardening your own.

10 Respect The Unrespectable

The head of the home is a God-given office. The person who holds that office deserves respect. A citizen of the United States can respect the position of the president even if the person in the Oval Office is unrespectable. A wife can respect the position given to her husband even if he's an unrespectable man.

I (Lenya) love submission! You may think I'm outdated or crazy, but I've learned that when I obey God's Word by relinquishing my rights to my husband, Skip, it gives God the opportunity to accomplish His will in my husband's heart. Submission means I get out of the way so God can get in the loop.

If Abraham is the "father of faith," then Sarah is the "mother of submission." She was willing to submit to Abraham, trusting God to get her husband's attention. Genesis 12 tells us that Sarah was beautiful to behold. Abraham knew foreign dignitaries would covet her and threaten his life, so he asked Sarah to bend the truth by telling them she was his sister. Genesis 20 reveals that she was his half sister—the daughter of his father but not his mother. Sarah submitted, and as a result a king took her into his harem. Sarah let her husband make a bad decision, knowing God would hold Abraham accountable. And He did. God tormented the king with nightmares and threatened him with death if he touched Sarah. All's well that ends well: Sarah remained chaste, Abraham was chastened for his lack of faith, and the king was restored.

When a wife doesn't submit, it's like a tug-of-war—husband on one end and wife on the other—both pulling with all their might. When a wife submits, she lets go and places her end of the rope in God's hands. No one wins in a tug-of-war against God—the person just gets dragged through the mud.

LISTEN TO ...

Respect a man; he will do the more.

—James Howell

Heart of Love

USA Today reported the story of a seven-hundred-pound lovesick moose that was courting a cow on a farm in Vermont. The Hereford cow apparently accepted the moose. "They've nuzzled like they're kissing, but I ain't seen no action," said the cow's owner, Larry Carrara. Curious spectators from all over have parked cars and pickups in front of the farmhouse to watch the strange affair. Can they mate? Yes, and fertilization is even possible. But reproductive physiologists say there would be no offspring because their chromosome numbers don't match.

A cow has a face only a mother cow could love, but somehow a tall, dark, and handsome moose fell head over hooves for Mr. Carrara's Hereford. The attraction compelled the moose to abandon his roguish ways for domestic bliss. It was a match made in green pastures. Today we learn about a match made in heaven. Jesus came to earth to find an unlikely bride—the church—and make her His own. He teaches men to leave their selfish ways and to love their wives the way He loves His church—by laying down their lives.

LIFT UP ...

Jesus, thank You for loving me when I was unlovely. I'm grateful that You left heaven to find me on earth. Your love has transformed my heart. Praise Your name. In Jesus' name. Amen.

LOOK AT ...

We have learned about the submissive role of the wife in the home. Now we turn our attention to the husband's role to love sacrificially.

READ EPHESIANS 5:25–28.

Husbands, love your wives, just as Christ also loved the church and gave Himself for her, that He might sanctify and cleanse her with the washing of water by the word, that He might present her

to Himself a glorious church, not having spot or wrinkle or any such thing, but that she should be holy and without blemish. So husbands ought to love their own wives as their own bodies; he who loves his wife loves himself. Ephesians 5:25–28

LEARN ABOUT ...

I Unconditional Love

The Greek word for love here is *agape*, a love that is the antithesis of selfishness. Husbands should love wives under one condition—unconditionally!—regardless of how she looks, acts, or submits. God loves the unlovely: "God showed his great love for us by sending Christ to die for us while we were still sinners" (Rom. 5:8 NLT).

4 Sanctify

The word *sanctify* means "to separate or set apart; to separate from the sinful in order to set apart for a sacred purpose." "May the God of peace Himself sanctify you completely; and may your whole spirit, soul, and body be preserved blameless" (I Thess. 5:23).

7 Love As Himself

The true spirituality of a husband is measured not by his church attendance or tithe record but by the way he treats his wife at home when no one else is around. The man who lacks love and care for his wife is guilty of self-neglect and spiritual fraud.

1. What does God command husbands to do?

2. Husbands should model their own love after Christ's love for the church. How did Christ show His love for the church?

3. How do you think a husband could treat his wife with this kind of love? Give some examples.

4. What two things did Christ do for the church by giving Himself?

5. How does He sanctify and cleanse the church?

6. Christ presented the church to Himself. What kind of church did He desire to present to Himself?

7. Husbands should also love their wives as they love their own bodies. What are some ways a man treats his body with love?

8. How might a man treat his wife in a similar way?

LIVE OUT ...

9. Actions speak louder than words. Jesus told us how to measure love: "There is no greater love than to lay down one's life for one's friends" (John 15:13 NLT). Your husband may be a man of few words, but his sacrificial actions can speak volumes. Check off the ways your husband has shown his love for you.

____ Coaches the team   ____ Pays the bills

____ Helps with chores   ____ Maintains the vehicles

____ Works in the yard   ____ Disciplines the kids

____ Does household repairs   ____ Manages crises

____ Protects the home   ____ Prays for the family

____ Gives me free time   ____ Plans for the future

____ Other:

LEARN ABOUT ...

10 Self-Love

Society elevates self-love, but God says loving others as ourselves is the highest priority. "The commandments ... are summed up in this one rule: 'Love your neighbor as yourself'" (Rom. 13:9 NIV). The Old Testament defined neighbor as one who lived nearby. In the parable of the good Samaritan, Jesus expanded loving your neighbor to helping anyone in need.

10. a. Today we learned that husbands should love their wives as they love themselves. This type of love needs to be reciprocal in marriage. List a few things that you do for yourself. (Example: exercise, eating, or entertainment.)

b. How can you sacrifice one of these things to show your "better half" that you care for him as much as for yourself? (Example: Cancel your workout time to free him up to go fishing.)

11 Everlasting Kiss?

Husbands and wives who kiss daily before leaving the house usually live five years longer than those who don't. They have fewer car accidents, lose nearly 50 percent less time at work because of illness, and earn 20 to 30 percent more money than nonkissers. "Let the husband render to his wife the affection due her, ... likewise ... the wife to her husband" (1 Cor. 7:3).

11. Husbands are to give their wives tender love and physical affection. Has your husband been trying to warm up to an iceberg? If you have been giving your husband the cold shoulder, it's time to open your arms for a warm embrace.

Draw a line to discover how to replace cold treatment with warm response.

COLD	WARM
Silent treatment	Tender touch
Cold shoulder	Warm embrace
Icy glare	Sweet nothings in his ear
Walking on thin ice	Glowing eyes
Pointing the finger	Paths of pleasure

○ ○ ● ○ ○

Theologian Charles Spurgeon retold a story about the deep love French soldiers had for Napoleon Bonaparte. It wasn't uncommon for a soldier on his deathbed to prop himself up and proclaim allegiance to his much-admired general. If the dying man happened to see Napoleon nearby, he would cry out, *"Vive l'Empereur!"* One of the most moving declarations of love came from the mouth of a soldier who'd received a critical chest wound. As the surgeon desperately attempted to remove the fatal bullet, the dying man whispered, "Go a little deeper and you will find the Emperor."[3]

The husband is the head of his wife, but she is his heart of hearts. The two have become one flesh. To injure one is to inflict pain on the other. No healthy human would intentionally harm himself. No healthy husband should ever intentionally wound his soul mate—it will cause heart damage.

LISTEN TO ...

He who does not honor his wife dishonors himself.

—Spanish Proverb

DAY 5

Heart of Unity

It's been said that there's "chemistry" involved in finding the right spouse. In chemistry, when two different yet compatible elements are mixed together, a whole new substance is created. Marriage is much the same: The blending of a man who is completely different yet wholly compatible with a woman creates a new compound—one flesh.

I (Lenya) read about a scientist in the field of chemistry who said that if you mix hydrogen and oxygen, the well-known components of water, you would get no chemical reaction and no water! But if you add a small amount of platinum to this stable mixture, things start to happen quickly. The hydrogen and oxygen begin to unite as a chemical change occurs, producing H_2O. Marriages, like chemical reactions, require an extra element for unification. In a Christian marriage, that extra element is God, the strongest bonding agent known. Two becoming one is good, but three bound together is better. Solomon said, "A threefold cord is not quickly broken" (Eccl. 4:12). The chemical compound for water is H_2O (two parts hydrogen plus one part oxygen), while the designation for a strong marriage is HWC (husband plus wife plus Christ). The new compound created is two hearts beating as one—a heart of unity!

LIFT UP ...

Lord, thank You for cementing my marriage together. Keep my heart inextricably bound to the husband You've given me. Don't allow any outside influence to corrode our commitment to each other. In Jesus' name. Amen.

LOOK AT ...

We have learned how a husband must love his wife both unconditionally and sacrificially. Now we discover that the bond between a man and a woman is meant to reflect the unity between Christ and His church.

LEARN ABOUT ...

2 Nourish And Cherish

To nourish means "to provide for someone's needs and give what is necessary for growth and maturity." To cherish means "to give tender love and physical affection with warmth, comfort, protection, and security." While some view nourishing and cherishing as feminine traits, these responsibilities are primarily directed to the husband for his wife.

7 Becoming One

Becoming one flesh is a process: leaving and cleaving. Leaving means you detach yourself from your parents in order to attach yourself to a marriage partner. Cleaving means to cement together in a permanent, unbreakable bond. This bond is a spiritual mystery and a physical reality from the bedroom to the birthing room.

9 Marriage Vows

Couples recite the familiar vows: "For better, for worse; for richer, for poorer; in sickness and health; to love and to cherish, until death us do part." Some people selectively hear "better, richer, and healthy." They ignore the "worse, poorer, and sickness" parts. Couples who cherish each other will take the bad, nourishing it until it becomes better.

READ EPHESIANS 5:29–32.

For no one ever hated his own flesh, but nourishes and cherishes it, just as the Lord does the church. For we are members of His body, of His flesh and of His bones. "For this reason a man shall leave his father and mother and be joined to his wife, and the two shall become one flesh." This is a great mystery, but I speak concerning Christ and the church. Ephesians 5:29–32

1. Yesterday we learned that a husband must love his wife as his own body. What reason did Paul give for this?

2. In what two ways should a husband show he loves his wife as his own flesh?

3. What perfect example should the husband follow?

4. Why does the Lord nourish and cherish the church?

5. What is Christ's body made of?

6. What are the two steps a man should take in the marriage process?

7. What supernatural event occurs between husband and wife?

8. What great mystery does marriage depict?

LIVE OUT ...

9. a. Review the sidebar that defines nourishing and cherishing. List the qualities that define each trait:

Nourish:

Cherish:

b. Describe a specific situation in which your husband has demonstrated these qualities toward you.

10. a. Fill in the chart below to discover how God displays these same traits toward His loved ones.

SCRIPTURE	TRAITS OF NOURISHING AND CHERISHING
Psalm 32:7–8	
Psalm 61:3–4	
Psalm 103:4–5	
Isaiah 66:13	
Philippians 4:19	
James 1:2–4	
1 Peter 2:2–3	

b. Journal a prayer asking God to help you see the ways He has nourished and cherished you. Thank Him for His tender care in your life.

11. Becoming one flesh in marriage is a two-step process: leaving and cleaving. Before you can firmly hold on to your spouse, you must let go of your parents. List the things you need to release and those you need to hold on to.

THINGS I MUST LET GO (LEAVE)	THINGS I MUST HOLD ON TO (CLEAVE)

LEARN ABOUT ...

11 Hands Off

Marriage is the birth of a family. The new couple releases old family ties in the realm of authority and responsibility. Leaving parents doesn't mean dishonoring them. Parents are to be respected, but after marriage they no longer exercise control over their children's lives. "Honor your father and your mother, so that you may live long" (Ex. 20:12 NIV).

○ ○ ● ○ ○

When Kerry and I (Penny) were first married, we didn't know that things would get *worse* before they got *better*. As newlyweds we experienced the *poorer* part when we were devastated by a lawsuit that cost us everything. As new parents we began to struggle with the *sickness* part when I began to suffer from debilitating migraines. That's when the *nourishing* and *cherishing* parts of our vows were put to the test. Kerry felt like a failure because we had to file for bankruptcy. I let him know that success in my eyes was measured by his godly attitude, not a giant bank account. At his lowest point, he confessed to me, "I don't know what to do." I lovingly embraced him and said, "We're in this together, baby; God will take care of us." Kerry has nourished me in physical struggles. Countless times I've interrupted his sleep, groaning, "Honey, we need to go to the ER. My head's killing me." When the migraines come, he cooks, cleans, and cares for me.

It's a mystery to me how deeply a married couple can feel and heal one another's deepest needs. But Paul revealed a greater mystery still: The bond between husband and wife reflects the bond between Christ and the church, His bride. He feels our pain and went to the cross to heal our wounds.

Listen To …

There can be no unity, no delight of love, no harmony, no good in being, where there is but one. Two at least are needed for oneness.

—*George MacDonald*

LESSON ELEVEN

((Work Ethic))
Ephesians 6:1–9

The book *The Day America Told the Truth* by James Patterson and Peter Kim claims,

> The so-called Protestant ethic is long gone from today's American workplace.
>
> Workers around America frankly admit that they spend more than 20 percent [seven hours a week] of their time at work totally goofing off. That amounts to a four-day work week across the nation.
>
> Almost half of us admit to chronic malingering, calling in sick when we are not sick, and doing it regularly.
>
> One in six Americans regularly drink or use drugs on the job.
>
> Only one in four give work their best effort; only one in four work to realize their human potential rather than merely to keep the wolf from the door....
>
> About one in four expect to compromise their personal beliefs in order to get ahead on their current job.[1]

Why the decline of the honorable work ethic in the United States? This week we will discover that honor and duty are learned long before a job interview. The Bible encourages parents to train their children in "Word ethics" that will influence their "work ethics."

Though there are no guarantees, children trained up in biblical values are more likely to become productive employees and employers, filling the workforce with men and women who can be trusted.

Day 1: Ephesians 6:1–3	ACCOUNTABILITY
Day 2: Ephesians 6:4	ADMONITION
Day 3: Ephesians 6:5	ATTITUDE
Day 4: Ephesians 6:6–8	ACTIONS
Day 5: Ephesians 6:9	AUTHORITY

Accountability

Lift Up ...

Father, thank You for my parents. Give me the wisdom to honor them in all that I say and do. In Jesus' name. Amen.

Look At ...

Having examined the marriage relationship in lesson 10, we turn our attention on the attitudes and actions of Spirit-filled believers at home and work. Today we look at the God-given responsibilities of Christian children.

Read Ephesians 6:1–3.

Children, obey your parents in the Lord, for this is right. "Honor your father and mother," *which is the first commandment with promise: "that it may be well with you and you may live* *long on the earth." Ephesians 6:1–3*

Learn about ...

I Obedience

To be obedient means "to carry out the word and will of another person." Obedience is "a positive, active response to what a person hears." There are three signs of disobedience: (1) delayed obedience, (2) partial obedience, and (3) resentful obedience.

4 Honor

Honor is respect mingled with reverence and love. Honor is more than obedience. Obedience is action-oriented; honor is attitude-oriented. As a child Jesus honored and obeyed His parents. "He returned to Nazareth with them and was obedient to them.... Jesus grew in wisdom and in stature and in favor with God and all the people" (Luke 2:51–52 NLT).

6 Reinforcements

God the Father promises either a positive or a negative reinforcement to train His kids. "I am giving you the choice between a blessing and a curse! You will be blessed if you obey the commands of the LORD.... You will be cursed if you reject the commands of the LORD" (Deut. 11:26–28 NLT).

1. What are children commanded to do?

2. How are children to obey their parents?

3. Why are children to obey?

4. Describe the attitude children are to exhibit toward their parents.

5. What Old Testament law did Paul quote?

6. What two things does God promise as a result of keeping this commandment?

7. Read Exodus 20:12. How did Paul change the wording of this commandment to include Gentile believers in the promise?

Live Out ...

8. How do you think an adult is to honor his or her parents?

9. Listed below are the three signs of disobedience found in today's lesson. Journal about a time when your children fell into each of these dishonoring behaviors. How did you discipline them?

Delayed obedience:

Partial obedience:

Resentful obedience:

10. Reflect on a time when *you,* as a child of God, fell into similar dishonoring behaviors in your journey of faith. Journal about how you disobeyed and how God corrected you.

Delayed obedience:

Partial obedience:

Resentful obedience:

11. Disobedience leads to God's loving discipline. The writer of Hebrews wrote encouraging words for Christians who are going through a season of discipline from the Lord. Rewrite these verses into a personal prayer to your heavenly Father, thanking Him for His loving correction:

Have you forgotten the encouraging words God spoke to you as his children? He said,

"My child, don't make light of the LORD's discipline,
    and don't give up when he corrects you.
For the LORD disciplines those he loves,
    and he punishes each one he accepts as his child." (Heb. 12:5–6 NLT)

○ ○ ● ○ ○

"How do you honor a dishonorable parent?" a young woman asked me (Lenya) in hushed tones. Though she was shy and fragile, her story took shape with patient coaxing: "My mother's not normal. She's mentally ill,

LEARN ABOUT …

10 Better to Obey

Peter's betrayal of Jesus was one of the worst forms of disobedience. "Jesus' words flashed through Peter's mind: 'Before the rooster crows, you will deny three times that you even knew me.' And he went away, weeping bitterly" (Matt. 26:75 NLT). Disobedience to God is a crying shame. But when godly sorrow leads to repentance, He'll wipe away your tears.

11 Consequences

Sin has consequences: Some are natural, and others are supernatural. Natural consequences are simple: Touch a fire, and you'll get burned. Supernatural repercussions are certain: "You cannot mock the justice of God. You will always harvest what you plant. Those who live only to satisfy their own sinful nature will harvest decay and death from that sinful nature" (Gal. 6:7–8 NLT).

and for as long as I can remember, I've been embarrassed by her. I never brought friends home from school. If she wouldn't go away, then I would disappear into a place of quiet shame. But now I'm grown with kids of my own. It's her birthday this week. Do I have to go? I'm a new Christian. How do I honor my mother?"

I ached for her lost childhood and longed to somehow make it better. I encouraged her: "You can't change *her,* but God can change *you,* from resentful to respectful. You can honor your mother's role as a parent without approving of her inordinate behavior. Focus on appreciating *who* she is instead of *what* she's done. She gave you life; you can offer her love—God's unconditional love. God loved us while we were inordinate, and He can teach you how to love her even if you can't change her. Go to her birthday, and offer her the gift of a blessing instead of a curse."

Honoring your parents is not a divine suggestion but one of the Ten Commandments. When you honor your earthly parents, it reflects a heart that honors your heavenly Parent. Obedience and honor bring great rewards: blessings on earth and treasures in heaven.

Listen To ...

To "honor" our parents means much more than simply to obey them. It means to show them respect and love, to care for them as long as they need us, and to seek to bring honor to them by the way we live.

—*Warren Wiersbe*

DAY 2

Admonition

A cartoon showed a father scowling over his son's bad report card. His son asked, "What do you think it is, Dad? Heredity or environment?" This kid was no dummy. Either way, the father would be forced to take the blame if his son didn't make the grade. What impact *does* a father have on his child? Consider the results of a study done on these contrasting parenting philosophies.

Max Jukes was a ne'er-do-well New Yorker who didn't believe in Christ or Christian training. At the time of a study of his family in the late nineteenth century, he had over one thousand descendants. Of these, over three hundred were professional paupers; fifty "lived lives of notorious debauchery"; seven were murderers; and sixty were "habitual thieves." Only twenty of his descendants learned a trade, and ten of those learned that trade in the state prison. According to the study, the family had cost the state in excess of $1,250,000. They made no noticeable contribution to society.

Jonathan Edwards lived around the same time as Jukes. He loved the Lord and saw that his children attended church every Sunday. At the time of the study, he had over one thousand descendants. Of these, over one hundred were ministers, missionaries, and theologians; over one hundred became university professors; thirteen became university presidents; one hundred became lawyers; sixty authored or edited books; several were elected to Congress and three to the Senate. One became vice president. At the time of this study his family hadn't cost the state one dime but had contributed immeasurably to society.

We know that not all children with good fathers become pastors or presidents, nor do all offspring of wicked fathers become pushers or parolees. Yet dads who provide a loving home where the Bible is taught and prayer is offered give their children everything they need to succeed.

LEARN ABOUT ...

1 Provoking

When you provoke someone, you stir up that person, making him or her bitter and angry. The term implies a long-term, repeated pattern of treatment that slowly forms a latent anger and resentment eventually manifesting itself in outward hostility.

---

4 Dad or Dictator?

A dictator uses his authority to throw his weight around, regardless of the feelings of others. An ideal dad throws his weight behind God's Word, elevating his children to greater heights, encouraging their emotional well-being.

---

6 Train a Child

Training: using fair, consistent discipline to raise children in a godly manner. "What son is there whom a father does not chasten? ... No chastening seems to be joyful for the present, but painful; nevertheless, afterward it yields the peaceable fruit of righteousness to those who have been trained by it" (Heb. 12:7, 11).

LIFT UP ...

Dear Father, I want to be a good daughter—one who listens to the good advice You give me. Help me to tune in my ears so I won't turn my heart from Your commands. In Jesus' name. Amen.

LOOK AT ...

So far we have seen God's requirements for Spirit-filled husbands, wives, and children. Now we examine God's requirements for Spirit-filled parents.

READ EPHESIANS 6:4.

And you, fathers, do not provoke your children to wrath, but bring them up in the training and admonition of the Lord. Ephesians 6:4

1. What negative command for fathers is given here?

2. Give some examples of actions that could provoke a child.

3. How do children respond to being provoked?

4. According to Colossians 3:21, what is another consequence of provoking children?

5. Rather than provoking their children, how should parents bring them up (Eph. 6:4)?

6. According to Proverbs 22:6, what is the promise for parents who train their children as God prescribes?

7. Read Deuteronomy 6:6–9.

a. What is the prerequisite for parents in teaching their children God's Word?

b. How thorough should parents be when teaching God's Word to their children?

LEARN ABOUT ...

8 Encouraging Words

Children, like tender seedlings, need to be fertilized with your favor, watered with your words of praise, and exposed to the light of your love. Overexposure to hot tempers, blustery attitudes, and cutting words makes them wilt. Encouragement is Miracle-Gro for the soul.

LIVE OUT ...

8. a. From the following list of words and phrases, separate those that tend to *provoke* children from those that *encourage* them: praise, favoritism, criticism, unconditional love, unfulfilled promises, acceptance, physical abuse, compliments, blaming, hugs, perfectionism, conditional love, comparisons, unfair punishment, consistent discipline, high standards, affection, undivided attention. Add your own words to each list.

PROVOKES   **ENCOURAGES**

LEARN ABOUT ...

9 Saying and Doing

Parenting balances words and deeds. As the father of the Gentile church, Paul was a good parent whose works and words matched up. "I ... [have brought] the Gentiles to God by my message and by the way I worked among them" (Rom. 15:18 NLT). Do what you say in order to bring your children to God.

b. Examine the list of provoking behaviors. Is there some way you are provoking your children? How is God asking you to change?

c. Examine the list of encouraging behaviors. Choose two ways to encourage your children this week, and journal about what you will do.

9. God wants His plan and His Word to be passed on to your children and the next generation.

Journal a prayer asking God to help you pass on His Word and His ways to the next generation.

· ○ ● ○ ○

In this passage the apostle Paul affirmed a father's authority in the home. He also warned that fathers who abuse their authority raise anger-filled children. Godly parenting can be a balancing act—seesawing between looking the other way and overlooking a child's feelings.

A 1986 Stanford University study of 7,836 high school students and 3,500 parents in the San Francisco area showed that children with either permissive or authoritarian parents tended to earn lower grades. However, parents who encouraged their children and were communicative enabled their children to get higher grades. Parents who balance punishment with praise really do make the grade!

LISTEN TO ...

Correction does much, but encouragement does more. Encouragement after censure is as the sun after a shower.

—*Johann Wolfgang van Goethe*

Attitude

"My boss is such a slave driver!" Oh, really? Roman slaves were treated with brutality. They had no legal rights and were treated like expendable commodities: bought, sold, traded, and discarded as if they were used cars. One Bible commentary notes that the Roman statesman Cato said, "Old slaves should be thrown on a dump, and when a slave is ill do not feed him anything. It is not worth your money. Take sick slaves and throw them away because they are nothing but inefficient tools."[2]

Unlike employees today, slaves had no coffee breaks, no paid vacations, no insurance plan, and no profit sharing. Their hours were 24/7, not 9 to 5. They worked hard for no money. They were the exclusive property of real slave drivers and had no rights to complain of wrong treatment.

Paul told the Ephesian slaves suffering under terrible tyranny to obey their masters as they would obey their Lord. If slaves could adopt a Christ-centered attitude in their work, so can you. Your boss is no slave driver to expect reasonable work for fair wages. Maybe *you* need a perspective check. Diligently work for your earthly employer, knowing the Supreme Supervisor will give you an eternal promotion.

LIFT UP ...

Father, when I am asked to serve You by serving others, help me to follow through with a sincere heart. Give me the strength to work faithfully until You return. In Jesus' name. Amen.

LOOK AT ...

We shift our focus from relationships in the home to relationships in the workplace. Though Paul addressed this section of Scripture to "bondservants" or slaves, we can logically apply his teaching to today's business relationships. Let's look at how Christian workers ought to respond to their "masters," or bosses.

LEARN ABOUT ...

1 Bondservant

A bondservant is a person who is bound to service without wages. Kids don't say, "When I grow up, I want to be a slave and earn no money." Yet, Peter, Paul, and James aspired to be "bondservants" of Christ, to be like Christ. "The Son of Man came not to be served but to serve others" (Matt. 20:28 NLT).

4 Sincerity

The word *sincere* comes from two Latin words meaning "without wax." Ancient potters repaired flawed statues by filling in cracks with wax, lowering their value. A perfect piece was labeled "sincere," meaning it was genuine, without pretense.

6b Poured Out

Made Himself of no reputation, from the Greek, means, "He emptied Himself." Literally, Jesus emptied Himself of self! He poured out the full benefits of deity, limiting Himself to flesh and bones, time and space. Jesus had all the rights of deity, yet during His incarnation He surrendered His right.

READ EPHESIANS 6:5.

Bondservants, be obedient to those who are your masters according to the flesh, with fear and trembling, in sincerity of heart, as to Christ ... Ephesians 6:5

1. How should bondservants respond to their masters?

2. Masters maintain authority according to what? What does this mean?

3. With what two attitudes should servants approach their masters?

4. In what condition should their heart be?

5. What attitudes do you think would be involved in obeying a master as we obey Christ?

6. The best masters lead by example. Our Master, Jesus, knew what it was like to be a servant during His earthly ministry. Read Philippians 2:5–9 to discover the example He set for all believers.

   a. Before He became a man, what form did Jesus have and to whom was He equal (v. 6)?

   b. Jesus emptied Himself of the prerogatives of His deity at the incarnation. What three transformations took place to make this possible (v. 7)?

   c. What two attributes made His transformation into a bondservant possible? And to what extent did He take on the role of servant? (v. 8)

d. How did God reward Jesus for His humble obedience (v. 9)?

LIVE OUT ...

7. Fill in the chart to discover who called themselves servants and how these servants of Christ behaved.

SCRIPTURE	SERVANT'S NAME	SERVANT'S BEHAVIOR
1 Samuel 3:9–10		
Psalm 78:70–72		
Galatians 1:1, 10		
Colossians 4:12		

8. Today we discovered that a bondservant is one who works without wages. The Bible teaches that all who call on the Lord become His slaves. "If you were a slave when the Lord called you, you are now free in the Lord. And if you were free when the Lord called you, you are now a slave of Christ" (1 Cor. 7:22 NLT).

   a. What have you done for Christ without receiving monetary compensation?

   b. What are you willing to do for Him without reward or recognition?

9. Slaves are called to serve with "sincerity of heart." We learned that a "sincere" statue was one without wax covering up weaknesses—pure and without pretense. Picture yourself as a statue. Acknowledge below any sinful cracks you may have covered over with pretense. (Example: Eyes: I act indignant about pornography but watch inappropriate movies.)

Eyes:

Ears:

Mouth:

Heart:

Hands:

Feet:

10. Reword the following psalm into a personal prayer of repentance and restoration: "Oh, give me back my joy again; you have broken me—now let me rejoice. Don't keep looking at my sins. Remove the stain of my guilt. Create in me a clean heart, O God. Renew a loyal spirit within me" (Ps. 51:8–10 NLT).

o o ● o o

Franklin Graham, president of the relief and evangelistic organization Samaritan's Purse, encounters people around the world who are willing to sacrifice the promise of gold for the kingdom of God. In his book *Living Beyond the Limits*, he tells of one such man, Steve Duncan:

Steve was a well-educated Boston man and a skilled surgeon. He was preparing to leave for Angola as soon as he could raise support and make the logistical arrangements. Steve made quite an impression on me as he told of his desire to serve the Lord in a foreign country. I knew he could be earning enough money to buy anybody's version of the great American Dream. Instead, all he talked about was taking God's gospel to Angola—a country that at the time was in the throes of a particularly vicious and ugly civil war.[3]

Steve, like Paul the apostle, is just one example of a modern-day bondservant of Christ. He works long hours in a dangerous place without financial compensation. He has given up boardrooms and surgical suites for bunkers and grass huts, living for eternal rather than temporal rewards. Where is God calling you to work for Christ instead of cash?

LISTEN TO …

The average church member would do well to look in his concordance and see how many columns it takes to list all the "serve," "servant," and "service" references.

—Vance Havner

DAY 4

Actions

"When the cat's away, the mice will play." When I (Lenya) was in high school, I worked at the local drugstore with two good friends. When the boss was gone, we goofed off: trying on the latest lipstick, reading magazines, and spiking our sodas on Friday nights. My friends and I were living proof that the Protestant work ethic was dying.

God breathed new life into my personal work ethic when I was born again. Later, on my first professional job at McLain Development Company in Newport Beach, even if the boss wasn't around I could be found doing the right thing. When my duties were done, I would offer to help my coworkers finish their work or straighten up the lunchroom. I never called in sick if I wasn't and didn't take long lunches.

How did I go from goof-off to Goody Two–shoes? It was through the influence of my pastor, Chuck Smith, who has the most amazing work ethic of anyone I know. He taught me that even when my boss didn't see me, God did. My work then became an act of worship. Your work should be worship as well: Your actions and attitudes at work reflect your service to God.

LIFT UP ...

Lord, help me to remember that whatever I do, I do for You. You are a Master who is just and gives good rewards to those who labor on Your behalf. In Jesus' name. Amen.

LOOK AT ...

Yesterday we looked at the godly attitudes of the Christian worker. Today we explore the righteous actions of Christian workers on the job.

READ EPHESIANS 6:6–8.

[Be obedient] not with eyeservice, as men-pleasers, but as bondservants of Christ, doing the will of God from the heart, with goodwill doing service, as to the Lord, and not to men, knowing that whatever good anyone does, he will receive the same from the Lord, whether he is a slave or free. Ephesians 6:6–8

1. What phrase lets you know that servants should not just be obedient only when the boss is watching?

2. Whom do those who work with eyeservice seek to please? What do you think is wrong with that?

3. In contrast, how are believers to work? What does this accomplish?

4. What do you think it means to do the will of God "from the heart"?

5. What do you think it means to do service "with goodwill"?

6. Once again, Paul reminds us that our service should be conducted as to _____ and not _____.

7. What does God promise Christian workers for the good they do?

8. What phrase lets you know that God rewards believers with servant hearts regardless of their position?

LEARN ABOUT …

1 Eyeservice

Eyeservice is working only under the "master's eye"; performance when the boss is looking, but neglect in the boss's absence. Out of sight, out of mind? While your boss is out of sight, you still have to mind because "the eyes of the Lord watch over those who do right" (1 Peter 3:12 NLT).

---

3 God's Will

Some Christians are obsessed with knowing the will of God and not concerned with doing the will of God. But when you actively do God's will, you'll automatically know God's will. "Continue to do God's will. Then you will receive all that he has promised" (Heb. 10:36 NLT).

---

8 Slave or Free

People may play favorites, but God levels the playing field. He treats all who follow Him with equality. "There is no longer Jew or Gentile, slave or free, male and female" (Gal. 3:28 NLT).

LEARN ABOUT ...

9 For His Pleasure

Pleasing others is not the Christian's aim. It can, however, become the means to an end. Pleasing others in order to please God puts you right on target. "Exhort bondservants ... to be well pleasing in all things, not answering back, not pilfering, but showing all good fidelity, that they may adorn the doctrine of God our Savior in all things" (Titus 2:9–10).

---

10 Secret Character

Reputation and character are different. Reputation is achieved in public—what others see. Character is cultivated in private—what God sees. Reputation is fleeting, for people are fickle. Character is forever, for God rewards the faithful.

LIVE OUT ...

9. a. Rather than trying to please people on the job, we must strive to please God. Fill in the chart below to discover some of the things that are pleasing to God.

SCRIPTURE	WHAT PLEASES GOD
Psalm 69:30–31	
Colossians 1:10	
1 Thessalonians 2:4	
Hebrews 11:6	
1 John 3:22	

b. Journal about when you know that you are pleasing God (based on the above passages). Then write about how you will try to please God in the areas where you fall short.

10. In Matthew's gospel, Jesus named three ways His disciples could express their devotion to God in a secret way, not to please people but to please God. How will you offer something in secret to God this week? Write about how you will follow through.

Financial Giving: "Give your gifts in private, and your Father, who sees everything, will reward you" (Matt. 6:4 NLT).

Praying: "When you pray, go away by yourself, shut the door behind you, and pray to your Father in private. Then your Father, who sees everything, will reward you" (Matt. 6:6 NLT).

Fasting: "No one will notice that you are fasting, except your Father, who knows what you do in private. And your Father, who sees everything, will reward you" (Matt. 6:18 NLT).

11. We also discovered that pleasing God takes more than eyeservice—it takes service from the heart. In which of the following ways will you, with goodwill, serve someone this week?

____ Do my chores while singing praise songs

____ Pay the bills with thanksgiving in my heart

____ Season dinner with love and serve it with kindness

____ Bless a fellow employee by pitching in and offering praise

____ Take my boss to an appreciation lunch

____ Other: _____

○ ○ ● ○ ○

One day a defiant child talked back to his mother when she asked him to do his chores. His dad scolded him and said, "Son, go sit in time-out for fifteen minutes." The strong-willed lad refused, clenching his fists and digging in his heels. His father insisted and threatened to take away TV privileges if he didn't get in that chair *now!* The little boy slumped, dragged himself to the chair, and sat down with a moan. As he crossed his arms he muttered, "I may be sitting down on the outside, but I'm standing up on the inside."

When your boss asks you to do your work, do you talk back? "That's not my job." Do you comply on the outside but complain on the inside? "I'll do it, but I don't have to like it." Your actions and your attitudes are inseparable—your heart and hands must work together to get the job done or, in God's eyes, it's not a job well done.

Listen To ...

There is no work better than another to please God; to pour water, to wash dishes, to be a souter [cobbler], or an apostle, all is one; to wash dishes and to preach is all one, as touching as the deed, to please God.

—William Tyndale

DAY 5

Authority

My husband is one of the best examples of a servant-leader I (Lenya) know. We moved from the sunny beaches of California to the desert sands of New Mexico to start a new church. When Calvary of Albuquerque began, Skip wore many hats: leading worship, keeping the financial records, and moving sound equipment, as well as teaching and counseling. As the church staff has grown, Skip has never lost his servant's heart. You can still find him picking up trash, clearing tables, or mopping floors.

As a boss, he responds to the needs of his staff. When one staff member's wife was diagnosed with breast cancer, Skip gave him time off, and the church paid some of their bills. When an employee's daughter couldn't afford her cheerleading uniform, Skip pitched in what was needed. One employee observed, "Working for Skip is a great adventure because of his predictable unpredictability. He's a visionary who encourages others to excel." A former youth director went to lead a Christian rock band. Several assistant pastors have gone on to pastor their own churches. Church secretaries have gone overseas to become missionaries. Skip's employer philosophy is simple: "Release people to reach their God-given potential."

You don't have to be a pastor to be a good employer. The book of Ephesians shows us that God sets high standards for all Christian employers.

LIFT UP ...

God, I want to help others reach their full potential by placing their needs before my own. Help me to do for others what I want them to do for me. In Jesus' name. Amen..

LOOK AT ...

We have seen how slaves or Christian employees ought to respond to those God has placed in authority over them. Today we examine the responsibility of masters—Christian employers.

READ EPHESIANS 6:9.

And you, masters, do the same things to them, giving up threatening, knowing that your own Master also is in heaven, and there is no partiality with Him. Ephesians 6:9

1. Paul told masters to do the same things to their slaves and servants. What things was Paul referring to (vv. 6–8)?

2. What are employers to give up?

3. According to Colossians 4:1, how are masters to treat their bondservants?

4. According to Colossians 4:1 and Ephesians 6:9, why should masters treat their servants well?

5. Fill in the chart below to discover how masters acquired their slaves in ancient times.

SCRIPTURE	BECAME SLAVES BY ...
Genesis 37:28	
Exodus 21:2, 4	
Leviticus 25:39–40	
Joshua 9:23–27	

6. Read Matthew 20:25–28. How was Jesus' standard for authority contrary to the world's view of authority?

7. Whom did He give as an example of leading through serving?

LEARN ABOUT ...

I Same Work

What's good for the goose is good for the gander. If employees must work sincerely, so must employers. If slaves were to be God-pleasers rather than men-pleasers, so should masters. Both blue- and white-collar workers should work with goodwill in their hearts.

---

4 God the Master

The buck stops here? Corporate executives, presidents, and managers may think they are the top dogs, but in fact, God is King of the hill—the Master of the universe. With God, you don't climb the corporate ladder; you meet on common ground—common people serving an uncommon God.

---

7 Become a Servant

If you're an employer, maybe you should institute "Show and Tell" at your place of business. The most effective bosses are those who are willing to roll up their sleeves and get their hands dirty. Are you willing not only to tell people what to do but to show them how to do it?

9 Threaten

To threaten means "to express an intention to inflict evil, injury, or damage." It implies alarming by a definitely hostile aspect or character. In modern terms, a person who threatens is a bully. Jesus was bullied, but "He did not retaliate when he was insulted, nor threaten revenge when he suffered" (1 Peter 2:23 NLT).

12 No Favorites

"Mom always liked you best." Comedian Tommy Smothers always got a laugh with this famous line to his brother. But partiality is no joke. God doesn't play favorites; He likes all of His children best. "There is no iniquity with the LORD our God, no partiality" (2 Chron. 19:7).

8. According to Ephesians 6:9, what two things do earthly masters know about their heavenly Master?

LIVE OUT ...

9. Christian employers ought to serve their employees, not threaten them. List some ways that employers in today's workforce might threaten their employees.

10. Fill in the chart below to discover three ways to serve those over whom you have some form of authority. Then journal about how you will serve someone under your authority (children, employees, ministry workers, etc.) this week.

SCRIPTURE	HOW TO SERVE	HOW I WILL SERVE
Luke 12:35–37		
Romans 1:9		
Galatians 5:13		

11. We've seen that Christian employers should treat their employees as God treats us, without partiality. Journal about a time when you played favorites or when someone played favorites with you. How did it make you feel?

12. Based on your experience, why are you grateful God doesn't play favorites?

○ ○ ● ○ ○

The legend is told of a desert wanderer who found a clear, fresh, crystal spring. The water was so pure he decided to bring some to his king. Hardly satiating his own thirst, he filled a leather bottle and carried it many days through the hot desert until he reached the palace. When he finally offered the king his gift, the water had become stale and rancid. But the wise king did not reveal to his faithful servant that it was unfit to drink. He sampled it with expressions of gratitude and delight, and the wanderer went his way, filled with gladness. After he had gone, others asked why the king pretended to enjoy the bitter water. "Ah!" said he. "It was not the water I tasted, but the love that brought the offering." Frequently our service is tainted by imperfections, but our Master sees our motives and says, "It is good."

This week we have learned that our motivation in serving others stems from our love for God and our desire to please Him. When you serve others—husbands, children, employers, employees—as you would serve Him, you can know that one day you will hear your heavenly Master say, "Well done, my good and faithful servant. You have been faithful in handling this small amount, so now I will give you many more responsibilities. Let's celebrate together!" (Matt. 25:23 NLT).

Listen To ...

A leader is one who knows the way, goes the way, and shows the way.

—*John Maxwell*

LESSON TWELVE

Stand Your Ground
Ephesians 6:10–24

Once upon a time in a distant kingdom, there lived a dreadful dragon. Its great wings could be heard flapping for miles around, striking terror in the hearts of the people throughout the countryside. With a single blow its terrible claws could kill an ox. Its nostrils billowed clouds of smoke and flame, bringing death to anyone who encountered the beast.

Each year a young girl was chosen as an offering to appease the dragon. One year the lot fell to the beautiful daughter of the king. Just as the dragon swooped in on the fair damsel, a valiant knight in shining armor rode to her rescue. Brandishing his gleaming sword, he struck the monster a mighty blow, wounding it so badly that the princess was able to wrap her sash around its head and lead it to the marketplace of her village. There amidst the cheering throngs, the knight slew the fearsome dragon. And they all lived happily ever after.

That story may be just a fairy tale. But the real story is that your heavenly Knight in shining garments has come to your rescue, delivering you from sin and transforming you from victim to victor. You are no longer a damsel in distress but have been clothed in His shining armor, ready to deliver others from Satan, the fire-destined dragon. This week you will learn about the dragon's devices, how to deploy your armor and artillery against him, and how to defend your spiritual treasures by standing your ground.

Day 1: Ephesians 6:10–13	BE POWERFUL
Day 2: Ephesians 6:14–15	BE PROTECTED
Day 3: Ephesians 6:16–17	BE PREPARED
Day 4: Ephesians 6:18–20	BE PRAYERFUL
Day 5: Ephesians 6:21–24	BE PEACEFUL

Be Powerful

LIFT UP ...

God, thank You for making me aware of the fact that I have an Enemy. Help me to be alert to his tactics and vigilant in my stand against him. In Jesus' name. Amen.

LOOK AT ...

In our exploration of Ephesians we have learned about the heavenly treasures God has in store for His children. Throughout the study we have learned to walk worthy of our position as His spiritual heirs. Now we come to the end of our journey, where we learn to stand "in the power of His might" against the enemies who would rob us of our inheritance. Today we learn how to stand powerfully against our spiritual enemies as we gain insight into God's battle plan.

READ EPHESIANS 6:10–13.

Finally, my brethren, be strong in the Lord and in the power of His might. Put on the whole armor of God, that you may be able to stand against the wiles of the devil. For we do not wrestle against flesh and blood, but against principalities, against powers, against the rulers of the darkness of this age, against spiritual hosts of wickedness in the heavenly places. Therefore take up the whole armor of God, that you may be able to withstand in the evil day, and having done all, to stand. Ephesians 6:10–13

1. As Paul drew his letter to a close, what two things did he urge his brethren to be strong in (v. 10)?

LEARN ABOUT ...

I Powerful God

Christians shouldn't rely on their own strength but must tap into the mighty power of the Lord. Human strength is impotent in opposing our supernatural enemy, the Devil. With the omnipotent God as our power source, even a little strength is sufficient for victory. "Remember the LORD your God. He is the one who gives you power" (Deut. 8:18 NLT).

---

4 Devil's Schemes

The word *wiles* refers to schemes or devices to deceive or ensnare; it is often used of predatory animals who cleverly stalk and suddenly pounce on their victims. The word *devil* literally means "slanderer" and refers to the personal supreme spirit of evil; tempter of humanity; and leader of apostate angels.

---

5 Rulers of Darkness

Principalities, powers, rulers, and spiritual hosts describe the different ranks of Satan's minions. The Devil's army is extremely organized and prepared for devastating battle. Their demonic influence spans time, from past to present, and space, from heaven to earth.

2. What equipment should the Christian "put on" in order to be strong in the Lord?

3. What parts of God's armor can you leave off?

4. Why do we need God's armor?

5. a. Paul acknowledges that we are in a battle. Why do you think it's important to understand that our battles are not physical in nature?

   b. What four enemies do we war against?

   c. Complete the phrases describing where these enemies are deployed.

   "of the darkness of _____"
   "hosts of wickedness in _____"

6. What will we be able to do by taking up the armor of God? (Compare verse 13 with verse 11.)

7. We need to stand strong in "the evil day." What do you think this means?

8. Paul gives assurance that, "having done all," we will not fall in battle. What is God's part in this? What is our part?

LIVE OUT ...

9. Paul has warned us about the wiles of the Devil—his cunningly disguised traps. One of his favorite traps is temptation. Temptation is often an attempt to fulfill our fleshly needs through inappropriate ways. How have you tried to get something right the wrong way?

   ____ I was hungry, so I stole bread.

   ____ I felt inferior, so I lied about my past.

   ____ I needed money, so I cheated the IRS.

   ____ I was lonely, so I dated an unbeliever.

   ____ I was depressed, so I drank.

   ____ I was bored, so I read a trashy novel.

   ____ I wanted children, so I settled for sex.

   ____ I wanted friends, so I gossiped about others.

   ____ Other:_____

10. Once a Christian succumbs to temptation, Satan takes on the role of an accuser, debilitating a Christian with recriminations of shame and guilt. "The accuser of our brothers and sisters has been thrown down to earth—the one who accuses them before our God day and night" (Rev. 12:10 NLT).

If you have been bullied by Satan's name-calling or buried under his shame, take the time to write out and confess your sins to God. Ask Him to wash your conscience clean with the blood of the Lamb. "They have defeated [Satan] by the blood of the Lamb and by their testimony" (Rev. 12:11 NLT).

11. Satan is persistent. If he doesn't get you now, he'll try again later. "Now when the devil had ended every temptation, he departed

LEARN ABOUT ...

6 Stand Strong

God wants you to be able to withstand and stand against the Devil's onslaught. *To withstand* means "to resist or oppose an evil influence." *To stand* means "to take a prolonged stance, to continue to hold up under pressure." Withstand for the moment; stand for a lifetime.

9 Resist

Temptations vary: toys for tots, sex for singles, or greed for the gray-haired. Satan is more persuasive than any ad campaign. The Bible says to run away from temptation and resist the tempter. "Resist the devil, and he will flee from you" (James 4:7 NLT).

10 No Condemnation

The difference between condemnation and conviction? The Spirit convicts of sin to bring forgiveness and fellowship. Satan condemns already confessed sin to bring shame and separation. But, "there is no condemnation for those who belong to Christ Jesus" (Rom. 8:1 NLT).

from [Jesus] until an opportune time" (Luke 4:13). Journal a prayer asking the Lord to make you strong in the power of His might, so you will be able to resist temptation today, tomorrow, and always. Make sure you are leaning on His everlasting arms.

○ ○ ● ○ ○

The city of Pompeii in southern Italy was destroyed in AD 79 when Mount Vesuvius erupted and covered the ancient city with molten rock. Pompeii's most amazing spectacle is the remains of a Roman soldier who stood his ground. On the fatal day when Vesuvius shook the earth, the guard kept watch by the gate that faced the burning mountain. Roman sentinels were trained to never abandon their posts unless relieved by a superior. To do so would blemish a soldier's reputation and end his career. This loyal guard was left to choose between death and dishonor. A picture of courage under fire, he stood by his post, slowly covered from sandals to helmet with hot lava.

Christian martyrs who stood against tyrants lost their earthly lives but gained an eternal reward. The Roman soldier who stood against a raging volcano lost his life but gained honor. As a believer, you stand against a formidable foe, and you, too, can gain ultimate victory in the power of God's might.

LISTEN TO ...

Stand still ... and refuse to retreat. Look at it as God looks at it and draw upon His power to hold up under the blast.

—*Charles R. Swindoll*

DAY 2

Be Protected

William Levine decided to buy a bulletproof vest after his butcher shop was robbed four times in a month. After hearing about Mr. Levine's purchase, other business owners began to ask him where they could get vests for themselves. Mr. Levine took orders, changed careers, and today is full-time president of Body Armor, International. He supplies forty sales representatives across the country and is selling five hundred to six hundred vests a month.

There comes a day when God's children, like William Levine, discover that life on earth can be a spiritual battle, not business as usual. Believers don't often encounter bad guys with bullets; they face Satan's artillery of temptations and accusations. William Levine's body armor may be an adequate defense against earthly ammo, but God's breastplate of righteousness is what you need to be protected from Satan's spiritual assault. If God is passing out spiritual armor, don't you want to try it on?

Lift Up ...

Lord, thank You for protecting me against my enemies. I know that part of Your protection requires me to take action. Help me to take up Your armor on a daily basis. In Jesus' name. Amen.

Look At ...

Paul urges us to wear God's armor as we fight against our spiritual enemies. Let's look at three pieces of the armor God provides.

Learn about ...

1 Gird with Truth

In Roman times, the girdle was a belt used to hold the armor together. The belt also gathered up a soldier's flowing tunic, enabling him to march unhindered. The truth in your life will keep you from falling apart or falling down. Don't let dishonesty trip you up.

---

3 Righteousness

A Roman soldier's breastplate was made of metal, leather, or animal horns and protected his vital organs. Your spiritual breastplate is impenetrable, made of "the righteousness which is from God by faith" (Phil. 3:9), protecting your soul from the assault of Satan's accusations.

---

6 Gospel Shoes

To stand and withstand requires the surefooted shoes of the gospel—the good news about Jesus Christ. The Christian who witnesses is the Christian who wins spiritual battles. Proclaiming the gospel defends your borders and conquers new territory for God's army! "The gospel of Christ ... is the power of God to salvation for everyone who believes" (Rom. 1:16).

Read Ephesians 6:14–15.

Stand therefore, having girded your waist with truth, having put on the breastplate of righteousness, and having shod your feet with the preparation of the gospel of peace ... Ephesians 6:14–15

1. What equipment is to go around your waist?

2. Fill in the following chart to discover where truth is found.

Scripture	Truth Found
John 14:6	
John 16:13	
John 17:17	
2 John 4	

3. What is the second piece of equipment believers should put on?

4. Read Romans 13:14. What more must we put on in order to wear the breastplate of righteousness?

5. According to Isaiah 64:6, what do we wear when we put on self-righteousness rather than the breastplate of righteousness?

6. As Christian soldiers, what should we wear on our feet?

7. The gospel is good news for everyone. Read Luke 4:18, and list the five groups of people Jesus reached with the gospel.

Live Out ...

8. a. We've seen that the belt of truth keeps a Christian soldier from falling down or falling apart. Listening to lies, and not truth, can do damage. Write down a lie you have been told and believed. (Example: "If you take this pill, you'll lose weight.")

   b. How did that lie trip you up or make you fall apart? (Example: "I didn't think the pills would keep me awake, make me irritable, and get me hooked.")

   c. Journal about how finding out the truth helped you get back on your feet or pull it together. (Example: "Those pills are full of caffeine. The healthy way to lose weight is to eat less and exercise more.")

9. To put on the breastplate is to live in daily obedience to God's Word through practical acts of righteousness. Satan can't bring accusations against a Christian who is living a righteous life. How do your words and deeds promote righteousness? What behaviors give a place for Satan to accuse you and make you feel ashamed? Write a few examples of these down in the columns below.

Produces Shame
(Example: When I'm petty, criticizing or treating others cruelly.)

Promotes Righteousness
(Example: When I tell the neighborhood kids about Jesus.)

Learn About ...

9 Righteousness
The word *righteousness* means "holy and upright living in accordance with God's standard; it comes from a root word that means 'straightness.' God's character is the definition and source of all righteousness. Therefore, people's righteousness is defined in terms of God's righteousness."

LEARN ABOUT ...

10 Gospel of Peace

Peace is not the absence of war but the presence of God. Isaiah said Jesus would be called the "Prince of Peace," bringing the gospel of peace. The Bible teaches that we are at war with God. But "there is peace with God through Jesus Christ" (Acts 10:36 NLT). Jesus is God's peace treaty with us.

10. The Christian's feet are to be adorned with "the preparation of the gospel of peace." Are you prepared to preach the gospel? Let's take a walk on the Roman road, learning the steps to help lead others to salvation. Read each passage, and describe the step in the space below. Then underline the passages in your Bible, writing the number of the step it is (1–6) at the beginning of each underlined passage. At the end of each underlined passage, write which passage to turn to next.

Step 1: Romans 3:10–12

Step 2: Romans 3:23

Step 3: Romans 6:23

Step 4: Romans 5:8

Step 5: Romans 10:9–10

Step 6: Romans 10:13

∘ ∘ ● ∘ ∘

A brother and sister visited their grandparents on the farm. Johnny was given a slingshot to play with in the woods. He practiced but couldn't hit the target. Discouraged, he headed home, and there he spotted his grandma's pet duck. On impulse, he took out the slingshot and killed the duck. In a panic, he hid the dead duck and then looked up to see his sister, Sandy, watching. Over the next few days, every time Grandma asked the little girl to do a chore, she'd boldly say, "Oh, Johnny said he'd do it!" then whisper, "Remember the duck?"

After several days of doing both his and Sandy's chores, Johnny had had enough, so he told his grandma about her dead duck. She knelt down, gave him a hug, and said, "Honey, I know; I was standing at the window and saw the whole thing. I forgive you. I just wondered how long you would let Sandy make a slave out of you."

I don't know what sin the Enemy keeps accusing you of, causing chinks in your armor. But whatever it is, you need to know something: Jesus is standing at the window and sees the whole thing. But because He loves you, He has forgiven you. Perhaps He's wondering how long you'll let the Enemy get past your armor and make a slave out of you.

LISTEN TO ...

Peace is not made at the council tables, or by treaties, but in the hearts of men.

—*Herbert Hoover*

DAY 3

Be Prepared

An ancient king of Sparta boasted about his mighty walls, which could thwart any invading army. An ambassador on a diplomatic mission came to view the famous city-state. The reputation of Sparta's strength was acclaimed throughout Greece, so he anticipated seeing great, fortified walls surrounding the town. He was shocked to discover no walls whatsoever. He chided the ruler, "Sir, I've seen no famed walls of defense. Where are they?"

"Come with me tomorrow, and I will show you the walls of Sparta," replied the king. The next day he led his guest to a field where his army was arrayed in full battle gear, their shields glistening in the sun. Pointing proudly to the columns of soldiers who stood at attention, he said, "Behold the walls of Sparta—ten thousand men, and every man a brick!"

The king of Sparta was prepared for battle. He had recruited and trained an army of men, supplying them with shields for defense and swords for combat. God is prepared for the battle of the ages: the forces of light against the powers of darkness. You've been enlisted as a member of His mighty army. You must be prepared for combat; so raise high the shield of faith, and unleash the sword of the Spirit on God's enemies.

LIFT UP ...

Dear God, the world is full of danger. My heart rejoices that You, O Lord, will shield me from the trouble that comes my way. I will trust in Your strength when I feel weak. In Jesus' name. Amen.

LOOK AT ...

We have studied about three pieces of spiritual equipment necessary for protection during spiritual warfare: the girdle, the breastplate, and the shoes. Ephesians continues with three more armor pieces necessary for Christians in battle.

READ EPHESIANS 6:16–17.

... above all, taking the shield of faith with which you will be able to quench all the fiery darts of the wicked one. And take the helmet of salvation, and the sword of the Spirit, which is the word of God ... Ephesians 6:16–17

1. What are believers to take into battle above all else?

2. a. In what way does this piece of equipment help us against the wicked one?

   b. How would you explain this in your own words?

3. How many fiery darts—attacks—will it quench?

4. What piece of armor should we wear figuratively on our head?

5. Read 1 Thessalonians 5:8–10. According to these verses, what additional benefits does the helmet of salvation offer?

6. What is the sword of the Spirit (Eph. 6:17)?

7. According to Hebrews 4:12, why is the Word of God such an effective weapon?

LIVE OUT ...

8. The shield of faith will quench Satan's fiery darts. Fill in the following table to discover some of the other "arrows" found in Scripture.

LEARN ABOUT ...

I Shield of Faith

United we stand! Shields in Paul's day had interlocking edges to enable soldiers to become a solid wall of defense. God fortifies Christian soldiers who unite their shields as one. "Where two or three gather together as my followers, I am there among them" (Matt. 18:20 NLT).

4 Salvation Helmet

The bronze helmet protected the soldier's head from harm. God's helmet of salvation protects the believer's mind from havoc. The mind controlled by God is safe from Satan's turmoil. "His peace will guard your hearts and minds as you live in Christ Jesus" (Phil. 4:7 NLT).

6 Spirit Sword

The sword of the Spirit is the only piece of equipment used for offense. Metal swords cut the flesh to maim and kill. God's sword, His Word, divides soul from spirit, bringing wholeness and life. Christians are to use this sword to slay God's spiritual enemies, not to hurt one another.

LEARN ABOUT ...

8 God's Arsenal

The Enemy is powerful, but he is not equal to God. God is eternal, but Satan is finite. God is omnipotent while the Devil is limited. Satan's weapons can wreak havoc, but they're no match for God's invincible arsenal. "We use God's mighty weapons, not worldly weapons, to knock down the strongholds" (2 Cor. 10:4 NLT).

9 Mind Games

"There is another power within me that is at war with my mind" (Rom. 7:23 NLT). The Enemy uses an arsenal to conquer the believer's mind. *Deception:* to mislead or cause to believe an untruth. *Distraction:* to turn aside or to stir up and confuse with conflicting emotions. *Disillusionment:* to disappoint, to let down, or to dishearten.

SCRIPTURE	ARROW USED BY	ARROW USED TO
2 Kings 13:17		
Psalm 64:7		
Proverbs 7:21–23		
Proverbs 25:18		
Jeremiah 9:8–9		
Zechariah 9:13–14		

9. A believer's helmet is necessary to guard the mind from dangerous beliefs. Our enemies—the world, the flesh, and the Devil—work together to *deceive* with half-truths, *distract* with competing loyalties, or *disillusion* with doubts about God.

a. Journal about a time when failing to trust in your helmet allowed the Enemy to strike a devastating blow that damaged your thought process in one or more of the following ways.

Deception:

Distraction:

Disillusionment:

10. Once you become aware of the mind games your enemies have used against you, God exhorts you to eradicate the stinkin' thinkin' with the truth. Journal the following passage into a personal prayer asking God to eliminate destructive thought patterns and to replace them with divine ones: "Do not be conformed to this world, but be transformed by the renewing of your mind, that you may prove what is that good and acceptable and perfect will of God" (Rom. 12:2).

o o ● o o

You wouldn't wear a bikini to the battlefield any more than you'd use a BB gun against a bazooka. A good soldier has the clothes and the gear to get the job done. When my son, Nathan, was small, he loved to dress up as a marine, a gladiator, or a cowboy. He was out to conquer any foe in our neighborhood or his imagination. One night when I (Lenya) came to tuck him in, I felt something hard underneath his covers. As I lifted his blanket, I discovered an arsenal: a plastic sword, a wooden gun, and a leather whip. I asked him, "Why did you bring your weapons to bed?"

He grinned and said, "Don't worry, Mommy, I'll protect you if any bad guys break into our house."

I smiled, kissed him good night, and said, "You're growing up to be such a big boy, but Daddy is bigger, and he'll watch over you while you sleep. And you know what? God is the biggest of all; He'll watch over all of us as we sleep."

Isn't it good to know that in battles, seen and unseen, you can rest assured that God is on your side? With His weapons and His wardrobe, you are prepared and invincible against the bad guys who go bump in the night.

Listen To ...

Satan's ploys are no match for the Savior's power.

—Unknown

DAY 4

Be Prayerful

Oswald Chambers said, "The armor is for the battle of prayer.... Prayer is the battle."[1] My husband, Skip, told me a story from his mission trip to the Philippines about a battle fought and won by prayer. Communist guerrillas in the Philippines, who were violently opposed to Christianity, were threatening and raiding small churches in remote jungle villages. In one village the church was assaulted by a band of armed guerrillas during a Sunday service. The guerrillas threatened the church members with death if they met the following week. The congregation decided to fight on their knees. All week they prayed, and when Sunday came, they met in church and continued to pray. The services ended without incident. Later the victorious saints discovered that the jeep full of armed rebels had crashed and flipped, defeating their wicked plans.

When you find yourself in a battle, don't just stand there—pray!

LIFT UP ...

Lord, teach me how to fight the good fight in prayer. Help me to pray for those in battles to be strengthened by Your Spirit and delivered from the Evil One. May I see Your mighty hand prevail. In Jesus' name. Amen.

LOOK AT ...

The whole armor of God is needed to stand against the wiles of the Devil. Paul reminds us that prayer is the secret weapon behind spiritual victories.

READ EPHESIANS 6:18–20.

... praying always with all prayer and supplication in the Spirit, being watchful to this end with all perseverance and supplication for all the saints—and for me, that utterance may be

given to me, that I may open my mouth boldly to make known the mystery of the gospel, for which I am an ambassador in chains; that in it I may speak boldly, as I ought to speak. Ephesians 6:18–20

1. When should believers pray?

2. How much and what kind of prayer did Paul specify here?

3. Which member of the Trinity empowers prayer?

4. What phrase reveals that we should be alert as we pray?

5. What phrase reveals that we should not give up in prayer?

6. For whom should we pray?

7. What did Paul ask would be given to him? Why?

8. Despite being in prison and in chains, what was Paul's heartfelt desire?

LIVE OUT ...

9. a. There are many ways to pray, and Paul encouraged his readers to use all forms. If you're in a praying rut, perhaps it's time to break free. Check off all the ways you have prayed in the past.

FORM OF PRAYER	POSTURE	TIME
___ public	___ walking	___ morning
___ private	___ standing	___ noon
___ loud	___ bowing	___ evening

LEARN ABOUT ...

3 In The Spirit

The Trinity asserts three requirements for prayer: (1) in the name of the Son: "If you ask anything in My name, I will do it" (John 14:14); (2) in the will of the Father: "Your will be done" (Matt. 6:10); (3) in the Spirit's power: "Pray in the Spirit at all times" (Eph. 6:18 NLT).

5 Perseverance

To persevere means "to continue persistently in a steadfast effort stemming from a faithful trust in God." Remember the poster with a kitten dangling from a bar? It read, "Hang in there, baby!" Persevering prayer is hanging on to God, knowing He won't let go.

9 Prayer Stair

If your prayer life is stuck, climb to the next level. Try STAIR. *Supplication:* Ask God for what you need. *Thanksgiving:* Thank God for what He does. *Adoration:* Praise God for who He is. *Intercession:* Stand in the gap for someone else. *Repentance:* Confess sin.

LEARN ABOUT ...

10 Patient Prayer

Prayer sows spiritual seed, planting a crop that takes time. The prayer warrior, like the farmer, must practice patience. "See how the farmer waits for the precious fruit of the earth, waiting patiently for it.... You also be patient" (James 5:7–8).

11 Pray for Me

Paul told the Ephesians, "I have not stopped thanking God for you. I pray for you constantly" (Eph. 1:16 NLT). Now Paul asks the Ephesians to return the favor. Praying for one another is a duty and a privilege.

___ silent   ___ kneeling   ___ in the night

___ structured   ___ sitting   ___ meal time

___ spontaneous   ___ lying down   ___ crisis

___ singing   ___ hands raised   ___ special occasions

b. Review the columns above. From each column choose an item that you have never experienced before. Journal about how you will incorporate this new method into your life this week. If possible, go ahead and practice this new method of prayer now.

10. a. We are instructed to persevere in prayer—never give up! Name a person or situation about which you have grown discouraged in prayer.

b. Take the time now to tell God about your frustration. Ask Him to fill you with new hope and vision to pray. Begin again by writing a prayer concerning this discouraging situation.

11. Who prays for you on a regular basis? Do you pray for them? If not, return the favor by journaling a prayer on their behalf.

○ ○ ● ○ ○

Life is full of unsung heroes—men and women who have given of themselves unselfishly for others without receiving recognition. I'd (Lenya) like to sing the praises of one of my heroes of the faith, Kay Smith. As wife of Pastor Chuck Smith from Calvary Chapel in California, she is the great woman behind a great man. An unpretentious woman with an unstoppable prayer life, her time spent on her knees helps others stand on their feet. I've heard many shipwrecked Christians express, "I was down for the count; everyone had given up on me. But Kay Smith never gave up in prayer for me. Through her intercession God rebuilt my broken life."

Southern California in the 1960s was a mecca for long-haired hippies on the pursuit to find themselves. It was a scene that was volatile, sensual, and psychedelic. Kay would drive with her husband down to the Huntington Beach pier and watch the hippies tune in, turn on, and trip out. Her heart was grieved by what she saw, so she began to pray and then found others to pray with her for that lost generation. As a result of their prayers the Jesus Movement took off—a generation of hippies were delivered from drugs and deception to devotion to God.

You, too, can become an unsung hero. Who knows what God will do when you go to the football game, the mall, the beach, the movies—wherever—and pray "always with all prayer and supplication in the Spirit" for this generation?

LISTEN TO ...

Satan trembles when he sees the weakest saint upon his knees.

—*William Cowper*

DAY 5

Be Peaceful

God's people are like sheep. David the psalmist found comfort in knowing that the Lord was his shepherd, who could make him "lie down in green pastures" (Ps. 23:2). Modern-day shepherd Phillip Keller wrote in his book *A Shepherd Looks at Psalm 23,* "Freedom of fear from the torment of parasites and insects is essential to the contentment of sheep.... Sheep ... can be driven to absolute distraction by ... flies ... and ticks. When tormented by these pests, it is literally impossible for them to lie down and rest."[2]

In the Christian life our most annoying pest is worry. It can drive us crazy with concern. My (Lenya) mother never slept at night until her three kids were home safe and sound. My son, Nathan, was unsettled at school when his father was traveling overseas. The apostle Paul knew it was natural to worry about those you love, so he wrote to the Ephesians in order to comfort their hearts and give them peace.

LIFT UP ...

Father, I praise You that You are the God of all comfort. I ask You to allow me to comfort others with the comfort I have received. In Jesus' name. Amen.

LOOK AT ...

This week we've learned to put on the armor of God and utilize the secret weapon of prayer. As we come to the end of our exploration of the book of Ephesians, let's study Paul's closing words to his friends and his prayer for peace.

READ EPHESIANS 6:21–24.

But that you also may know my affairs and how I am doing, Tychicus, a beloved brother and faithful minister in the Lord, will make all things known to you; whom I have sent to

you for this very purpose, that you may know our affairs, and that he may comfort your hearts. Peace to the brethren, and love with faith, from God the Father and the Lord Jesus Christ. Grace be with all those who love our Lord Jesus Christ in sincerity. Amen. Ephesians 6:21–24

1. Why did Paul send Tychicus to the Ephesians?

2. How did Paul describe this messenger and his message?

3. What two reasons did Paul give for sending Tychicus?

4. For what two blessings did Paul pray?

5. From whom do these blessings come?

6. What was Paul's final benediction to the Ephesians?

7. Whom did Paul pray would receive this blessing?

LIVE OUT ...

8. Paul called Tychicus a beloved brother in the Lord. Write down the names of three people who, though not born into your earthly family, have become beloved members of your heavenly family.

9. Paul sent this letter because he wanted to comfort and encourage the Ephesians. Choose one of the people from your list above, and send that person a letter offering words of comfort or encouragement. Share what you've learned about God and His spiritual treasures from this study in Ephesians.

LEARN ABOUT ...

2 Beloved Brother

As members of God's family, we acquire brothers and sisters, not by physical birth, but by the new birth of the Spirit. Jesus said, "Anyone who does the will of my Father in heaven is my brother and sister and mother!" (Matt. 12:50 NLT). It's all in the family!

3 Comfort

The Greek word for *comfort* means "to call alongside, or to help." The English definition is "to give strength and hope to; to ease the grief or trouble of." Comfort combines cheer with consolation. "The Lord comforts us, not to make us comfortable, but to make us comforters."[3]

6 Grace to You

We might close a letter with "Sincerely yours." Paul concluded his letter encouraging his readers to be "Sincerely His." When we genuinely belong to God, we experience peace, love, faith, and grace "from God the Father and the Lord Jesus Christ." Amen!

10. Using Paul's benediction as a model, write a prayer of blessing for your beloved friends.

11. a. In his final words Paul bestowed blessings on his beloved friends: peace, love with faith, and grace. Journal about which of these things you need most in your life right now. Why?

    b. Journal about the ways God has blessed you throughout your study of Ephesians.

· ○ ● ○ ·

The television game show *Who Wants to Be a Millionaire?* captured network ratings and the hearts of Americans. If this slick show tapped into the pulse of current society, then we find ourselves living in a world obsessed with material wealth—and a world where many people are spiritually bankrupt. A million dollars sounds great—but you can't take it with you!

Living for the here and now and not for the hereafter is a risky game. Jesus said, "What do you benefit if you gain the whole world but lose your own soul? Is anything worth more than your soul?" (Matt. 16:26 NLT). You're in the hot seat, and you're gambling with your soul. The all-important question is "What will you do with Jesus?" Host Regis Philbin offered three flimsy lifelines. Will you risk your spiritual inheritance on a fifty-fifty chance, the opinion of an audience, or the advice of a friend on the phone? Or will you confess "your faith in the Lord Jesus" (Eph. 1:15) and be a real winner?

God wants to know, "Is that your final answer?" If you answer the question correctly, you'll inherit much more than a mere million dollars—you'll gain eternal life and spiritual treasures that are "exceedingly abundantly above all that we ask or think" (Eph. 3:20).

LISTEN TO ...

To forsake Christ for the world ... is to leave a treasure for a trifle; ... eternity for a moment; reality for a shadow.

—*William Jenkyn*

Bibliography

The authors have used the following books and electronic sources in preparing the illustrations and sidebar material for this book.

Barclay, William. *The Letters to the Galatians and Ephesians.* Philadelphia: The Westminster Press, 1954.

Bible Illustrator for Windows. CD-ROM, version 3.0F. Parsons Technology, 1998. Illustrations copyright © 1998 by Christianity Today, Inc.

Braude, Jacob Morton. *Complete Speaker's and Toastmaster's Library.* Upper Saddle River, NJ: Prentice-Hall, 1965.

Chambers, Oswald. *So I Send You.* London: Simpkin Marshall, 1930.

Criswell, W. A. *Ephesians: An Exposition.* Grand Rapids: Zondervan, 1974.

Gandhi, Mohandas. *Autobiography.* Mineola, NY: Courier Dover Publications, 1983.

Graham, Billy. *Just As I Am.* New York: Harper Collins, 1997.

Graham, Franklin. *Living Beyond the Limits: A Life in Sync with God.* Nashville: Thomas Nelson, 1998.

Halley, Henry H. *Halley's Bible Handbook.* Grand Rapids: Zondervan, 1978.

Harrison, Everett F., and Charles F. Pfeiffer, eds. *The Wycliffe Bible Commentary.* Chicago: Moody Press, 1962.

Henry, Matthew. *Matthew Henry's Commentary on the Whole Bible: One Volume Edition, Complete and Unabridged.* Peabody, MA: Hendrickson, 1991.

Hewett, James. *Illustrations Unlimited.* Wheaton, IL: Tyndale House, 1988.

Hodge, Charles. *Ephesians.* The Crossway Classic Commentaries. Edited by Alister E. McGrath and J. I. Packer. Wheaton, IL: Crossway, 1994.

INFOsearch™, Illustrations data and database, The Communicator's Companion™, P.O. Box 171749, Arlington, Texas 76003, www.infosearch.com.

Jowett, John Henry. *The Silver Lining.* Boston: Grossett and Dunlap, 1907.

Kafer, Donna. *Women of Courage.* Alachua, Florida: Bridge Logos, 2007.

Keller, W. Phillip. *A Shepherd Looks at Psalm 23.* Grand Rapids: Zondervan, 2007.

Lewis, C. S. *Letters to Malcolm*. Orlando: Harcourt, 2002.

MacArthur, John. *Ephesians*. Chicago: Moody Press, 1986.

―――. *The MacArthur New Testament Commentary: Ephesians*. Chicago: Moody Press, 1986.

―――. *The MacArthur Study Bible*. Nashville: Word, 1997.

Marshall, Catherine. *A Man Called Peter*. Grand Rapids: Chosen Books, 2002.

McAuley, Jerry. *An Apostle for the Lost*. New York: George H. Doran Company, 1907.

McLellan, Vern. *The Complete Book of Practical Proverbs and Wacky Wit*. Wheaton, IL: Tyndale House, 1996.

Merriam-Webster's *Collegiate Dictionary*, 11th ed.

Meyer, F. B. *Devotional Commentary*. Wheaton, IL: Tyndale House, 1989.

Morris, Leon. *Expository Reflections on the Letter to the Ephesians*. Grand Rapids: Baker Books, 1994.

Nelson's Quick Reference Topical Bible Index. Nashville: Thomas Nelson, 1996.

Patterson, James, and Peter Kim. *The Day America Told the Truth*. Upper Saddle River, NJ: Prentice Hall, 1991.

Ruskin, John. *Modern Painters*. Vol. 5. New York: John Wiley & Sons, 1885.

Salt For Sermons, http://www.saltforsermons.org.uk.

Selzer, Richard. *Mortal Lessons: Notes on the Art of Surgery*. Orlando: Harcourt Brace, 1974.

SermonCentral.com, http://www.sermoncentral.com.

"Sermon Illustrations," Net Bible, http://www.sabda.org/netbible5/illustration.php.

Sermon Illustrations, http://www.sermonillustrations.com.

Spurgeon, Charles H. *Spurgeon's Sermon Illustrations*. Edited by David Otis Fuller. Grand Rapids: Kregel, 1990.

Stott, John. *The Message of Ephesians*. Downers Grove, IL: InterVarsity Press, 1984.

―――. *Your Mind Matters*. Downers Grove, IL: InterVarsity Press, 1972.

Unger, Merrill F., and R. K. Harrison, eds. *The Unger's Bible Dictionary*. In *PC Study Bible*. CD-ROM, version 4.2b. Seattle: Biblesoft, 2004.

Vine, W. E. *Vine's Expository Dictionary of New Testament Words*. In *PC Study Bible*. CD-ROM, version 4.2b. Seattle: Biblesoft, 2004.

Walvord, John F., and Roy B. Zuck. *The Bible Knowledge Commentary: New Testament*. Colorado Springs: David C Cook, 1983.

Wiersbe, Warren. *Be Rich*. Colorado Springs: David C Cook, 2009

Winship, Albert Edward. *Jukes-Edwards*. Harrisburg, PA: R. L. Myers & Co., 1900.

Youngblood, Ronald F. *Nelson's Bible Dictionary*. In *PC Study Bible*. CD-ROM, version 4.2b. Seattle: Biblesoft, 2004.

Notes

INTRODUCTION

1. "Celebrating Solutions," United Way of Pierce County, accessed September 16, 2006, http://www.uwpc.org/News&Events/DOCs/CelebratingSolutions1003.pdf#search=%22found%20an%20uncashed%20check%22 (site discontinued).

LESSON ONE: ARE YOU IN THE WILL?

1. Henrietta Mears, quoted in Donna Kafer, *Women of Courage* (Alachua, FL: Bridge Logos, 2007), 105–6.

LESSON TWO: SECRET TREASURE

1. David Jeremiah, *Begging Children,* DavidJeremiah.org, http://www.davidjeremiah.org/site/magazine.aspx?id=3602 (accessed June 17, 2011).
2. Steve Raymond, "Season of Hope," *Sports Illustrated,* July 20, 1981, http://sportsillustrated.cnn.com/vault/article/magazine/MAG1148137/2/index.htm (accessed December 10, 2010).
3. Frank Waldman and Blake Edwards, *Return of the Pink Panther,* directed by Blake Edwards (1975; New York: Universal Studios, 2006), DVD.

LESSON THREE: THE GREATEST GIFT

1. "Conversion to Hindu Faith Is Tortuous," *Grand Rapids Press,* December 1989.
2. John Stott, *Your Mind Matters* (Downers Grove, IL: InterVarsity Press, 1972), 52.
3. "Featured Use Your Life Award," *Oprah's Angel Network,* May 15, 2000, http://www.oprah.com/angelnetwork/Beas-Kids-Use-Your-Life-Award.

LESSON FOUR: SHARE THE WEALTH

1. Mohandas Gandhi, *Autobiography* (Mineola, NY: Courier Dover Publications, 1983).

2. Peter Marshall, quoted in Catherine Marshall, *A Man Called Peter* (Grand Rapids: Chosen Books, 2002), 343.

LESSON FIVE: TRUSTEE OF GOD'S WILL

1. Jerry McAuley, *An Apostle for the Lost* (New York: George H. Doran Company, 1907), 118.

2. Ibid., 143–44.

3. Robert Nemiroff and Jerry Bonnell, "Doomed Star Eta Carinae," Astronomy Picture of the Day, NASA, March 26, 2006, http://apod.nasa.gov/apod/ap060326.html.

4. Robert Garner, ed., "Eta Carinae" NASA, last modified September 9, 2009, http://www.nasa.gov/mission_pages/hubble/multimedia/ero/ero_eta_carinae.html.

5. Don Edward Fehrenbacher and Virginia Fehrenbacher, eds., *Recollected Words of Abraham Lincoln* (Palo Alto: Stanford University Press, 1996), 105.

6. Warren Wiersbe, *Be Rich* (Colorado Springs: David C Cook, 2009), 85.

7. "TIME 100 Persons of the Century: Heroes and Icons," *TIME*, June 14, 1999.

8. Billy Graham, *Just As I Am* (New York: Harper Collins, 1997), 120–21.

LESSON SIX: EXCEEDINGLY ABUNDANTLY MORE

1. Leon Morris, *Expository Reflections on the Letter to the Ephesians* (Grand Rapids: Baker Books, 1994), 104.

2. Richard Selzer, *Mortal Lessons: Notes on the Art of Surgery* (Orlando: Harcourt Brace, 1974), 45–46.

LESSON SEVEN: COMING OF AGE

1. John Clardy, "As the Eagle Stirs Up Her Nest," Everyone's Apostolic, http://www.everyonesapostolic.org/articles/568/1/As-The-Eagle-Stirs-Up-Her-Nest/Page1.html (accessed December 13, 2010).
2. C. S. Lewis, *Letters to Malcolm* (Orlando: Harcourt, 2002), 75.
3. Leonard Ravenhill, "Prayer," 1994, http://www.ravenhill.org/prayer.htm.

LESSON EIGHT: DRESS FOR SUCCESS

1. "Imelda Marcos' Shoe Collection Continues to Grow," CBC News, http://www.cbc.ca/world/story/1999/08/18/Imelda990818.html, updated November 10, 2000 (accessed December 13, 2010).
2. Johnny Cash, "I Walk the Line," *With His Hot and Blue Guitar* © 1956 Sun Records.
3. Nancy Sinatra, "These Boots Are Made for Walkin'," *Boots* © 1966 Boots Enterprises.
4. Mark Twain, quoted in Jacob Morton Braude, *Complete Speaker's and Toastmaster's Library* (Upper Saddle River, NJ: Prentice-Hall, 1965), 43.
5. John Ruskin, *Modern Painters,* vol. 5 (New York: John Wiley & Sons, 1885), 268.
6. James Patterson and Peter Kim, *The Day America Told the Truth* (Upper Saddle River, NJ: Prentice Hall, 1991), 45.
7. Bernard Brunsting, "The Lord's Laughter," *The Joyful Newsletter.*

LESSON NINE: IN MY FATHER'S FOOTSTEPS

1. James Hewett, *Illustrations Unlimited* (Wheaton, IL: Tyndale House, 1988), 282.
2. Josh McDowell (lecture, Moody Founder's Week, February 1986).
3. James Dobson, *Focus on the Family* (Waco: Word Educational Products: 1986), VHS.
4. Warren Wiersbe, *Be Rich* (Colorado Springs: David C Cook, 2009), 138.

LESSON TEN: CHANGE OF HEART

1. William Barclay, *The Letters to the Galatians and Ephesians* (Philadelphia: The Westminster Press, 1954), 208–15.
2. John Stott, *The Message of Ephesians* (Downers Grove, IL: InterVarsity Press, 1984), 218.
3. Charles H. Spurgeon, *Spurgeon's Sermon Illustrations,* ed. David Otis Fuller (Grand Rapids: Kregel, 1990), 15.

LESSON ELEVEN: WORK ETHIC

1. James Patterson and Peter Kim, *The Day America Told the Truth* (Upper Saddle River, NJ: Prentice Hall, 1991), 155.
2. John MacArthur, *Ephesians* (Chicago: Moody Press, 1986), 323.
3. Franklin Graham, *Living Beyond the Limits* (Nashville: Thomas Nelson, 1998), 1.

LESSON TWELVE: STAND YOUR GROUND

1. Oswald Chambers, *So I Send You* (London: Simpkin Marshall, 1930), 129.
2. W. Phillip Keller, *A Shepherd Looks at Psalm 23* (Grand Rapids: Zondervan, 2007), 50.
3. John Henry Jowett, *The Silver Lining* (Boston: Grossett and Dunlap, 1907), 124.

About the Authors

Born in a small town on the shores of Lake Michigan, Lenya Heitzig moved to beach cities in California and Hawaii before settling into the mountainous terrain of Albuquerque, New Mexico, where she now resides. Whether majoring in fashion merchandising, or serving as a missionary with YWAM, or being a cancer survivor, Lenya thrives on adventure. As executive director of *she* Ministries at Calvary Albuquerque and coauthor for two Bible study series—the Fresh Life series, which includes *Live Intimately: Lessons from the Upper Room, Live Fearlessly: A Study in the Book of Joshua, Live Deeply: A Study in the Parables of Jesus, and Live Relationally: Lessons from the Women of Genesis;* and the Pathway series, which includes *Pathway to God's Treasure: Ephesians, Pathway to God's Plan: Esther,* and *Pathway to Living Faith: James,* published by Tyndale and soon to be part of the Fresh Life series through David C Cook—she delights in seeing God's Word do God's work in the lives of women. Her first book, *Pathway to God's Treasure: Ephesians,* received the Gold Medallion Award. She also contributed a number of devotionals to the *New Women's Devotional Bible,* which was a finalist in the 2007 Christian Book Awards. Her semi-biographical book, *Holy Moments,* published by Regal, enlightens readers to see God's hand of providence move miraculously in daily life. Her husband, Skip Heitzig, is senior pastor of a fourteen-thousand-member congregation. Their son, Nathan, and his wife, Janaé, have one child, Seth Nathaniel.

Penny Rose is a Gold Medallion Award winning author. She is the coauthor of *Live Intimately: Lessons from the Upper Room, Live Fearlessly: A Study in the Book of Joshua, Live Relationally: Lessons from the Women of Genesis,* and *Live Deeply: A Study in the Parables of Jesus.* She was the general editor and a devotional writer for Zondervan's *New Women's Devotional Bible,* a finalist for the Christian Book Award and contributed to Zondervan's *True Identity: The Bible for Women.* She wrote *A Garden of Friends,* published by Regal, as an ode to biblical friendship. Penny lives in Albuquerque, New Mexico, with her husband Kerry, a pastor at Calvary Albuquerque. They have two daughters, Erin and Ryan; a granddaughter, Charlotte; and one son, Kristian.

With Gratitude

Lenya—Heartfelt appreciation to my family for imparting faith to me: Thanks to my father, Rod Farley, for introducing me to the faith; to my mother, Helen DeBeck, for her unconditional faithfulness to me; to my husband, Skip, for being an example of unshakable faith; to my son, Nathan, for showing me childlike faith; and to all the women at Calvary for faithfully serving God side by side with Penny and me.

Penny—Many thanks to those who have shown me such love: Thanks to my parents, Jack and Janelle Pierce; to my husband, Kerry, who loves me even though he knows everything about me; to my children—Erin, Kristian, and Ryan—who fill my heart to overflowing with love; and to the women at Calvary for loving God's Word.